A PSYCHOANALYTIC ODYSSEY

A PSYCHOANALYTIC ODYSSEY

Painted Guinea Pigs, Dreams, and Other Realities

Eugene J. Mahon

KARNAC

First published in 2014 by
Karnac Books Ltd
118 Finchley Road
London NW3 5HT

British Library Cataloguing in Publication Data

A C.I.P. for this book is available from the British Library

ISBN-13: 978-1-78049-144-8

Typeset by V Publishing Solutions Pvt Ltd., Chennai, India

Printed in Great Britain

www.karnacbooks.com

For Delia
For Eugene, John and Emer
And in memory of Sabrina

To follow knowledge, like a sinking star,
Beyond the utmost bound of human thought.

—Ulysses, Alfred Lord Tennyson

CONTENTS

ACKNOWLEDGEMENTS

First I want to thank Delia Battin for so many years of a rare quality of devotion, influence, and inspiration; she also was the co-author of early versions of Chapter Seven on Screen Memories and Chapter Eight on Symptom as Irony. It would be difficult for me to say whether her influence and my own insights were ever truly individuated or merely complementary reflections of each other.

Next I want to thank Salman Akhtar who not only suggested the writing of this book but also enthusiastically introduced me to its publisher, Oliver Rathbone. I want to thank Robert Michels for reading an early version of the manuscript, sharpening its *voice*, and suggesting judicious editing where necessary. Walter Troffkin also read the manuscript with great care and made invaluable suggestions as to the content and its most likely audience. My thanks to Phillip Freeman who read the manuscript: his critique was insightful, supportive, and helpful. Again I want to thank Delia Battin for reading the manuscript carefully many times. Its content and style were edited by her with great skill and erudition.

I want to thank all those who have influenced my education from the earliest years to the present, beginning with what I like to call the little academy of childhood where siblings (Jim, Tom, Paul, Chris, and

Maeve) played such a crucial emotional and intellectual role. There were many extra-familial teachers of course: Robert Michels, Eugene Feigelson, Alexander Beller, Herbert Hendin, Loretta Bender, Margaret Mahler, Marianne Kris, Peter Blos, Peter Neubauer, John Sours, Lionel Ovesey, Clarice Kestenbaum, Richard Druss, Ethel Person, Helen Meyers, Donald Meyers, Jerry Wiener, and Alberta Szalita. All the members of The Center for Advanced Psychoanalytic Studies, Princeton, Group IX have been part of the internal theatre of ongoing education since 1978. It has been and continues to be a collegial, intellectual ferment of inestimable value. There were and are many colleagues and friends whose imprint is lasting: Steve Ablon, Charles Affron, Mirella Affron, Jacob Arlow, Sheldon Bach, Christianne Baudry, Francis Baudry, Phyllis Beren, Maria Bergmann, Martin Bergmann, Charles Brenner, Arnold Cooper, Lucy Daniels, Peter Dente, Nathaniel Donson, James Egan, Carolyn Ellman, Steve Ellman, Frederic Ewen, Cecily Firestein, Stephen Firestein, Clara Genetos, Miriam Gideon, Philip Ginsburg, Rachel Ginsburg, Arnold Goldberg, Constance Goldberg, Paul Gray, William Grossman, Irene Guttman, Samuel Guttman, Helen Halverson, Richard Halverson, Jim Herzog, Lila Kalinich, Donald Kaplan, Louise Kaplan, Lydia Katzenbach, Nicholas Katzenbach, Anton Kris, Donald Kuspit, Patrick Leyden, Rosemary Leyden, Gordon Lish, Miriam Mahon, Michael McAuliffe, Virginia McAuliffe, Fred Pine, Sandra Pine, Warren Poland, Arlene Richards, Arnold Richards, Samuel Ritvo, Robert Rodman Noah Rosoff, Lynne Rubin, Jonah Schein, Lester Schwartz, Mara Schwartz, Len Shengold, Mark Silvan, Abby Silvan-Adams, Martin Silverman, Henry Smith, Al Solnit, Vann Spruiell, Carole Stacks, John Stacks, Lucille Stein, Martin Stein, Irving Steingart, Joyce Steingart, Toby Troffkin, Ed Weinschel, Fred Wiener, Mary Wiener, Len Brown, Magda Brown, Mark Brown, Sandra Brown, Geoffrey Brown, Olivia Brown, Paul Mahon, Sharon Mahon, Sean Mahon, Jason Mahon, Jim Mahon, Margaret Mahon, Dominic Mahon, Rosalind Mahon, Christopher Mahon, Maeve Mahon, Patrick Ferriter, Elizabeth Gero-Heymann, Felix Pick, Nella Pick, Milka Toya, Carlo Gragnani, and Josef Yerushalmi.

I want to thank Sophia Rosoff for teaching me that music and psychoanalysis share a deep basic rhythm that transcends the surface reality of notes and words.

I also want to thank Lucio Amadio for his patient skillful cyber-education of a Luddite in the preparation of this manuscript.

I also want to thank Kate Pearce and Rod Tweedy at Karnac for their dedicated, thoughtful shepherding of the whole manuscript from start to finish. My debt to Oliver Rathbone and all at Karnac is great.

Permissions and copyrights

I would like to thank Yale University Press for their kind permission to excerpt, modify, revise, or reprint the following articles from *The Psychoanalytic Study of the Child* (*PSOC*).

Battin, D. & Mahon, E. J. (2003). Symptom, screen memory and dream. *PSOC 58*: 246–266.

Mahon, E. J. (1992). Dreams—A developmental and longitudinal perspective. *PSOC 47*: 49–65.

Mahon, E. J. (1992). The function of humor in a four-year-old. *PSOC 47*: 321–328.

Mahon, E. J. (2000). Parapraxes in the plays of William Shakespeare. *PSOC 55*: 335–370.

Mahon, E. J. (2001). Anna Freud and the evolution of psychoanalytic technique. *PSOC 56*: 76–95.

Mahon, E. J. (2002). A joke in a dream. *PSOC 57*: 452–457.

Mahon, E. J. (2002). Dreams within dreams. *PSOC 57*: 118–130.

Mahon, E. J. & Battin-Mahon, D. (1983). The fate of screen memories in psychoanalysis. *PSOC 38*: 459–479.

Mahon, E. J. & Simpson, D. (1977). The painted guinea pig. *PSOC 32*: 283–303.

I would like to thank John Wiley & Sons, Inc. for their permission to excerpt, modify, revise, or reprint the following papers from *Psychoanalytic Quarterly*.

Battin, D. & Mahon, E. (2009). Seeing the light. *Psychoanalytic Quarterly 78* (1): 107–122.

Mahon, E. J. (1991). The "dissolution" of the Oedipus Complex: A neglected cognitive factor. *Psychoanalytic Quarterly 60*: 628–634.

Mahon, E. J. (2004). Playing and working through: A neglected analogy. *Psychoanalytic Quarterly 73*: 379–413.

Mahon, E. J. (2005). A parapraxis in a dream. *Psychoanalytic Quarterly 74*: 465–484.

Mahon, E. J. (2005). To repress: A note on an ambiguity of meaning. *Psychoanalytic Quarterly 74*: 1053–1068.

Mahon, E. J. (2007). A pun in a dream. *Psychoanalytic Quarterly 76*: 1367–1373.

Mahon, E. J. (2012). The uncanny in a dream. *Psychoanalytic Quarterly 81*: 713–725.

Mahon, E. J. (2013). Mourning, dreaming and the discovery of the Oedipus Complex. *Psychoanalytic Quarterly 82* (4): 877–895.

This material is reproduced with permission of John Wiley & Sons, Inc.

ABOUT THE AUTHOR

Eugene J. Mahon, MD, is a Training and Supervising Analyst at the Columbia Psychoanalytic Center for Training and Research and at the Contemporary Freudian Society. He is also a member of the Center for Advanced Psychoanalytic Studies, Princeton, New Jersey. He won The Alexander Beller Award of Columbia Psychoanalytic Institute in 1984, and has been on the editorial boards of the *International Journal of Psychoanalysis*, the *Journal of The American Psychoanalytic Association* and he is currently on the editorial board of the *Psychoanalytic Quarterly*. He has published articles in all the major psychoanalytic journals on a great diversity of topics: memory, dreams, mourning, repression, the dissolution of the Oedipus complex, play, working through, prejudice, the golden section. He has published poetry, plays, and applied analytic essays on Shakespeare, Anna and Sigmund Freud, Beckett, Bion, Vitruvius, Oscar Wilde, and Samuel Taylor Coleridge. One of his poems, "Steeds of Darkness", was set to music by the American composer Miriam Gideon. He practices Child Analysis and Adult Analysis in New York City.

INTRODUCTION

This is a book about psychoanalysis in general and psychoanalytic process in particular. Psychoanalysis, though difficult to describe intellectually, is a visceral, emotional, thoughtful, sometimes exasperating, precarious relationship between an analyst and an analysand. It "is not about something" as Beckett famously observed of Joyce's Finnegan's Wake, "it is the something itself." I have conceptualized it as an odyssey, a journey through the uncharted regions of the mind every daring analysand must make. The analogy of psychoanalytic process as an odyssey first came to me through child analysis. In the midst of a child analysis, which was a most creative hybrid of play and language, Alexander, aged five, having enacted a drama of a storm-tossed ship at sea, built a terminal for the ship to return safely to. Stepping out of this engrossing play and stepping into the transference insightfully, interpretively Alexander said: "maybe you can become a person terminal for me." In a few words the child had captured some of the key ingredients of psychoanalysis, its creative energies (person terminal is an amazing condensation of play and transference), its therapeutic momentum, its capacity to transform storm and fear into trust and engagement. Alexander also made boats out of wood, painted them and gave them very significant names. In mid-analysis a boat was called The Catch-Up, as if the child sensed he had much to catch up on, emotionally and developmentally; at the end of analysis a boat was given a code name of letters and numbers that signified the analytic consulting room where the odyssey had ended and begun. Again, it was the same child, in the midst of engrossing play, who demonstrated a rudimentary understanding of the interpretive process itself when he remarked, "you like to make things out of what I say." I believe nascent insight, therapeutic alliance, and object relationship are all represented with eloquent subtlety in such remarks.

An odyssey is a journey of excitement, discovery, danger and daring. "All serious daring starts from within" Eudora Welty commented in *One Writer's Beginnings*. She might have been talking about the odyssey of each analysand and the intrapsychic process of analysis, given the serious daring it takes to begin a journey of free associative exploration into the unknown within. It is the excitement of such psychoanalytic odysseys *within* that I will be stressing in this book even though conflict, compromise, anxiety and resistance cannot be left out of the reckoning either. I remember the excitement I felt as a young psychoanalyst-in-training when a three-year-old child asked, "who painted him?" when confronted with a substitute pet (of a slightly different color) a few days after his beloved guinea pig died. He was one of thirty nursery school children trying to process their first confrontation with death. "Who painted him?" was a question that seemed to emanate from the depths of a very young soul indeed as it tried to take the measure of one of life's inevitable existential assaults on the short lived Edens of childhood experience. The child's question lodged in my own mind, demanding to be addressed as seriously, as scientifically as its own quite serious spontaneity and curiosity insisted upon. It is the excitement of questions such as these that inform all psychoanalytic odysseys, an excitement I want to try to capture in the pages of this book.

I am a child psychoanalyst and an adult psychoanalyst: play, dreams, transference, free associations, fantasies, screen memories, resistance, insights, interpretations and excitement have been the raw material of my professional engagement for the last forty years. Excitement can be pleasurable, or challenging or even precarious as the mind tries to take the measure of its immediacy. "Who painted him?" is exciting and baffling all at once as the mind tries to do justice to its creative spontaneous energies. Children's play in general can be fascinating and baffling nowhere more so perhaps than accounts of children playing in the Holocaust. When Jan Karski, a Polish diplomat, visited the Warsaw Ghetto and saw children playing amidst the disease and stench and degradation of the wartime ghetto experience, he remarked with shocked spontaneity: "They only make believe it is play" (Brenner, 2012). Questions such as "who painted him?" or statements such as "They only make believe it is play" shake the mind out of its complacency into a state of intellectual and emotional excitement that will not rest until their troubling urgencies are engaged with passionately.

That level of excitement cannot be sustained throughout a book perhaps but I do believe that the raw materials of psychoanalysis are endlessly exciting as analytic process engages them day after day. In Chapter One, I address the controversial issue of mourning in childhood, a topic I return to again in Chapter Nine when I address the mourning of Sigmund Freud and suggest that mourning and dreaming may have been the key triggers of a remarkable period of creativity that led to *The Interpretation of Dreams*. In the intervening chapters I address repression, insight, transference, child analysis (where play is introduced, not only in its tragic manner as in the Warsaw Ghetto, but in all its protean manifestations, as the great hybrid of fantasy and reality that in fact it is throughout childhood, not to mention its important extensions into the world of adulthood), children's and adults' dreams, screen memories, and insight again in a more ironic iteration of itself than introduced in Chapter Three.

Throughout the book I engage with issues that every analyst deals with every day, as the table of contents briefly referred to earlier suggests. But the contemplation of the most classical topics always seemed to me to have facets of the unknown embedded in their certitudes and therein lay the possibility of renewed excitement as opposed to reverential acceptance of received conventional wisdom. For instance why has insight become a less than inspirational topic at the moment in psychoanalysis? Could it be that its extraordinary initial promise left one, and still leaves one, disappointed, as insights, which began with such exuberance, quickly seem to lose their nerve, so to speak, and retreat into repression or resistance again, their initial expectations never realized? I address this seeming lack of resilience on insight's part: I personify the issue, so to speak, suggesting that insight is always transgressive, always challenging the psychic status quo of superego authority and intimidation and that the ensuing anxiety often leads to a quick retreat from its initial clarity and verve. I rely on a biblical etymological definition of the expression "ahah" (as in the "ahah" phenomenon that usually announces insight's bold entrance) and a clinical case example to suggest that insight is always transgressive and therefore always questioning its own authority and even abandoning it altogether.

In Chapter One as mentioned earlier, I address the issue of children and mourning. The conventional wisdom had for years suggested that young children do not, or cannot, mourn. It was implied that the immaturity of their egos could not sustain such a complex process as mourning. Children "mourning" a school pet made me realize that their emotional reaction, by whatever name we call it, is a phenomenon worthy of study. Painting over, or ignoring the reality of their conflicted suffering seemed like the wrong psychoanalytic attitude to me. I went on to conclude that mourning is possible in childhood as long as the adult observer does not insist that it mimic adult mourning rather than expressing its grief in its own unique way.

Repression is the cornerstone on which the whole theory of psychoanalysis rests. A clinical case in which the word re-press (as in the making of multiple copies of a disc in the recording industry) figured at first in dreamtime, and subsequently in the excitement of analytic process itself, introduced an ambiguity into the term repression which illuminated the concept in novel ways. The return of the repressed had always suggested that the repressed does not subside, but returns symptomatically when the ego's repressive energies falter. But I wanted to stress the idea that the ego's function was not merely to exclude turbulent issues from consciousness but to find ways to re-introduce the repressed in adaptive ways, to re-press them, so to speak, back into service in a more functional, resourceful, resilient consciousness. I address these ideas more completely in Chapter Two.

The concept of transference is almost as fundamental a psychoanalytic concept as repression itself. I try to see it in a new light by approaching the topic developmentally. I consider the necessary developmental achievements required before the mind would be capable of engineering an act of transference in the first place. In other words, if transference is defined as a displacement of affects from one object relationship (usually a most significant genetic component of the facilitating environment) to another, more recent one, differentiated self and object representations would have to be established in the mind before such a transfer could be even conceptualized. This is not just a theoretical splitting of hairs with no clinical relevance. With borderline patients it can be difficult to ascertain whether precise differentiation of self-representations and object-representations has actually been accomplished intrapsychically. A lack of differentiation between analysand and analyst can therefore masquerade as transference when in fact something far more primitive needs to be addressed clinically. I engage this issue more fully in Chapter Four.

In Chapter Five I introduce child analysis, emphasizing play as one of its core features. Freud suggested that a child's play and fantasy were basically the same except for the fact that play relies on practical, concrete objects (toys, playthings) to express its interiority. I have always found this definition of Freud's to be illuminating and exciting and I expand on it by suggesting that playing and working through are analogous in ways that have not been appreciated. This neglected analogy between play and working through dissolves unnecessary boundaries between the essentials of child analytic and adult analytic process. I state very briefly en passant that an adult's capacity to play is an important ingredient of parenthood, a crucial skill that is largely unacknowledged, despite its central role in maintaining the fabric of society.

Since 1900 dreams have been considered as fundamental to any in-depth understanding of the unconscious mind. I have tried to bring attention to certain features of dreams not emphasized by Freud or subsequent scholarship. Freud was fascinated by children's dreams, given how transparently they seemed to corroborate his basic theory of dream as the disguised fulfillment of an infantile wish. The infantile wish seemed so undisguised in children's dreams it did not take so much to convince the dubious of its obvious role in the formation of the dream. To my knowledge Freud did not study children's dreams from a developmental point of view. I had an opportunity once to study three dreams from different developmental epochs in the same child as he grew from five years of age to twenty. I was practically able to see the infantile wish get modified as it moved through developmental phases and altered the manifest appearance of dreams accordingly. Freud mentions dreams within dreams quite briefly in *The Interpretation of Dreams*. He argues that if something appears in a dream within a dream one can be sure that that is a sure sign that it really happened and that its reality is being denied vehemently by being embedded so deeply. I was struck not only by Freud's ingenious explanation but also by his neglect of the bi-sectional structure of a dream within a dream. Clearly there are two compartments in a dream within a dream, two reels of film, so to speak, from a cinematic point of view. I suggest that there is a key dynamic connection between the two cinematic dramatizations that should not be neglected. The complex story is told in all its detail in Chapter Five. I also personify a "cunning artistry of the dream work" as I try to explain the many ingenious disguised inclusions it is capable of inserting into the manifest content of a dream. I bring particular attention to dreams where a parapraxis, a joke, a pun or even an uncanny proper name is inserted into the manifest content in the interest of disguise. I argue that the latent content is being protected in secrecy while all of this beguiling display is going on in the manifest limelight.

I have always found screen memories as intriguing to contemplate and work with analytically as dreams themselves, which they resemble. I bring special attention to one feature of screen memories that has not been accentuated heretofore. When an analysis nears termination the screen memories that have been worked on directly and indirectly throughout the course of the analytic process can sometimes undergo a remarkable, subjectively perceivable, change in their appearance. They tend to lose the luminous "halo" effect that is sometimes (not always) so characteristic of them. I have argued that this noticeable change in the structural façade of a screen memory can be one indicator of a readiness for termination. I also suggest that it is not only termination that can be illuminated by the analysis of screen memories but the ongoing analytic process as well. I describe a case in which symptom, screen memory and dream seem to engage with the same genetic material over time suggesting how organic and integrated analytic process is as it tries to take the measure of genetic conflict and experience throughout all the phases of analysis.

In the last three chapters I bring attention first to a symptom that seemed to mock the very processes of insight that human development depends on. If "seeing the light" usually refers metaphorically to the acquisition of insight itself, I argue that seeing the light literally, as opposed to figuratively, can be a troubling symptom. From symptom I turn to character, in Chapter Nine, arguing that the distance between the two may not be as great as nosology insists. Then in a final chapter I return to the topic of mourning, this time not painted over, but actually used by Freud to pry open one of the great psychological mysteries of the human mind. I am referring to Freud's discovery of the Oedipus complex in 1897 and the critical role mourning and dreaming may have played in it. It is a triumphant note to end an odyssey on, an odyssey that began with mourning but ends in triumph as insight, schooled in the existential lost and found shops of human experience, extracts gain from loss and finds resilience in the deconstruction of its own conflicts, going beyond transgression toward transcendence.

It is a conceptual psychic odyssey I am imagining of course and a most arbitrary one at that. I link together the concepts of mourning, repression, insight, transference, play, working through, dreams, screen memories and the Oedipus complex as if they were co-ordinates on some map that lead toward a reachable destination but a destination that is, in fact, not attainable at all. Objection sustained. The mind is not a region whose concrete co-ordinates can be mapped out. And yet my design, such as it is, is not completely arbitrary. There are linkages between the various concepts that might not seem obvious at first. For instance if play is defined as fantasy that needs to link itself to child-hood toys and other concrete objects in order to give expression to itself, transference could be conceptualized as unconscious genetic fantasy that insists on linking itself to the person of the analyst. Dreams could be defined as unconscious latent desires that need to link themselves to manifest imagery in the service of evasion of censorial detection; screen memories could be defined as the infantile amnesia maintain-ing its unconscious privacy by highlighting one luminous moment of memory while repressing all the rest. Repression could be characterized as insight in flight from itself, yet always trying to retrieve its status by re-pressing itself back into adaptive functioning. Insight in conflict with its transgressive nature could be viewed as a confused hybrid of bold defiance and fearful retreat. Mourning and the Oedipus complex could be seen to share an internal structure that is not immediately visible in the manifest activities that define them. So in a way all the concep-tual ports-of-call of this psychoanalytic odyssey are linked. I hope that at least a few significant cross sections of the mind are illuminated as the unconscious mind is mapped in this idiosyncratic manner and one human, limited odyssey proceeds.

CHAPTER ONE

A painted guinea pig

All that lives must die
Passing through nature to eternity.

—*Hamlet*, Act One, Scene Two, William Shakespeare

At the end of the prologue I introduced an analogy: children painting over some aspect of psychological life that was too painful for them to process consciously could be compared to the unconscious act of repression in general, or indeed, all defensive strategies of the mind. The death of their school pet, a beloved guinea pig, was perhaps the first taste of tragedy most of these three year olds had ever experienced, and it might have gone unnoticed had the curiosity of one child not brought attention to the slightly different color of the pet's replacement. When the child asked "who painted him?" a process of rudimentary mourning was set in motion, tragedy, with the assistance of a sensitive school teacher, addressed as opposed to denied. It may seem excessively morbid to begin a psychoanalytic odyssey with mourning, loss and cover up, rather than joy, expectation and optimism as the oars of momentum launch the developmental vessel toward its goal and ultimate destination. And yet from a historical

1

developmental point of view life's journey does start out breathlessly in the womb and ends breathlessly in death; it begins its post-uterine existence in helplessness and total dependency but then gradually embraces pre-Oedipal attachment, individuation, independence, the industry of latency, the challenges of adolescence, the fulfillments and disappointments of adulthood; and all along the way loss and gain stamp experience with their indelible affects, shaping the mind's character and identity as nature and nurture, constitution and environment alloy themselves in the conflicted alchemy of development. So if I begin with sorrow and loss, there is a resilience of the mind I am also stressing, a resilience that characterizes the childhood odyssey that not only thrives on love and nurture but also learns to master adversity and turn it to its developmental advantage. There is no need to romanticize this resilience, this dogged sense of momentum and courage, since psychopathology often illustrates how regressive defeat and failure can also characterize experience as much as courage and success can. But psychoanalysis takes human experience as it finds it, and has been instructed and enlightened by psychopathology as much as by normal development. It has learned from Virchow and from Freud. Virchow believed that death dissected, pathology investigated, could instruct health about what led to death and pathology, if science was not afraid to grip the scalpel of investigative daring in its hands. And Freud taught us that childhood was not all Victorian innocence, but that its polymorphous nature, its sexualities and hatreds, could help us understand our adult selves, our life instincts, and death instincts if we did not deny the developmental complexities we sprang from. And so I begin with thirty three-year-old nursery children trying to understand their complex reactions to a new sudden addition to their school curriculum, the concept of death. A child will lead us, so to speak, into the later, deeper waters this book attempts to navigate.

Guinny, (aka Betsy) as he was affectionately called, a pink-eyed guinea pig who made a squeaking noise that endeared him to the children, died in February of the school year. He died in the home of one of the children (each weekend a different family took the guinea pig home to return him each Monday morning, when he took up his residence as school pet for another week). The initial reaction of this child's mother was denial: she immediately wanted to buy a new guinea pig exactly like the old one. The teacher explained to her that the guinea pig had died and that it was unwise to try to cover it up; but a new guinea pig could be bought sometime in the future. The mother agreed. The children were told in class that their pet had died. Their initial reactions were not easy to measure. However, when a new guinea pig was brought to the classroom a few days later, many interesting reactions were observed. The school teacher had decided to get a new guinea pig that did not look exactly like the old one, but was of a slightly different color. When the children first saw the new guinea pig, one asked and a chorus of others chanted: "Who painted him?"

But initial curiosity turned to denial and avoidance. The children shunned this new pet like the plague for three weeks. The children who used to bring food for the old pet every day and hold and touch him incessantly did not touch the new pet at all; nor did they bring him any food. Some of the children took food from home for the new guinea pig, but lost it on the way to school. Other children pinched the new guinea pig. One girl who had always brought carrots for the old pet would think of bringing a carrot for the new pet, but then close her refrigerator, saying, "I'll bring something tomorrow." Clearly the children were angry at their old pet for leaving them and took it out on the new one.

The teacher was at all times sensitive to the feelings the children were struggling to express, as the following example illustrates.

TEACHER: You loved Guinny very much, but he isn't here anymore.

CHILDREN
(IN A CHORUS): No, he died.

PHILLIP: Where is he dead?

NICKY: He is thrown away.

ROGER: Thrown away in the sandbox.

POLLY: In the Zoo again.

TEACHER: No, Guinny died and he was buried in the park. I know you loved him and it is sad, but he will never come back.

RUTHERFORD: I don't love him because he is dying and going away.

TEACHER: I think you're angry, Rutherford, because he died. It's all right to be angry. (As the discussion turns to the new pet:) Remember you said you wanted a new guinea pig?

CHILDREN
(IN A CHORUS): Yes.

TEACHER: Well, you haven't been taking care of him.

NICKY: But he is a little shy.

BROOKE: I didn't like my guinea pig to be sad.

TEACHER: I think you are the ones who are shy and sad because he isn't here, your old guinea pig. That's all right. You can still play with this one and care for him. You don't have to love him yet. You loved the old guinea, cared for him and had a good time with him.

JENNIFER: My goldfish died.

ANDREW
(POINTING TO
THE NEW GUINEA): He won't die because we love him.

TEACHER: Even when we love something it may die. We loved Guinny and he died. But it's all right to love another pet. Are you afraid that if you love this new guinea it will die too?

ELIZABETH: He needs to be in my arms.

TEACHER: Maybe you think you shouldn't love this guinea because you loved the other guinea pig and he went away.

CHILDREN
(IN A CHORUS): No, no.

TEACHER: Well, you haven't been caring for him. What does he need?

CHILDREN: Blankets, blankets, breakfast, some food, lunch, he needs to go home, he needs a basket, celery and carrots.

The teacher (in consultation with a psychoanalyst) had such conversations with the children in small groups, allowing them to express their feelings about the old pet and helping them to understand their reactions to the new one. She did not push the children into a grief they were unable to handle, but her influence was a crucial determinant of their reactions. For instance, when they saw pictures of pets in books and became sad, the teacher identified this affect and discussed it to the limit of the children's wishes. Then the matter was dropped until other verbal or nonverbal cues alerted the teacher to pick it up again. Gradually the children became a little freer in discussing their feelings. In a general conversation about pets one day Cathy said, "Guinny died. That was Betsy (another name for the old pet)."

NICKY: I only like little guinea pigs.

TEACHER: You loved Guinny very much. You miss him, I know. You don't have to like this new guinea pig right away.

NICKY: It doesn't squeak like Betsy. I like to hear squeaking.

TEACHER: I know, that's one of the good things you can remember about Guinny.

NICKY: Yes, Guinny had pink eyes.

TEACHER: Yes, you have so many good things to remember.

A few days later in another discussion about pets Phillip started to say, "We don't have a guinea pig anymore; Betsy died," but Rutherford interrupted: "Phillip is sad because Guinny died." When Phillip denied this, the teacher asked, "Well, what are you, Phillip?" With what seemed like a concrete nonsequitur, Phillip announced: "I'm a boy." (Perhaps this was not a nonsequitur, but Phillip's way of expressing his feelings that boys were not supposed to show sadness and cry.) The teacher responded, "Yes, Betsy is dead, but we have a new guinea pig to care for." Phillip said, "He needs love. I do that when I hold him."

On another occasion, the boy in whose house the school pet had died expressed his worry by asking, "Why did Guinny die? Maybe he died because we fed him too much. Maybe he died because I loved him too much." The teacher tried to correct such guilt-ridden distortions.

Here are the children's reactions to the death of the guinea pig in chronological sequence. On February 19th, the children were told that the guinea pig had died. On February 22nd, a new guinea pig was brought to the classroom. By March 15th, none of the children had brought the new guinea pig any food or held him except for Polly, who on March 8th sat quietly holding and petting the new guinea pig in her lap. By April 9th, the children had passed through their grief for the old guinea pig and were ready to accept the new one in his own right. They were assisted in this "mourning" by the auxiliary ego of a very sensitive schoolteacher. They called the new guinea pig Piggy on April 9th, and by April 11th the children were heard to say, "We have a pet, Piggy."

The children's initial reactions were denial and displacement, which can be seen in part as a refusal to accept reality, a refusal to "mourn" the loss of their pet. With the teacher's help, these eventually gave way to more appropriate expressions of grief for their lost pet, their generic sounding "Guinny" or their more intimately loved "Betsy." Finally, when the period of grief and "mourning" had elapsed, the children were able to accept their new pet, not as a painted ghost of an object they were unwilling to relinquish, but as a pet in his own right.

The teacher also dealt with the reactions of individual family members. One mother complained that all this talk about burying the guinea pig ran counter to her religious beliefs. She believed that cremation was a more appropriate form of burial. On the surface this sounded like a religious issue, but the teacher sensed that there were other more important worries at the root of her attitude. The real issue was, in fact, that the grandmother in this family was old and the family felt very uncomfortable discussing anything that pertained to death. The teacher was able to help this family understand that denial was not the most adaptive way of dealing with painful concerns. Another child in the class had "lost" her mother when she was six months old and ever since had been cared for by her uncle. The teacher sensed that the guinea pig's death and the classroom discussions of death had a very special meaning for this child and her family.

The child's and the adult's conception of death

It is obvious that these children did not wish to accept the death of their pet as a fact, even though it was explained to them rather graphically, by the nursery schoolteacher. But let us begin with an adult's conception of, and reaction to, death. In 1917 Sigmund Freud described the normal psychological mechanisms at work in mourning, comparing them to the pathological mechanisms at work in melancholia. Since then the psychoanalytic literature has reflected a continuing interest in the mourning of adults and children. Despite a wealth of literature, we do not have a clear picture of the psychological building blocks that the developing mind uses to attain the ability to mourn. We do know that adults mourn. We have Freud's unequaled classical description of the processes of mourning. We do know that children react to the loss of important objects, but that the reaction is phenomenologically and descriptively different from that of adult mourning. If Helene Deutsch (1937) is correct in her notion that children do not grieve because their immature egos cannot sustain the difficult task of mourning, then it would seem that there must be developmental steps in the acquisition of these ego functions that seem to be lacking in children but are present in adults. How do children who cannot mourn become adults who can? Wolfenstein (1966) states that children cannot mourn until adolescence. In adolescence the normal task of object removal (Katan, 1937), the detaching of the libido from the primary objects and investing it in non-incestuous objects outside the family, is a kind of trial mourning (Freud, 1958). Wolfenstein believes that until this trial mourning has been accomplished in adolescence, mourning in the adult sense is not possible. She observed that prior to adolescence the opposite of mourning is the rule in children: the lost object is hypercathected in fantasy. There is a refusal to let go. Nagera (1970) reiterates Wolfenstein's hypothesis when he argues that children cannot mourn for fear of the developmental vacuum that acceptance of the loss would entail. Nagera maintains that the child needs the psychic representation of the lost important object to foster normal development.

Erna Furman (1974) disagrees with authors who say that young children cannot grasp the meaning of death. "In our experience, normally developed children above the age of two years could achieve a basic understanding of 'dead' if they had been helped to utilize their daily experiences with this goal in mind" (p. 50). She believes that the child will be able to comprehend the reality of death if the adults do not misrepresent or obscure the objective facts. She illustrates her argument with poignant case material:

Susie was barely three years old when her mother died. After being told this sad news, Susie soon asked, "Where is mommy?" Her father reminded her of the dead bird they had found and buried not too long ago. He explained that mommy, too, had died, and had to be buried. He would show her where whenever Susie wished. One month later Susie reported to her father, "Jimmy (the neighbor's six-year-old son) told me that my mommy would come back soon because his mommy said so. I told him that's not true because my mommy is dead, and when you're dead you can't ever come back. That's right, daddy, isn't it?" (p. 51).

One feels like applauding Susie for her ability to maintain her newly found reality testing, in the face of great temptation from Jimmy and his mother.

Primary and secondary objects

If these children's reactions constituted mourning, such a conviction needs to be reconciled with the objections of Wolfenstein and Nagera and others who contend that children cannot mourn important objects until the trial mourning of adolescence has been negotiated. The word important, and the concept of need-satisfying object seem crucial as this discussion is engaged. The child may not be able to mourn an object of such critical importance as mother or father or other substitute caretaker without the help of adults (Furman, 1964a). But a pet that is dearly loved but not as critical an object in the development of the child as mother or father can be mourned precisely because of this relative diminution in importance. The pet is a trial object, so to speak, which the child can learn to love or to mourn before he loves or mourns "in earnest" after adolescence. The word pet, the dictionary says, is of unknown origin, but petting is, as in foreplay, a kind of preliminary trial lovemaking. This suggests that we may not be incorrect in seeing the pet as a trial object, a transitional toy, so to speak, half human, half plaything, from which the child can learn some awesome existential lessons.

If a transitional object is the first not-me possession (Winnicott, 1953, 1971) which helps a child to define his body boundaries and separateness from mother and which provides an important self-soothing link to her when she is absent, we can conceptualize the pet as a not-me "living" possession of the child. Abrams and Neubauer (1975) have pointed out that beginning at birth, children have highly individualized approaches to "persons" as opposed to "things", certain children being more interested in people, others being more fascinated by mobiles and other inanimate objects. The quality of the attachment to persons and things is modified by development but continues to be a characteristic trait of a child's object relatedness. It would seem that a pet, neither person nor thing, can serve an important function for the child in his mastery of object relatedness and reality testing.

A six-year-old boy in analysis, struggling with murderous Oedipal hatred of his father, was very sad when his school guinea pig died. "I'm sorry for guinea," he said. "The one thing I'm not sorry for is ants. You can kill one without feeling guilty." Then he turned his attention to some metallic cars he had brought with him as substitutes for the guinea pig. One can sympathize with his struggle to find an object, human or animal or metallic, with which to play out his Oedipal wishes and master his sense of guilt. The ant can be dispatched without guilt, but not the beloved guinea pig, nor the beloved father, for that matter. The availability of objects (be they father or friend, guinea pig or ant, metallic car or other toy) and his relationship to them will influence the variety of his solutions as he struggles with his wishes and affects.

In a sense, the child is the first human "possession" of adults, the primary objects who care for him. He is a citizen without rights in a world of adults. Many factors will determine his growth and development, from possession to human being in his own right—full citizenship, so to speak. The child's own possessions (animate and inanimate) provide him with a secondary world, where he is master. The pet, for instance, can be loved, hated, lost, mourned, but always from the point of view of the child as active owner of the pet, as opposed to the child as a dependent possession of the parents. While the concepts of the child as a possession of his parents and the pet as a possession of the child are gross oversimplifications of the over-determined, complicated ways in which children relate to parents and pets, nevertheless one senses that the child's modulation and mastery of his impulses and affects in the secondary world of pets help his adaptation and development in the primary world of his relations with parents and peers.

I suggest that because the child's dependency on the primary objects is so great, their loss generates affects, which threaten to overwhelm the child, but similar, though attenuated, affects can be mastered and studied in the secondary world of pets, toys, and imagination. A pet can be more easily mourned than a mother. A child's reactions to the loss of secondary objects are easier to observe because they are less overwhelming and less defended against. The secondary world offers the child's ego a playground for Greenacre's (1957) "love affair with the world," Mahler's (1968) "practicing" sub-phase of individuation, or Winnicott's (1971) "potential space" between the baby and the mother where "cultural experience or creative playing" can take place. The territories of the secondary world need not be restricted to issues of separation-individuation and "transitional" experiences: the six-year-old boy, mentioned earlier, was struggling with Oedipal conflicts in which a guinea pig and an ant had significant roles. W. H. Auden (1968) has described a primary world of objective reality ("We are born into it and by death disappear from it without our consent" p. 51) and secondary worlds that the poet creates out of his imagination. I would like to suggest that a pet is one of the important dramatis personae of such secondary worlds. The child has this living theatre at his disposal to help his psychological growth and development.

In the attempt to understand a child's "mourning," we may have to distinguish between this secondary world and the primary one, and separate the reactions to the death of primary objects from reactions to the death of secondary objects such as pets or friends. The literature has almost exclusively focused on children's reactions to the loss of primary objects. This may have given us a skewed definition and description of mourning in children, with the result that Nagera can say that mourning is impossible and inconceivable because of its threat to development; and Erna Furman, that it is possible only when adults help the child achieve it. The study of children's reactions to the loss of other than primary objects allows us to see mourning from another vantage point and describe it from a different angle. It seems reasonable to suggest that it will be easier for a child to recognize and describe his reactions to the loss of a guinea pig than it will be for him to recognize his reactions to the loss of a mother.

Mourning in children and adults

Another reason for the conventional wisdom (Miller, 1971) that children do not mourn may be that the extrapolation from adult phenomenology to child phenomenology has led us astray. Just as we were unable to find schizophrenia or depression in children as long as we looked for adult "symptoms" and used criteria gained from observations of adults, we may have been unprepared to recognize mourning in children because we were looking for the adult model, rather than observing children's reactions to loss and trying to understand them in their own right.

For example, a ten-year-old boy, on hearing of the imminent death of his grandfather, rode his bike and played with his skateboard all day. He had been told a few weeks earlier that his grandfather would probably die, but he put it out of his head. Now he had been told that it was cancer and that the grandfather would be dead in a few weeks. He rode his bike for hours and played with his skateboard for days. When his grandfather died two weeks later, the boy walked in a park and played ball for a while. He sat down and penciled the names of all his living relatives on a bench. Later he sat on a rock and pensively asked what was the best way to stop a ball from rolling down a hill. He explained how he would pursue the ball and place his shoe in front of it and stop it. Throughout this time, he was playing a game with a quarter, which he placed on his elbow, flipped, and caught before it reached the ground. At this point, he described to his analyst how his grandfather had been cremated. Later he found a strip of caps from a gun and used a quarter to ignite them. As they exploded and the smoke curled upward, he inhaled it through his mouth and nostrils and then exhaled. When the analyst suggested to him that the cremation had made his grandfather go up in smoke and that he was playing inhalation peek-a-boo to master his feelings about cremation and the death of his grandfather, he genuinely agreed. Two days later, he seemed to be in a better mood. While he avoided questions about his grandfather, he returned to the same rock, lay down and slept (or seemed to sleep) for a while. Days later when his mourning seemed complete, the analyst told him that he had the feeling children and adults "mourn" differently: adults seemed to slow down for weeks or months, look sad, and go over it in their memory. The boy explained that children had not known the lost object as long as the adults had and that was the reason for the shorter period of mourning in children. He went on to explain that adults did not have bicycles and skateboards to express their feelings with, and that was why they appeared so inactive and depressed. When asked what children would do if for some reason they were unable to be active in mourning and could not use their skateboards and bicycles, he replied that they would break out of their restraints and steal and rob.

Can one conclude from this brief vignette that the child is mourning in his own way? Children are more active than adults, and therefore also need the motor discharge pathways in mourning. Moreover, children have a different sense of time. What is a short time span to the adult seems like a very long one to the child. Freud (1917) suggested that a prerequisite for mourning is the narcissistic affirmation by the living of their own vitality compared to the dead and that this sense of healthy narcissism allows the ego to mourn: "the ego … is persuaded by the sum of the narcissistic satisfactions it derives from being alive to sever its attachment to the object that has been abolished" (p. 255). This child writes the names of himself and his living relatives on the bench to assure himself that he and the survivors are well. His affect is one of sadness and bereavement, but in the period of anticipatory mourning, he celebrates his aliveness on the skateboard; later, when confronted with actual loss, he is sad. He knows his grandfather has been cremated. He contemplates repair of his loss by stopping a ball from rolling downhill, or catching a falling coin, or inhaling and exhaling smoke. Obviously, one can say this is the opposite of mourning: a manic celebration of oneself on a skateboard, the denial of death with olfactory peek-a-boo, and the retrieval of lost objects; or one can say the child is fully aware of his grandfather's cremation and has a sense of loss, experiences the sadness, and handles his memories and affects in play and motor activity, all of which constitute his mourning. The child attempts to undo death in symbolic action as adults so often do in fantasy. Adult mourning is clearly different from this "active" mourning of the child, but we should not equate activity with absence of mourning. If we take the child's level of development and psychic organization into account, mourning on a skateboard begins to make sense. The adult has solidified and de-personified his internalizations so that his psychic structure is cohesive and well established, its stability being relatively independent of primary object attachments. He mourns in one way: he withdraws into himself and reviews his memories and affects in a quiet, slow, sad, contemplative, and motorically inactive way. The child's internalizations are still relatively dependent on the primary object attachments; his development, far from settled, continues to pull in the direction of growth and maturation. He will mourn in another way, commensurate with his level of development and psychic organization: he will be sad, in an active way. He will "surround" his sadness with current developmental issues. He will mourn on a skateboard.

Reflections on the psychic fate of a painted guinea pig

The children are now grown-ups and one wonders what residue of their nursery school experience informs their consciousness or unconsciousness after all these years. I myself have a screen memory that dates (or so it seems) from my second year of life. The family had moved from one location in the city of my birth to another and my grandmother returned a pair of red pull-ups (rudimentary childhood trousers) that had been forgotten in transit. The color and the scene of the event in the garden of my new home have remained with me ever since, not unlike the significance of colors in Freud's celebrated 1899 paper on screen memories. I introduce my own memory by way of speculating about the fate of the painted guinea pig (or at least its psychic representation) in the older minds of the children described in this study. (The fate of screen memories in psychoanalysis is a topic I will address in greater detail later in Chapter Seven.) At this juncture I will only speculate briefly on what their experience must have meant to the children and how it might have affected their subsequent development. A school curriculum for very young children does not often include lessons about sorrow and loss, death and sexuality, life instincts and death instincts, Eros and Thanatos. It would be perverse, even insane, to manufacture tragedy as a way of enriching a child's curricular experience, but when loss and death occur it would be equally inappropriate to leave children unassisted as they struggle to come to grips with their emotional reactions. One would like to think that what these children experienced in nursery school may have been of benefit to them as they met with subsequent inevitable losses and hardships along the way. If mourning represents the human mind at its most realistic and courageous, it seems wise to come to the assistance of children when they first encounter it and struggle to manage it. If they paint over it at three, or mourn on a skateboard at a later age, they are also able to address it more directly if adults do not mistake paint and skateboards for callousness or absence of an emotional reaction. Later in this book, the play of children of the Shoah will be mentioned, children whose tragic curriculum included playing with death, not as concept but as reality, and their extraordinary attempts to deal with it; and in the final chapter I will address mourning once again and the critical role it may have played in Freud's masterpiece *The Interpretation of Dreams*.

I have begun this book with loss and the initial reaction of self-deception that attempts to ignore the impact of loss. But the mind that wants to deceive itself is also the mind that is eager to enlighten itself. If repression is the initial instinctive reaction to psychic pain, banished insight is not content to remain in exile forever. The tension between the psychic force that opts for repression, and the psychic force that insists on insight and enlightenment, will be the subject matter of the next two chapters, as the odyssey proceeds, propelled by the forces that advance it, and obstructed by the forces that impede it.

CHAPTER TWO

Repression and its vicissitudes

"But of the tree of the knowledge of good and evil,
thou shalt not eat of it."

—Genesis 2: 17

To my knowledge Freud never used the concept of painting over to signify the act of repression, but I have no doubt that his poetic soul would have empathized with the nursery children who, at first, hid their grief with a perceptual distortion of reality. It was Freud after all who said of his indirect analytic work with Little Hans that he never had a finer glimpse into the soul of a child. "Who painted him?" in its stark simplicity gives us a glimpse into a young child's mind also as the question reveals some nascent knowledge of death and loss even as it insists on repressing it. "The theory of repression is the cornerstone on which the whole structure of psychoanalysis rests" Freud wrote in his *History of the Psychoanalytic Movement* (1914). In the index of Freud's writings (Standard Edition XXIV, 1974) there are several hundred references to the word repressed, not surprising perhaps since the subject occupied him throughout his psychoanalytic life. Freud claimed at first (1914) that "the theory of repression quite certainly came to me independently of any other source" and later in 1925 that "it was a novelty and nothing like it had ever before been recognized in mental life." However when Otto Rank showed him a passage in Schopenhaur's *World As Will And Idea*, which "coincided with my concept of repression so completely" Freud had to concede that he owed the "chance of making a discovery to my not being well read." What philosophy recognized by intuition Freud arrived at through "laborious psychoanalytic investigation" (Freud, 1914).

Initially repression and defense were synonymous for Freud but the need for conceptual specificity would gradually modify his concept of defense. In 1897 he had introduced the concept of projection and in 1909 he had spoken of "two kinds of repression", one being the complete expulsion of the idea from consciousness in hysteria, as opposed to the defensive mechanism in obsessional neurosis whereby the emotional cathexis from an objectionable idea is not completely expelled but merely displaced. Later he proposed to restrict the concept of repression to the mechanism of complete expulsion from consciousness that occurs in hysteria, using the word "defense" as "a general designation for all the techniques which the ego makes use of" in dealing with conflicts.

Brenner (1957) described the evolution of Freud's ideas on repression, four fertile periods of Freud's creativity needing to be differentiated (1894–1896, 1900–1906, 1911–1915, 1923–1939) to do anything close to justice to the elegance, depth and originality of Feud's ideas. Between 1894 and 1939 the conceptualization of what was being repressed and of what agency was responsible for instigating and maintaining it, would undergo drastic revisions as Freud's clinical experience and theoretical insights cross-fertilized each other. If memory was the original target, eventually instinctual drive would be identified as the provocateur that stirred up anxiety, thereby signaling the ego to discharge countercathexes which attempt to keep the anxiety-provoking sexuality or aggression out of consciousness. Summing up the fourth phase of Freudian thought, Brenner writes: "the effects of repression are twofold. In the first place, the drive and its derivatives are excluded from the ego ... However, the repressed drive persists in the id and exerts a persistent pressure in the direction of emergence into consciousness and of gratification ... The return of the repressed implies a failure of repression." In 1933 Freud suggested that "symptoms are derived from the repressed, they are, as it were, its representatives before the ego" (p. 57). The additional feature of repression which I want to emphasize suggests that there are perhaps a myriad of representatives of the repressed that parade themselves before the ego with a subtlety that renders them practically invisible to the ego's radar system. These representatives are not as ego-dystonic as symptoms and when they present themselves "before the ego" the court of the ego may not even recognize the presence of these ambassadors of the unconscious. In a reversal of the emperor's clothes story, they are the clothed representatives of the repressed, but the ego may be totally unaware of such a subtle wardrobe. The classical depiction of repression seems to need the concept of a "failure of repression" to account for the psychic manifestations of the reappearance of what was expelled, what Freud called the "impulsion to break through into consciousness." Is there no way to dramatize this feature of repression from a more active, more functional point of view than portraying it as a failure? I believe there is, and in this chapter I want to introduce the idea that repression does not only expel ideas from consciousness, it seems to struggle to recycle them back into consciousness in many derivative forms. "The return of the repressed" captures some of my meaning but not all since I believe "the return of the repressed" has a pejorative ring to it as if the objectionable expelled guest was crashing a party and making an unwelcome re-entry into a psychic space where it did not belong. The idea for a more adaptive return of the repressed came to me when an analysand used the word "re-press" in a dream. This was a pun and not a pun all at once since on one level it referred to the music industry's craft of re-pressing multiple discs from one original master disc, while on an another level it "played" with the classical Freudian concept of repression. Let me describe these clinical events in more detail so that the concept I am introducing will be clearer.

As mentioned already I was surprised when an analysand used the word "re-pressed" in a dream. It was used in a way I had never heard before or at least had never really considered before. The word appeared in a dream in which the analysand had stolen some records in a music store, thinking them to be original discs. But they turned out not to be originals: they were re-pressed. A pun in waking life is a clever exploration of ambiguity in the service of humor. When it occurs in a dream, (see Chapter Six for a more detailed discussion of a pun in a dream) one can assume that the manifest ambiguity has some connections to deeper meanings in the latent realm of the psyche as well, bringing to mind Empson's argument that the multiple ambiguities of a literary text are legion and probably can never be mined in toto. Psychoanalysis is not a literary text of course, but an ongoing experiential collaboration where multiple meanings are dissected in the service of the mental health of the analysand. If a pun in a dream is riddled with ambiguities, as just mentioned, both products, (pun and dream) occurring in the context of an unfolding transference neurosis have even more subtleties and meanings and days' residues informing them than would be the case in a non-analytic context. Since the analysand in question was an avid rare record collector and therefore very interested in the music industry's constant production and reproduction of discs and records, the word re-pressed seemed to have little ambiguity to it for him at first. Records were re-pressed all the time. Nothing unusual about that. However, given that this word appeared in a dream in mid-analysis where records of the past are constantly being scrutinized and where the word repressed, if not used every day is never that far removed from the awareness of both parties to the analytic dialogue, this "new" word and its multiple ironies could not be denied. At first the analysand with a very characteristic dismissiveness, pooh-poohed the excessive Freudian interest in such masturbatory word games, but gradually the psychoanalytic play with the concept proved most fruitful. At least three meanings of the word repress began to gradually become familiar shorthand concepts of a unique collaborative language, the sort of shared linguistic intimacies that are probably the hallmark of all intense analytic dialogues. One meaning was the classic psychoanalytic meaning: to bar or rid something from consciousness. Another was the music industry concept: to re-press an original vinyl mold thereby making multiple copies of an original piece of music. The third meaning was however the most therapeutically fruitful, a meaning that developed over time: re-press began to mean pressing that aspect of conflict which had been initially repressed (in the psychoanalytic sense of the concept) into the new service of insightful reconsideration, a thoughtful rehashing rather than a dismissive unconscious action that makes conflict assessment impossible.

This rehashing or pressing of the formerly repressed into new service could not be called "working through" which is surely a later phenomenon but rather a "working into," so to speak, as the return of the repressed, that the free associative process facilitates, gets reconsidered and made use of in a new way. The formerly repressed psychic content is "worked into" the ongoing psychoanalytic process the way an artist analogously works one pigment into another to get the results he needs. This seems a more active way to conceptualize the opportunity the ego has when the return of the repressed offers it a chance to rework conflict in a more adaptive way. The idea of a failure of repression, which is the traditional way of describing these dynamic events, seems too passive a depiction of this opportunity for redress of the neurotic or the habitual. This third meaning of re-press seemed to quickly oust the second meaning almost completely (the music industry concept) so that from a clinical point of view, conflict, subsequently, seemed to be a choice between pressing something out of awareness (the usual psychoanalytic sense of repress) or pressing something into the new service of conscious insight, where it can be played with until the most adaptive resolution of conflict can be arrived at. This third meaning of repress may have co-opted its terminology from the music industry definition of the word but it had altered the meaning significantly, if not totally. The new meaning, after all, did not imply a slavish reproduction of an original created by someone else, but an exploration of variations on one's own themes, the analysand championing his own artistry rather than recycling someone else's. In a sense the collaborative work had "invented" a sort of primal word with an antithetical meaning: repress could mean any psychic avoidance of conflict or re-press could mean the constant attempt not to avoid any affect, no matter how painful, but to try to learn to use all affect and conflict as a signal, a signpost that would allow the mind to continue its exploratory journeys rather than abandon them.

Let me describe the analytic process in more detail so that the reader has more than abstraction to guide him as he considers the clinical legs of the argument this presentation stands on.

Clinical section

Jeremy C was a thirty-year-old Russian expatriate, an Oxford graduate who declined all invitations to join mainstream culture in any conventional manner. Having inherited great intelligence and wealth, he seemed to defiantly use the latter to minimize the former, or at least to make it seem so to family and peers. He did not seek to have his thesis published since this might have propelled him toward an academic career that would have bored him. In fact, he left his newly adopted country behind when conventional success seemed certain, and settled in New York instead, where he wrote music and poetry but seemed totally disinterested in having either published. He had a devoted cama- raderie of male friends but his heterosexual relationships seemed to last six months and then get disbanded, the unconscious agency completely unknown to him until analytic insights would subsequently make him aware of the hidden motivational system that pulled the strings and shaped behavior. An intense relationship with a woman had floundered in his mid-twenties. She subsequently married and Jeremy continued to carry a torch, aware that he was licking old wounds rather than allow- ing any healing to occur. Subsequent short-lived relationships seemed to reflect this bitterness about the lost love, earlier genetic antecedents completely out of awareness until analysis jogged some memories that had been long dormant.

Jeremy sought analysis when he began to realize that life was passing him by: he found himself much too comfortable with intense marijuana intoxication which tended to isolate him with his music and poetry and even began to alienate him from his male peer group. Added to this was a grief following his father's death that began to feel more like a linger- ing depression than a normal reaction to loss. Despite his great skepti- cism about all things intellectual, he seemed to be genuinely interested in analysis particularly since his great cynical humor was welcomed as part of the analytic process. It was after all the characterological raw material that fueled not only resistance, but revealed the genetic path- ways into the repressed core of the dynamic past as well.

The clinical hour in which Jeremy used the word repress in an unu- sual way (at least to a psychoanalyst's ears) will now be reported in detail. It is the third year of analysis. Analysis has allowed Jeremy to enter a long-term relationship with a woman without bolting after the customary six months. A new symptom emerged however: intimacy, which seemed genuine and intense, could not include sexual pleas- ure after about one year into the relationship. The brother-sister con- notation seemed odd to Jeremy since he had no female sibling. Any incestuous implication relating to his mother seemed like farfetched psychoanalytic cliché rather than any psychological concept Jeremy could associate to profitably. Jeremy sensed that there must be genetic antecedents. He was just unable to fathom the depth psychology that may have spawned him but also eluded him. The genetic past had been recounted but could not be seen as formative in any genetic dynamic way at least at this stage of the analytic process. Jeremy's mother was a novelist who had married a man twenty years older than her who was a respected journalist with an international reputation. The mother's cocaine addiction led to divorce. There followed a subsequent reconciliation after a two-year period of joint custody. While the divorce and reconciliation were "civilized" there was a turmoil and an uncertainty that left serious emotional scars. The period between Jeremy's fourth and tenth years of age were volatile. Jeremy's main defense seemed to have been isolation in his own room, an adaptation that fostered passivity, denial, disavowal and a sense of helpless fatalism.

The hour began with a dream, which has been mentioned earlier but will now be examined in detail.

> I am in a record store in London. I am trying to curb my manic habit of buying everything in sight. However I see some discs I cannot resist and I pocket them surreptitiously. They are original vinyl from the fifties and I am excited about my find even though I am guilty about the method of acquiring it. When I get home to my apartment, my friends point out that these are not the original discs I took them for. They are *re-pressed* records rather than the real thing.

Associations to the dream suggested that he is very guilty no matter how he tries to represent his wishes, foiled or satisfied. There is a kind of despair in the notion that the original record of emotional discourse with mother or father can never be retrieved, no matter how crucial the lost information. The best we can come up with are re-pressed records of lost originals. This sense of fatalism was an entrenched character trait that had multiple genetic determinants. One meaning considered was identification with a father who had remarried at a late age, his inevitable death leading to early abandonment of the analysand. The anger was muted by this defensive identification, which embraced the fatalistic, rather than railing against the father's shortsightedness. Another meaning was an identification with the mother who had curbed her appetites eventually and conquered her addiction. He too had curbed his marijuana use and his manic "consumption" of records, but the sense of "what's the use, the originals are irretrievable, only re-pressed, pale imitations of the past", dulled the joy of any achievement. Life, like analysis itself, is a lost cause, a disheartening pursuit of repressed meanings when all that can be realistically achieved are replicas, re-pressed vinyl imitations of an irretrievably lost childhood.

Jeremy had always made fun of interpretations, seeing them as "far-fetched" attempts to connect current reality with "clichés" from the past. He became aware over time that his "teasing" of the analyst was not without significance. As a child, he did not feel safe criticizing either parent, the mother's addiction and the father's advanced age, making both authorities seem too austere or too vulnerable to be "used" adaptively in the Winnicottian sense of the word. Allowing some humor, sarcasm, teasing, playfulness to emerge in the transference took courage and eventually became appreciated as an achievement. The double meaning of the word repress, at first sneered at as the kind of Freudian masturbatory word play that analysts get off on, came to be admired as an idea that had emerged in one of his own dreams and need not be demeaned so quickly. In fact, the obligatory demeaning of his own creativity, whether it be a university thesis or insight extracted from dream, was a form of neurotic cliché that attempted to downplay and numb all spontaneity. Labeling interpretative or reconstructive analytic work as cliché or farfetched theorizing was a form of resistance that could eventually be identified as such.

As he began to realize that his own insight into the nature of repression need not be ridiculed, he became deeply interested in his own dreams as uncanny records of the past, an amalgam of current realities and ancient memories that could ironically point the way into the future even though they seemed to obscure the blueprints of the past. His wish to curb his appetite for acquiring records, a greed to possess all the records in the world, could be accomplished in daylight perhaps, but sleep had its own rules. In the dream, he "appropriates" the "original" record he coveted but tried not to buy, but ironically, on arriving home with his stolen goods, he discovers it's not the original at all, it's a disc that was re-pressed. His associations make it clear that his feelings for the analyst are replicas of his feelings for his parents. Are the feelings that are generated in analysis real at all or cheap re-pressed records of forgotten memories? This questioning of the genuine nature of his feelings for the analyst was a transference of his mistrust of the primary caretakers and an abiding sense of his own passivity. His childhood solution to psychological conflict had been to retire to his room and attempt to disavow and deny all that he felt. The adult version of this habit led to loneliness, isolation, marijuana, pornography and the total decline of sexuality in his intimate relationship with his girlfriend. Analytic insights began to help him to understand the transference and its origins in the genetic records that shaped his childhood. His mistrust of analyst and girlfriend led to the insight that he shuts us out to make us feel what as a child he felt when his mother seemed to abandon him in a cocaine induced altered state of consciousness. He was aware that he was treating his girlfriend like a sister, the incestuous implication of his depriving her and himself of sex very disturbing to him. That should remain repressed in the old sense of the word, the original destroyed, never to be re-pressed into some current version of itself. A dream represented these ideas graphically and strikingly.

> I am in Paris, close to the Eiffel Tower. I am with an old girl friend who has a fictitious name, Mimi Seulement. She is so petite as to seem doll-like. By contrast I have an enormous dick and I feel triumphant as I ignore her.

This dream was analyzed from many vantage points. The relevant associations in this context referred to Mimi, which he believed to be a reference to "me me", the two aspects of his own self we had been focusing on. From a genetic point of view, he believed that the dream recaptured the ancient conflict of child and mother. He is angry with mother for turning away from him, finding cocaine more "attractive" than her own child. But he is unable to articulate any of his feelings toward her since he does not trust her as witness or custodian of his challenging affects, nor does he feel safe turning toward father for explanations and redress of the traumatic ambience much of his childhood was imbued with. By depriving his current girlfriend of sexual pleasure, he realizes that he is playing both parts of the sadomasochistic enactment: he is a version of Mimi, one me cruelly withholding love, the other me the perplexed victim of the deprivation.

In another dream:

> I am riding on an elephant and a long-necked monstrous creature appears. Suddenly his mother, in the guise of some Hollywood monstrous diva, appears out of nowhere and hacks the neck of the long-necked creature off. The whole thing is terrifying, one monster attacking another.

Jeremy was amazed that he had depicted the saving mother in the dream as no less monstrous than the long-necked creature that was threatening him. In genetic memory and its replay in transference, the invocation of parental or analytic goodwill could turn monstrous with an alacrity that not only alarmed Jeremy but alerted him also to the repressed lairs of his unconscious underworld where confounding convictions were spawned and then went into hiding. The analytic process seemed to have become more and more of a laboratory where unconscious danger could be studied: leaving the office after the session about the long-necked monster, Jeremy lingered to look at the miniature sculptures on the analyst's desk. Pointing to a figurine with its mouth open Jeremy joked, "Maybe you should cover it up. Better still, maybe you should put my records there in stacks instead of the sculptures." Could transference and analytic process be better characterized than this wish to put all unconscious records on the drawing board, the originals and the repressed replicas, the intricate archeology of repressed original memories and the re-pressed, recycled psychic derivatives that constitute the complexity of a human mind struggling with its conflicts?

I would like to close this clinical section with one further excerpt from the analytic process, which highlights again the concept of original records and how they get repressed in both senses of the word. Jeremy reported a dream:

> I am driving on a highway. I come to a large warehouse, a cave-like building. I feel lonely inside the sheer size of it. I see that there are stacks of records. I'm rummaging through them: lots of useless stuff, some good things. I find a record by Gran' Piccolo (a rapper). Even in the dream I seem amused by this condensation of "Big" and "Small." There are younger people around. They are record hunting too. I feel competitive with them. I get the Gran' Piccolo record for Jill (his girlfriend).

His first association suggests that he feels more generous with his girlfriend lately and he is proud of this achievement. Giving her things is starting to please him more. "Positive shit like that." Further associations to shit lead to the concept of shit as "an original record" of love (a gift to the parents) and hate (a hatred of being socialized, conventionalized). This is followed by a memory of a potty and a nursemaid and a triumphant bowel movement. "A gift to the mother," Jeremy sneers. He starts to ridicule these genetic "clichés" and how the analyst has contaminated him "with all this Freudian bullshit." But he goes on to remember a dream about an old girlfriend "shitting her pants" and his "getting off on it." After a period of teasing the analyst about interpretations as clichés, a more sober mood takes over. Is the dream a return to the mother-child dialogue as opposed to isolating himself in his room and cutting himself off from her? In the dream is he returning to bring her a gift, a reversal of what he really seeks, a replay of the wish that she would now and in the past have always given him the gift of maternal stability and love, without substance abuse coming between them? He begins to think of his nephew, a child of recently divorced parents. His mother and brother are both against providing analysis for the nephew and Jeremy plans to challenge both of them. He will stick up for his nephew, the way he wishes someone had for him and provided him with analysis as a child, not just as an adult. His association to Gran' Piccolo (the aforementioned rapper) was very significant. Earlier in the analysis he had dreamed about two warring rappers and his wish "to bring them together." In that same dream a new born child with placenta still attached was thrown carelessly at the bottom of his bed. Should he rush it to the hospital or forget about it? The condensation of Giant and Dwarf (the rapper Gran' Piccolo) in the current dream seemed like a continuation of this theme. He is bringing a record by Gran' Piccolo (a representation of himself as baby and grown-up) to his mother. He has repressed this record, dwarfed it for years. Now as a Giant (grown-up man) he insists that his dreams and his analysis in toto will re-press that original record of shit, and love, and hate, and straight talk turned crooked, into a new active image of himself, a free associating rapper who is not afraid of his own original records, nor all their derivatives and replicas in the conflicted music of everyday life, that "dance to the music of time" that characterizes the fugal complexity of the human condition. "I repress, therefore I am," Jeremy chortled, very much aware of the ambiguities that had once shackled him, but now could set him free.

Discussion

Marcel Proust would argue that while the past is within the present, "all the efforts of our intelligence are futile" in evoking it. "The past lies hidden beyond the mind's realm and reach, in some material object (in the sensation that material object gives us). And it depends entirely on chance whether or not we encounter that object before we die" (Proust, 2003). Freud, less fatalistic than Proust perhaps, argues that the repressed past is accompanied nonetheless by "a strong upward drive, an impulsion to break through into consciousness." (Freud, 1933)

Where Proust views chance and the sensations aroused by material objects as the royal road to recovery of the past, Freud exploited this "impulsion to break through into consciousness" which free associations, transference and their analysis makes possible, not leaving it to chance, therefore, but creating and cultivating the scientific situation and atmosphere that would best "recapture" it.

If the mind can re-press as well as repress, the dream in which the pun made its appearance seemed to have the defensive strategy of seducing the censor, and even the analyst perhaps, into believing that the manifest declaration of innocence (an "original" sin has not been committed, only a copy has been made off with) absolves the dreamer from the implication or examination of any of his latent wishes. This would seem to be an example of self-deception insisting on the unique meaning of re-press as a mere copy of an original (the music industry definition). I will suggest in Chapter Six that when a well constructed joke or a parapraxis takes center stage in the manifest display of a dream, these extra "manifest" flourishes are designed to throw the censor off the scent of urgent instinctual expressions clamoring for prime time offstage, so to speak, in some latent theatre of the mind. Jeremy's dream pun suggests a similar intent perhaps: to beguile the censor with manifest content, the better to deflect attention from the latent.

In Jeremy's case the latent incestuous wish is denied: he cops a lesser plea by admitting that he only made off with a replica. Jeremy's insistence that he merely re-pressed the original, nothing more than that, does expose however, as analysis proceeds, that the unconscious wish for total incestuous possession of the wayward mother, and triumph over the father, is not about to relinquish its unconscious Oedipal monopoly: there is a stubborn refusal to settle for the re-pressing of the old and primitive into the new developmental adaptations reality testing calls for. Only the original repressed can satisfy this incestuous hunger. The return of the repressed merely rubs salt in the narcissistic wounds of this "jilted" lover. At this juncture one could argue that the three meanings of repress mentioned earlier are jockeying for power as the conflict has revealed more of its facets in the analytic situation. The classic psychoanalytic meaning of repress (to shun from consciousness) would seem to have most power as the incestuous wish to make off and make out with the "original" object of desire is rejected, on the one hand, from a conscious point of view, but secretly enjoyed, however, from an unconscious point of view. The music industry's definition of re-press offers an appealing self-deceptive defensive strategy: "I never touched the original. It was a mere replica. I am not guilty." But a third meaning of repress is beginning to find a foothold as clinical process presses forward however haltingly, allowing a regressive pathway, ironically, to eventually lead it toward its progressive goals. Jeremy is beginning to sense that if his clever pun could be exploited by the dream work for neurotic purposes while he was asleep, he could put this playful creative potential to work when he's awake also! In that spirit, he did playfully suggest that the analyst could replace the figurines on his desk with stacks of Jeremy's old records, an obvious assertion of his sense of possession of the analytic space, his personal records more important than inert archeological replicas of the past.

It could be argued that the thesis of this entire chapter rests upon the shaky foundation of puns and word-play. But if one acknowledges that the essence of all conflict has to do with original records and how they were repressed in an early context and pressed back into service in a later context (re-pressed in the new sense) the complexity of these dynamics of obfuscation and disclosure are further layered when one considers the etymology of the word "record." Partridge (1958) reminds us that the word record comes to us by way of OF-MF (old French-medieval French) record, which meant memory. It was derived from OF-EF (old French-early modern French) "recorder", to remember for oneself, to recall to another. The earlier Latin recordari (re=back, cor=heart or mind, -ari=the infinitive i.e. to bring back to mind), reminds us that heart and mind, affect and intellect are integral to memory and all records of it.

I have argued that Jeremy has learned and is continuing to learn how to extract meaning from unlikely sources, how to mine the ambiguities of old records and their derivatives in dreams and puns and all aspects of character, symptom and behavior. I have emphasized how the mining of the multiple meanings of a pun in a dream led to a kind of dialectical discussion of an antithetical way of thinking about repression (at least in one analytic context). This emphasis on one word, one defensive concept and its ambiguities is not meant to demean or diminish the over-determined complexities of the rest of this particular analysis or all analyses in general for that matter, but merely to suggest that each clinical moment is part of a multi-textured fabric, each thread an integral part of a whole. If one thread can unravel the whole cloth, it can also instruct us, if pursued with care and respect for the loom and the fabric-maker, how the complex stitchery of the whole enterprise got started.

I have described how two psychical forces inform the structure of repression itself. In the next chapter insight will be conceived of as an act of transgression that is forever trying to reconcile itself with the sense of authority it insists on challenging. In the subsequent chapter on transference two psychical forces can be seen again: the wish to reveal and the wish to conceal all at once manifested in a single attitude toward the analyst. The whole book is a reflection of these conflicted psychical forces that seem to be reflected in infancy as the child turns curiously toward the desired perception, and away from the less desirable or threatening one, the wish to sleep, the contrary wish to be ever alert, a conflict as old as biology itself. We have just reviewed the contribution of these inherent attitudes to repression; later we will see them at work in dreams and transference, but now let us proceed to a chapter on insight, where an act of transgression tries to constantly reconcile itself with an act of compliance as the mind struggles to enlighten itself and keep itself ignorant all at once.

CHAPTER THREE

Insight as an act of transgression

Know Thyself

—Ancient Delphic Inscription

To thine own self be true and it must follow as the night the day
thou cans't not then be false to any man.

—*Hamlet*, Act One, Scene Three, William Shakespeare

Introduction

If the theory of repression is the cornerstone upon which the whole
structure of psychoanalysis rests, insight could be described as a censored trove of information hidden beneath the cornerstone. However,
when the cornerstone gets lifted by interpretations, insight does not
always emerge as a sturdy conviction, a profound truth, that once established, retains its affirmative sense of selfhood restored. On the contrary,
insights that begin as epiphanies quickly become co-opted back into the
neurotic status quo again. Why? Surely the truth should be made of
sterner stuff. I want to examine this paradox in this chapter and offer an
explanation for it. Why would insight begin in a flash of recognition and

29

then just as quickly seem to recede back into the background from which it emerged? I have often wondered why an insight that seemed to begin with such enthusiasm, often within a few days seemed to retreat from its original enlightened, assertive position. Could it be transference I wondered, the mind retreating from its own knowledge in deference to parental authority? "Who am I to know anything in here?" as one analysand recently described the intimidating atmosphere of the consulting room. I was aware of many analysands' needs to qualify any statement with an immediate undoing of its intent, every assertive comment followed by the immediate qualifier "Well who can be sure of anything in a world so full of uncertainty?" There are other patients of course for whom insight really seemed to imply a need to correct the neurotic point of view their insights had exposed. They seemed healthier, more courageous, as if the "ahah" of their epiphanies, the "explosion" of insight, (as one analysand characterized his experience) had more follow through than those analysands whose insights seemed initially compelling, but then quickly lost their motivational momentum. Recently reading Yochanan Muffs book on *Love and Joy: Law, Language and Religion in Ancient Israel* I had a sort of epiphany of my own. Insight has often been referred to as an "ahah" phenomenon, a eureka of intuitive understanding that suddenly makes a bewildering complexity understandable. Muffs wrote about the biblical usage of the word "ahah" by the ancient prophets. Whether the biblical use of "ahah" can be equated with the modern English usage of the term "ahah" is an etymological question I do not feel equipped to answer. But my reading of Muffs did lead to some insights of my own that have informed the thesis of this theoretically speculative, yet clinically informed communication.

Muffs described how in the Bible it is not uncommon for the prophet, interceding on behalf of his people, to challenge God. At first he may pray and plead that God's wrath not be visited upon the people despite the depth of their sins. But when prayer and pleading fall on deaf ears, the prophet will criticize what seems to him to be the irrationality of God. When the prophet assumes this feisty, challenging attitude his address to the Godhead begins "AHAH", as in the following example from the book of Jeremiah, (Jer. 4: 9–10 as cited by Muffs (1992, p. 29). "Behold, on that day, says the Lord, the king and the priests will be shocked …. And I said "Ahah, Lord God. Is it you who have misled this people … by saying, "Peace is yours?" There are other examples that begin with this threatening Ahah: From the Book of Ezekiel (Ezek: 11:13, cited by Muffs 1992, p. 32). "Ahah, Lord God, are You about to destroy the remnant of Israel?" Or from the Book of Joshua (Josh 7: 6–7, cited by Muffs 1992, p. 32) "Ahah, Lord God, why have You brought this people across the Jordan only to give them into the hands of the Amorites to destroy us?" If the Bible is read as a clash between Divine Justice and human intervention, a clash, in more psychoanalytic terminology between the irrational, id-driven absolutism of the Superego and the more adaptive, compromise seeking, conflict-resolving ego, the "ahah" that begins the prophetic, challenging intercession is not too dissimilar from the ego's tactics when, in its moments of insight, it challenges the ferocity of the justice-hungry, God-like Superego, insisting that it assume a more rational, human, and humane resolution of psychological conflict.

I am indebted to Muffs not only for these Biblical references but also for his astute etymological clarification of the expression "Ahah." "Biblical dictionaries do not clearly distinguish the three particles hoy, oy, and ahah, but each word has its clearly defined semantic field. Hoy is not an expression of pain as much as an exclamation: Pay attention! Listen to what I have to say! For example, "Hoy, sinful people, nation heavy with iniquity! (Isa 1: 4). Oy is an expression of pain and fear: "Oy (woe is me), for I am finished" (Isa 6: 4) "Ahah expresses prophetic opposition to a divine decree: "I fell on my face and cried out, Ahah, Lord God, are you going to destroy the whole remnant of Israel by pouring out your wrath on Jerusalem?" (Ezek, 9: 8) as cited by Muffs, 1992, p. 29). One is tempted to suggest that the "ahah" phenomenon of psychoanalytic insight is as precarious as its Biblical counterpart as it confronts and deconstructs the complexity of over-determined conflict. It is as if insight as messenger or prophet is always in danger of being over-ruled by God-like Superego decree, its initial shout of protest (Ahah) become a wail of woe (Oy!), the joy of insight transformed regressively into despair. It is as if insight has exposed more than the mind is ready to integrate. Courage is quickly reined in by fear, fear disguised as indignation or outrage, perhaps, as it assumes the mask of God-like authority, and re-instates the status quo by decree. How insight becomes less and less intimidated by such Superego decrees, making such hauteur of conscience the raw material of fresh deconstructions and incremental insights is the story of psychoanalytic process, a story we turn to now as we leave the biblical context, enriched of course by some of its ancient insights.

Clinical section

In psychoanalytic process it is not uncommon for an interpretation to be met by insightful recognition, a collaborative affirmation that the analyst has indeed exposed an unconscious motif that had made its way into preconscious territory. The analyst's formulation has shone a light into depths that were not initially obvious to the analysand but quickly became accessible with this additional verbal nudge from the analyst. The resultant "ahah" of recognition is a joyful moment for both parties to this psycho-archeological excavation. Such moments of insight are not being glorified here since resistance to insight or outright rejection of an insightful interpretation can be crucial stepping-stones in and of themselves as the complex journey toward insight is traveled by both parties to the exploration. However, moments of insightful clarity do occur and their appearance and disappearance, their genesis and vicissitudes are the subject matter of this chapter. I could choose any number of clinical examples to illustrate this thesis but I will focus on only one. I will describe the moment of insight, the "ahah" phenomenon, and the fate of the "conflicted" insight over time.

Rebecca

Rebecca was a woman in her fifties, whose myth of the birth of her self seemed one-dimensional to the point of caricature. She believed that her mother had favored her younger brother from the time of his birth. A genetic narcissistic injury had been delivered her, but she "milked" it for complex developmental reasons throughout her life. When her own children were born she re-created this narcissistic injury in a most perverse manner: the birth of her two children were not greeted as "mitzvahs" but rather as a confirmation of her belief that she was "all washed up" as the new generation was being "favored" and displacing her. Her misanthropic view of procreation was that it was "favoring" the child and not the mother, youth being bestowed on the one and stolen from the other. This neurotic attitude often made it impossible for her to enjoy her considerable intellectual talents, her professional achievements, her status as beloved wife and mother. Over time she became able to laugh at her insistence on what she termed "the woe is me refrain," and develop a good-enough working alliance with the analyst. Like all working alliances it was not perennially stable, but subject to the vicissitudes of transference and the conviction that the analyst often "favored" other analysands over her. These clinical storms could be weathered however as psychological insight gradually gained ground and entrenched pathology receded.

I want to describe one moment of insight. Rebecca had developed the habit of trying to control the people around her, a habit that could alienate not only professional colleagues but her own children and in-laws as well. The ensuing alienation was often misperceived by her as proof of her theory that others were "favored" while she was ignored or abandoned. The genetic roots of this symptomatic and extremely maladaptive behavior were gradually being exposed in the free-associative process of analysis. She was beginning to understand that her mother was an envious, competitive woman who could not feel joy as her children met the challenges of developmental life successfully. The mother always implied that ambition was an affectation of the upwardly mobile, who "did not know their place." These assaults were leveled at the social upstarts all around her, but these maternal barbs did find their way of course into the developing unconscious ideals of her children. The analysand was beginning to realize that the mother she so loved and idealized had indeed planted some very undermining seeds in the depth psychology of her child. Empathy was allowing the analysand to recognize the depths of deprivation and low self-esteem her own mother's attitudes sprang from. Empathy was also allowing her to individuate and take some distance from this kind of maternal malnutrition, but not without great psychic pain and guilt of course.

It is the symptom of trying to control those around her that I wish to focus on. For instance she would insist that her own grown married children should read the books she read or attend the theatre rather than watch "trash" on television. She would insist they attend synagogue services when she did, even though they had outgrown many of their original religious beliefs. This habit of trying to control others led to the exact opposite of the intended goal, leading to alienation rather than secure attachment. It had been examined from many vantage points, and while some progress had been made in understanding its genetic roots and modifying its current manifestations, the analysand would often complain that the analyst had not helped her to explore the depths of it enough yet. This complaint was an exact replica of course in trans-ference of the maternal neglect she felt in childhood, the analyst not as deeply informed about her hidden needs as he should be. At this point in the analytic process, one interpretation, which seemed no different from many other formulations we had explored together, produced an "ahah" phenomenon. The analyst said: "You need to control the outside because you feel so out of control inside." This may not have been the actual wording but this was the essence of what I was trying to communicate. The analysand reacted excitedly, saying: "Ahah, that's it. That's it", with a whoop of recognition, as if all the previous analytic spade-work had cleared the sand off one archeological artifact that could now be seen in full exposure, as if for the first time. One insight seemed to spawn several others. She went on to recognize that she imagines that any assertion of desire or disappointment leads to loss of maternal love, and the only way she knows how to deal with such psychic terror is by pre-empting it: she crawls into a metaphoric cave of alienation and this self-administered exile protects her from maternal rejection. When she dares to emerge again from the cave, she is in an alien world that she must control dictatorially or all is lost.

By the next session she had retreated from this insightful state of enlightenment, describing her wish to control her daughter and have her parent her child the way the dictatorial grandmother insisted, as if the previous session had never happened. When we explored the "ahah" moment and the rather sudden repression of it, she said: "It was too much to hold onto." She went on to describe her mother's typical reaction to any ambitious developmental progress, any ambitious yearning in children, friends, or neighbors: "Who do they think they are?" This maternal contempt for assertion of any kind had a tendency to "shrivel the soul" to use the analysand's poignant words. When I invoked the transference with the suggestion that the same hostile reaction might be her expectation in the analytic process itself, she said: "But I need you to be yourself" and before these words were half out of her mouth she began to weep.

Subsequent years of this most productive analysis would return again and again to this moment of insight, how transgressive it seemed of a maternal authority that had been so slavishly identified with, and how essential it was to repudiate the characterological "Oy" that constantly sought to undermine the exultant "ahah" of individuation. In the transference neurosis that dramatized this conflict in a most transactional manner, the analysand became convinced that the analyst, like the mother, was envious of all her achievements. The reactive "oys" that sought to undermine the "ahahs" of experience were repudiated eventually as interpretation exposed transference as merely another iteration of a "protective" neurosis that believed that repetition and identification had to be slavishly adhered to forever. The working through of any insight is not accompanied by the same initial "ahah" of recognition perhaps, but without it, insight could not sustain its own daring to transgress against the internalized structures of prohibition that neurosis has built so cunningly and maladaptively throughout the past. As the analysand put it succinctly and humorously: "It's a great mitzvah that you are not really my mother!"

The initial "ahah" that heard the analyst's comment "you need to control the ouside since you feel so out of control on the inside" seemed so important to the analysand because it brought a new focus on intra-psychic life as opposed to the world of displacements, projections and externalizations Rebecca usually inhabited. "It was like being on the Titanic and seeing the tip of the iceberg in the distance" she would later explain. Neurosis tries to blind the ego's perception of reality, sensing correctly that seeing the tip of the iceberg is a call to arms. One must rush to the helm, advise the captain of the danger, get him to change course immediately, avoid crashing into the iceberg and steer the Titanic safely to port in New York instead. In terms of changing or dismantling the genetic architecture of her neurosis, Rebecca would have to con-front mother, father, grandfather, grandmother, and instead of identify-ing slavishly with their tyrannies, develop her own voice and spunk instead. All of this would have to take place in the newly discovered intrapsychic theatre of her mind that the "ahah" of recognition brought attention to. Controlling the outside was not nearly as daunting a task as entering the fraught theatre of conflict and chaos, trauma, affect and instinct within. Insight demanded a sweeping revisionism of past his-tory that seemed too much to ask of a child. "I see myself as a child con-fronting these issues" she said "rather than a grown woman. How can you ask a child to rewrite history? You can't put an old head on such young shoulders." The analyst's empathy for such states of resistance is crucial as the vessel of insight charts its course tentatively, daringly, and eventually successfully as analysis proceeds toward termination, ana-lyst and analysand, Titanic and person terminal, negotiating the rapids of transference and counter-transference all the way.

Discussion

The insight that Rebecca embraced with such an "ahah" of recognition suggested that the conscious need to control the objects in her life was directly related to an unconscious instability or chaos, an out-of-control state that she had lived with intra-psychically since early childhood.

I chose this particular moment of insightful recognition, not because of its extraordinary nature. On the contrary, it represents a rather ordinary clinical moment in the flux of analytic process. I believe I could have chosen from a selection of many others, some more dramatic in presentation and form; I believe any analyst would be able to choose from a similar collection of examples from his/her own experience. What I wanted to illustrate was not so much the drama of the "ahah" epiphany, but the regression from the moment of insight that seems as clinically significant as the "ahah" phenomenon itself. Why does the mind need to pull back from the precipice of its own daring? Why is courage so often only a preamble to the re-instatement of fearful, neurotic inhibition? In Rebecca's case I believe we need to reflect on the two images, one conscious, the other unconscious, that the insight connected with a whoop of recognition. The conscious image was Rebecca's habit of controlling the people around her, as if they were pawns in her chess game, a tyrannical game in which only Rebecca could make any moves. The more hidden image was Rebecca's conflicted, unconscious mind, and the genetics and dynamics that structured it. As a child Rebecca suffered from elective mutism for a few months until her first bout of psychotherapy restored her voice to her. The mutism was an elective silence she had imposed on the screaming match of her dynamic interior. She wanted to speak her mind and feel comfortable expressing herself emotionally to her mother. But her father was overseas for years, working as a foreign correspondent. Rebecca interpreted his absence as an affront to her self-esteem. Had she been loveable he would have stayed home. She didn't feel safe being angry with him and she felt she could not be angry either with her mother or grandparents. The risk of abandonment was too painful to consider. To survive, she must comply, "I erase myself: therefore I am", her rendition of the Cartesian principle. As described earlier, that meant complying with and identifying with mother's insecurities, envies, and prejudices. She pictured her mind as a dangerous place, a mined, condemned playground. This emerged most dramatically in a dream. She is in a coffin, not dead but alive. However she cannot find the key to release the lid and escape from her captivity. To escape seemed more dangerous than to insist on release from captivity in a coffin of her own making. To play dead was one way of avoiding the threat of living. In pseudo-death danger was ironically defeated. In life, safety lay in maintaining a low profile, or no profile at all. She must hide her identity to preserve it. It was more of a hidden self than a false self, but it was very unstable since Rebecca's anger was almost always on the verge of exploding inappropriately, in a controlling or sarcastic way with friends or professional colleagues.

The insight that seemed so welcome at first suddenly began to seem like a most transgressive proclamation, a Lutheran tract of defiance pinned to the door of some unconscious church, an act of transgression that would surely lead to excommunication. In psychodynamic terms, such was indeed the conflict that raged inside her unconscious mind, a conflict that had to be worked through in the transference, as described earlier. Insight, no matter how enthusiastically embraced at first, needs the laborious subsequent work of analysis to midwife it through the neurotic aftermath that tries to silence it. One act of transgression doth not a revolution make, and psychoanalysis can be characterized as a revolution that seeks to rid the mind of a hegemony of fear and inhibition that rules by constant intimidation. If insight seems to falter in its resolve after its initial spurt of enlightenment, it nevertheless does represent a call to arms, but both parties to the nascent revolution must not confuse the subsequent back pedaling with total defeat. The analysand needs the analyst's support at this crucial juncture. The key that opens the coffin of self-confinement is at hand, but the neurotic hand cannot or will not reach for it. The "ahah"of insight catches a glimpse of the key; the insight-squelching unconscious agency of neurosis keeps the key hidden. The analyst is and must remain the witness of the significance of what has transpired in the "ahahs" of recognition even when the analysand needs to deny that anything significant has happened at all. Working through is another name for the analyst's dual resolve not to lose sight of the patient's courage and his own responsibility to champion it, even when insight loses its nerve. If insight is momentary key-finding, working through (a topic I will devote much more time to later in Chapter Five) insists on holding onto the key and using it to get out of the coffin and staying out. Rebecca's dream confines her in a coffin and denies her access to the key that could release her. Waking insights locate the key, expose the neurotic structure of the dream; working through insists that insight is not a murderous transgressive mental activity that is forbidden. Insight exposes the backlash of defense that tries to silence it immediately, claiming that such insight is transgressive. Defense tries to maintain and perpetuate the neurotic conviction that meekness is essential and that insights need to be abandoned. The tree of knowledge belongs to the Yahweh of neurosis alone. The Adams and Eves of insight must remain locked up and keyless forever in the coffins of ignorance.

It is interesting to consider the fate of insight in psychoanalytic theory since "the talking cure" began. Initially it seemed like one of the cornerstones of psychoanalysis and what used to be called insight-oriented psychoanalytic psychotherapy. Nowadays it seems to be hardly even mentioned whenever the essential ingredients of psychoanalysis are being considered. This fall from grace is one aspect of my central thesis that I want to draw attention to. I have argued that if insight is defined as an essentially transgressive act, then by definition, it is only one aspect of a conflict that can perhaps never be settled or resolved once and for all. One transgresses, then reflects and reconsiders and eventually opts for compromise. Let us consider the genetic origins of such transgressions, reconsiderations and compromises. Whereas Freud initially conceptualized a "dissolution" of the Oedipus complex, subsequent psychoanalytic explorations would stress a more modest conclusion: dissolution seems impossible and probably even undesirable; resolution and compromise, repression and identification seem to have replaced the decisive absolutism that Freud's term "dissolution" implied (I have addressed this issue elsewhere: Mahon, 1991).

Insight is impossible to talk about without considering the structural "enemies" of insight. If neurosis begins with repression, insight begins when repressive tyranny is ousted and the mind takes stock of its contents from a more expansive point of view. In this brave new world of retrieved insight, where id was ego shall be and where superego was ego also struggles to be. It is not easy to imagine a total psychic truce between these warring entities, whether one speaks topographically or structurally. Tension, conflict, transgression, and compromise formation may all eventually lead to an adaptive détente, but lasting peace is a pipe dream. As humor (Woody Allen's) suggests "the lamb may lie down with the wolf, but the lamb won't get a good night's sleep!" In Chapter Two I have even suggested that repression itself is better conceptualized ambiguously: one mental force (to repress) wants to remove psychic contents from consciousness, another (to re-press) wants to return the repressed to active duty, so to speak, in the field of psychic combat and adaptation. Freud had considered all of this, made room for it, so to speak, in the notion of "the return of the repressed" but I am stressing a more complex adaptive return of the repressed than a purely symptomatic reprise of the unconscious entities. If insight is conceptualized as "transgressive" and repression itself conceptualized as bipolar or ambivalent, the ensuing conflict between the two is even more dynamic and unstable than previously recognized. In the experience of many psychoanalysts, this depiction of clinical process reflects the reality of the consulting room and its shifting instabilities of affects and conflicts more than theoretical absolutism does.

In the case I described, what began as epiphany quickly lost its "halo" of insightful brightness, (the "light bulb effect", the "ahah" feeling of having stumbled on something new), suggesting that one flash of intuition does not a lasting insight make. The short life span of this halo effect in the epiphany of insight can be compared to the seemingly opposite phenomenon that characterizes a screen memory. The brightness of the halo effect in a screen memory seems to last throughout a lifetime until analysis of the screen diminishes the brightness as analytic work "removes" the psychic energy from the screening function and makes it available elsewhere in the mind. This change in the subjective inner experience of the screen memory can even be used as one indication among many of a readiness for termination of psychoanalysis (see Chapter Seven for a far more detailed account of this intriguing subject). The comparison between screen memory and insight would suggest that insight's loss of its epiphanic brightness is an example of the transgressive nature of insight losing its nerve, so to speak, and backsliding defensively to a less transgressive stance of ignorant passivity. In other words, the screen's retention of its bright halo reflects its essential, central defensive self-deceptive nature. On the other hand, insight's refusal to maintain its epiphanic glow is a reflection of its fear of being too transgressive. In both instances, absolute enlightenment seems to be the casualty.

From a developmental point of view, one could argue that the first six years of life culminate ideally in a robust Oedipus complex, an instinctual robustness that does need to be tamed, however, for society's sake. The Oedipus complex is a description of love and transgression, of course, and the "solution" as opposed to "dissolution" that adaptation opts for at age six is détente. The six year old "agrees" to repress unruly, instinctual desire, identify with the authority of both parents, thereby resolving positive and negative Oedipal conflict, and settling in to the relative quiescence of latency. *Sturm und drang* is traded in for schoolbooks. Peers replace parents as the central protagonists in schoolboy and schoolgirl conflicts. What I am stressing of course is the precarious stability of this "dissolution" of the Oedipus complex. Latency may well be calmer than pre-latency psychology, but it is short lived. Adolescence will eventually arrive and transgression will resume with full force. Adulthood will eventually arrive. Adolescent storms will recede as the new challenges of adulthood are engaged with. But the clash between transgressive and appeasing forces in the human mind is hardly over. Psychic conflict merely shifts from one psychological venue to another. If psychic structure is the heir of the Oedipus complex, peaceful adaptation is the great structural goal. If society begins with the renunciation of instinct, renunciation is not absolute and at any moment may yield to transgressive desire. Insight is a witness of this never-ending conflict, this uneasy renunciation of instinct that structural civility demands. Neurosis, or any psychopathology, is a compromise formation. When the patient feels too compromised by the contractual arrangements neurosis depends upon (symptoms etc.) or insists upon, he seeks analysis. The analytic free-associative process begins to expose the enormous psychic price being paid to maintain certain contractual arrangements. Developing insights blow the whistle on some of the structural defects that threaten the stability of the psychic edifice. These are transgressive in the sense that they challenge complacencies, self-deceptions, and the status quo. Superego threats intimidate the ego's transgressive insights. Transgression has disturbed the peace. Transgression reconsiders, waffles, regresses. Sometimes it stands its ground. The drama of transgression and regression, courage and cowardice, insight and repression, and challenge and appeasement characterize clinical process throughout the analytic experience. Eventually insight is less willing to cave in to intimidation. Psychic structures become less dictatorial, less absolute. Compromise formation becomes less compromising. A healthy active adaptation replaces the passivities of neurosis.

This brief excursus into psychoanalytic developmental psychology was an attempt to emphasize that insight must not be thought of as a momentary epiphany that lights up the psyche, once and for all, ridding the mind of neurotic darkness forever. I believe it is wiser to think of insight as a transgressive phenomenon, an "ahah" to be sure, but an "ahah" in the biblical sense depicted by Muffs, that I referred to earlier. The biblical "ahah" is transgressive. As Muffs put it: "Ahah expresses prophetic opposition to a divine decree". It is interesting to reflect on the psychology of the prophet. Although "prophet" (pro-phetes) literally means to speak for God, or to interpret God's decrees, the prophet is not passive when he challenges or opposes divinity. I have been suggesting that insight also is transgressive as it opposes a psychic status quo. Its "ahah" reflects not just one moment of epiphany but an enduring struggle with the complexity of psychic structure as insight seeks to change the status quo, and prepare the mind for a more liberal, expansive vision of itself than what neurosis had settled for. Insight is transgressive to be sure, but its ultimate goal is a mind that is not neurotically compromised by its own restrictive, fearful structures.

The etymological distinction Muffs emphasizes between "ahah, hoy, and oy" in Biblical times finds a resonance in modern ears. "Oy" has retained its doleful cadence as an expression of woe, and the assertive "ahah" seems to be the chant of non-verbal affect whenever the mind connects the dots it had not focused on before, and comes up with a new discovery. Since reading Muffs I have become more attentive to nuances of speech sounds in the consulting room, my own and the analysand's. Before the analysand reaches the "ahah" moment or the analyst concurs with an affirmative, complementary grunt (Hmm, hmm) it seems that there are many non-verbal sounds emitted along the way toward insight as the two excavators proceed with their work and working through. "Huh" often seems to be a grunt of partial insight. I once questioned an analysand about the meaning of several non-verbal expressions. "Huh", which could mean that the scent of insight seems closer, could also mean the opposite, a feeling of being stumped. At times the same analysand would emit a series of "huh, huh, huh, huh" as if stumped but close to insight at the same antithetical moment. If primal words can have antithetical meanings (Freud, 1910) primal grunts can be over determined or antithetical also; which raises the issue of Spitz's global words, and even global non-verbal precursors of words. Spitz (1957) described an archaic dialogue between mother and child, a pre-verbal dialogue in which the devoted mother is forever responding to the feel of the infant's smiles, cries and voicings of all decibel range. "Ma, ma, ba, ba, da, da" sounds can have "global" meaning, according to Spitz, by which he means something akin to over determination at a much later stage of development. The mother must intuit what the preverbal sounds mean. Does it mean "I want milk" or does it mean "I'm happy and expressing joy"? In this archaic dialogue the mother is the first interpreter. Peter Wolff (1959) has described a similar phenomenon in regards to crying. An infant has a repertoire of cries, some wild (a scream of pain followed by a bone chilling long silent inspiration (of breath) or some simply fussy. The attentive, devoted mother becomes an expert interpreter of these cries.

The devoted analyst (is there not an arresting analogy between the analyst's evenly hovering attention and the alert attention of the astute mother who is neither over-protective nor negligent as she responds selectively and judiciously to the infant's expressions, always mindful of her great role as facilitator of the child's development?) is heir to this affective trove of preverbal communication. It is a trove that is repressed or at least unregistered in any linguistic form, an inaudible, invisible ghost of what Alvin Frank (1969) has called "the unrememberable and the unforgettable." One senses that it may be partially reregistered in the *nachtraglicheit* of the grunts of puzzlement or insight that can become the ground bass of free-associative linguistic analytic process, a non-verbal accompaniment of the major themes of the uncovering process keeps developing. I want to stress the idea that one runs the risk of not hearing all the music, all the voices of the fugal analytic communication if one's evenly hovering attention ignores the contribution of the guttural.

An argument can be made that affect, before it links itself to language and becomes social and communicative, is a non-verbal private process of intense emotion. Surely the pre-verbal infant must express this private world of pain or joy with non-verbal gestures, cries and gutturals. The older child has play and language to help him as does the adult. But is the first expression of affect not entirely somatic, and is its first social communication not non-verbal in smiles and tears and laughter and grunts that bridge the gulf between private emotional worlds and the eloquence of their later expression in a world where language and its great symbolic hoard takes over?

My focus in this chapter has been on insight and how its quest for knowledge can seem transgressive in the eyes of structural judicial aspects of the mind. Transgression is not its primary function of course, enlightenment is, and it is ironic that enlightenment should be proclaimed by a non-verbal "ahah" of affirmation, as if the gut feeling were the final arbiter of the mind's judgments, the somatic and all the sublimated hierarchies of the structural mind in agreement as the enlightened moment of insight arrives, the somatic having the last non-verbal word nevertheless.

Throughout this book one focus that will recur often is the sense of two opposing forces in the human mind. Conflict is one way of conceptualizing the two forces: Brenner has even conceptualized psychoanalysis itself as the "Science of Mental Conflict." I am focusing on two psychical forces since I believe it allows us to conceptualize the microstructure of conflict in psychic phenomena whose structural integrity might seem incapable of any further reducibility. Shafer has made a similar point in his study of defense. He shows very insightfully how defense, which seems to want to thwart desire, also expresses the wish itself albeit very indirectly. The projections of a paranoid who fears that a man will penetrate him, also expresses the wish to be penetrated. In the previous chapters we have seen how repression and insight need not be considered as only seamless psychic phenomena but can be viewed as the interplay between two mental forces. In this next chapter on transference I will continue this theme showing how transference can be conceptualized as an act of revelation and resistance all at once.

CHAPTER FOUR

Transference: the past in the present, the present in the past

In looking at objects of nature ... at yonder moon dim glimmering through the dewy window pane, I seem rather to be seeking, as it were asking, a symbolical language for something within me that forever and already exists, than observing anything new. Even when that latter is the case yet still I have always an obscure feeling, as if that phenomenon were a dim awakening of a forgotten or hidden truth of my inner nature.

—*Samuel Taylor Coleridge*

HAMLET: Methinks I see my father
HORATIO: Where, my lord
HAMLET: In my mind's eye, Horatio"

—*Hamlet*, Act one, Scene two,
William Shakespeare

Transference was one of the pivotal discoveries of Sigmund Freud. It allowed the past to invade the present: such invasions, seemingly disruptive at first, came to be recognized as crucial portals of enquiry into the mind. But it took genius to characterize such invasions as

45

discoveries as opposed to intrusions. Let us review some of the basics of clinical process so that the discovery of transference can be appreciated in context. Freud's discovery of how a free associating mind, following the fundamental rule of psychoanalysis could eventually unlock the secrets of its own symptoms and dreams, not to mention its own character and personality and all aspects of psychopathology, was the basic insight that led him to abandon the hypnotic method. Hypnosis could unlock the doors of the unconscious to be sure but Freud wanted the patient to be wide-awake as the process of self-discovery advanced. There was only one main obstacle, namely resistance. You could lead the analysand to the font of free associative knowledge, but you couldn't make him drink. Why not? The mind that at first seemed willing to comply with the common sense logic of the fundamental rule and "say whatever comes to mind," no holds barred, so to speak, would eventually refuse to go on. The refusal did not seem to be a conscious decision. Some part of the mind, too schooled in "social hypocrisy" as Freud once called it, begins to object to the airing of all its dirty linen in public, or even in the privacy of the consulting room. This force was called resistance and one facet of resistance was transference.

I have used the concept of resistance to introduce another concept called transference. This is not the only way to introduce the concept, since transference is not all resistance. A major component of it is revelation, which could be called the opposite of resistance. Like many psychic concepts it can be one and the other at the same time. I have introduced this kind of duality in preceding chapters on repression and insight. It is a duality that will weave its way throughout this whole book in fact. But let me introduce transference as I had begun to, since it is true that transference often announces itself as resistance. Let us look at a typical clinical example: the analysand's free associations are flowing without resistance; after a while the analysand falls silent, imagining what the analyst's reaction must be to all that has been revealed. "If the analyst is anything like my father then I can expect criticism at this juncture" the analysand muses. This musing is unconscious of course. The silence represents it in its non-verbal form. This is a moment of transference. An attitude from a past relationship with a father has invaded a current dialogue with an analyst. An analyst's respectful silence is being confused with a father's criticism. The past has invaded the present. Its profound irrational influence silences a rational analysand. Freedom of speech has become tongue-tied. If the analyst interprets what has just happened as an inappropriate transfer of emotional experience from past to present and if the analysand can identify with the logic of the interpretation, a new conviction about the power and therapeutic possibility of analytic process is born. "Nothing is so convincing to a patient as a transference interpretation" to paraphrase Freud.

A more formal definition of transference may be in order. Transference is the unconscious displacement of a genetic relationship onto a current relationship. In its most classical terms current relationship means the relationship with the analyst in the analytic situation. An analyst is being confused with a father, (or any other significant figure from the genetic past e.g. mother, grandparents, teacher, pediatrician, etc.). Transference does exist of course in all walks of life outside the consulting room. But in the consulting room the anatomy of transference is laid bare: the analyst can bring it to the attention of the analysand repeatedly, and this focus of attention on the transference is one of the major pools of information the two parties to the analytic dialogue study over and over.

Since transference is one of the oldest psychoanalytic concepts, in this chapter I want not to merely describe it or define it. Freud and many others have done that already. What I plan to do is to reimagine transference as a developmental phenomenon. I also want to compare the concept of transference and the concept of the genetic hypothesis in psychoanalysis. Let me be clearer about both of these approaches.

Transference and development

How soon could we expect the child's mind to be able to use transference as yet another facet of its cognitive-emotional repertoire? We can rephrase the question in more psychological terms. When is the nascent ego able to differentiate separate categories of object relatedness, and having differentiated them, confuse one with the other again in an act of transference? Stranger anxiety at five to eight months of developmental life is an expectable emotional reaction. The child who has seemed to be well at ease with mother and several others in his/her milieu begins to notice at about six months that mother is exclusively mother. This act of growth and differentiation begins to define mother as highly familiar and all others as highly strange. This important developmental achievement announces itself dramatically as stranger anxiety. I have always found the term to be misleading, as if the tip of the psychological iceberg was claiming all the attention and the less visible bulk of the meaning was being ignored. Ideally stranger anxiety would be called "recognition anxiety," "now I know who my mother is anxiety" or "get this stranger away from me anxiety." In other words the ego of the child has made a most significant leap of cognition and recognition and the attendant anxiety illustrates that this perceptual acuity is not merely an abstract achievement, but a highly emotional breakthrough as well. In terms of insight as an act of transgression (the topic of Chapter Two) one could argue that the infant is saying: "Aha, now I really know who my mother is and it sure as hell is not this stranger who assumes that I am an undifferentiated object of sentimentality that can be swooped up in strange arms, without my making any objection to this violation of my achievement of a special new sense of intimacy and familiarity with my mother!" Stranger anxiety ideally would be named identity anxiety: "I know who I am becoming. I know one unique person whose love can help me to define who I am." As Augustine puts it: "Love made me what I am that I may be what I was not before" (1974). It is amazing how the seeds of love as the most significant issue of life sustaining object relationships begin to get established already at six months!

If differentiation begins to be clinically visible between five to eight months, transference as an observable psychological phenomenon certainly is not. The ego's capacity to differentiate objects in its facilitating environment may begin soon after birth. It is possible that the infant's relationship with mother has a different quality to it than the relationship with father and siblings. The ego's sophistication makes its presence felt in these psychological acts of discrimination and differentiation. By the second and third years of life the ego's repertoire has advanced in an extraordinary manner and a differential relationship with several discrete objects of the facilitating environment is the norm. As the act of differentiation identifies these objects as distinct and unique, the concept of transference in childhood certainly becomes a theoretical possibility. The actual observable appearance of transference in the child analytic situation has been a subject of controversy however. Initially (1927) Anna Freud believed that the occurrence of transference in child analysis was unlikely since children lived with their parents all day long and their need for transference would therefore be minimal. Later Anna Freud's clinical experience proved to her that transference was not as rare as she had posited earlier in her clinical career. Melanie Klein did not share Anna Freud's initial skepticism about transference in children, but gradually their points of view began to coalesce, at least on that subject.

From a theoretical point of view one could argue that as soon as the child's mind has a relatively stable internalized world of object representations and self representations (from about age three onwards) transference as a phenomenon is at least conceivable. A three to six year old in analysis will often mistakenly address the analyst as Mum or Dad and then correct the parapraxis, if indeed the child notices it at all. That is a simple example of transference: there are much more profound examples that could be cited. But I want to continue outlining the developmental sequence with broad strokes at first. As the child passes through Oedipal development, latency and adolescence, his/ her sense of integration and differentiation becomes more mature and more complex. By adulthood, the ego's reality testing and capacity to differentiate are, ideally, as completely developed as possible. But this normal developmental ideal is an abstraction and most human beings are not models of ideal development. They are complex mixtures of normality and pathology, their developmental goals achieved in some ways, not in others. "Out of the crooked timber of humanity nothing straight can ever be made" to quote Kant again (Berlin, 1998). Let us picture a borderline patient whose sense of an internal representational world has never progressed beyond the separation-individuation phase of development. Emotional object constancy has never been completely achieved. The self has never achieved a relaxed integrated sense of comfort with love and aggression. Splitting is the essential defense mechanism that keeps the divided house of the mind somewhat stable. Aggression and love have never been adequately fused into an intimate integrated object relationship that is sustaining and nourishing. Picture such a patient in analysis or therapy. Let us imagine that from the beginning of the analytic relationship the analyst has never been completely identified as a separate human being, a professional that the patient sought out as a differentiated other that could help the self of the analysand to analyze itself. This hypothetical patient, ab initio, might be assuming that the analyst is not a differentiated entity at all, but another version of the all understanding, all-forgiving, unconditionally loving mother. Is it best to conceptualize this as intense transference that has an immediacy that knows no bounds, or should it be conceptualized as an expression of a developmental lack, an ego's deficiency in the act of differentiation? An immediate objection might be raised to this kind of spurious diagnostic categorization: why invoke deficiency at all, when this could be cited as an example of primitive self-object transference that is a manifestation of a primitive ego's repertoire? Should such an objection be rejected or sustained? One could argue that one conceptualization is psychodynamic, the other developmental, and that both can help the clinician to understand the clinical complexity of the analytic situation. Empathy has been stressed as the key therapeutic ingredient of the analyst-analysand relationship, an empathy that must mirror the exquisite sensitivity of the patient's self-image at every juncture of the analytic process. Throughout the therapeutic process the patient's self-image will reflect precarious states of imagined humiliation, rejection, neglect and loss of safety in the face of "empathic failure" as the analyst's silence or interpretive comments are being judged and misjudged. The developmental point of view focuses as much on the ego and its immaturities as on the precarious state of the self and its struggles for maturity. These two points of view (the developmental and the psychodynamic) though complementary rather than mutually exclusive, are important to differentiate, since I believe they can augment the empathic repertoire of the analyst as he/she tries to be in touch with every facet of the analysand's affective experience.

The genetic hypothesis in psychoanalysis

Freud believed that adult analysis and child analysis, combining their complementary approaches to understanding the complex development and psychodynamics of each human being, could jointly offer the most comprehensive vision of the totality of mental phenomena. Six years after Freud's death, in the first volume of the Psychoanalytic Study of the Child, Hartmann, and Kris (1945) demonstrated with great clarity how the genetic life of the mind is exposed in analysis and how the exposure of genetic "mistakes" make "correction" possible. If Franz Alexander conceptualized analysis as an emotionally corrective experience, Hartmann and Kris's conceptualization stresses a more collaborative deconstruction of the genetic flaws that at first engineer and then sustain neurotic thinking. The transference neurosis lays bare the genetic blueprint of the original reasoning that glued together a makeshift neurotic philosophy out of magical defensive concepts. The original "flawed" blueprint gets modified through the interpretive work of analysis, a collaborative venture that charts a process that goes from self-deception to insight, and from conflicted insight back to self-deception again as the mind tries to exorcise itself of its beloved demons. If insight is always experienced as a form of transgression, as stressed earlier in Chapter Two, psychological truth is arrived at incrementally and slowly, since interpretation and working through are always trying to find their bearings in a constantly conflicted psychic milieu.

One could argue that the genetic past is forever being transferred into the present, distorting it until interpretation and insight sort out the pedigree of all the various components of current experience. There is no other way of getting to know the unconscious past perhaps except when it is transferentially relocated, so to speak, into the present. When an analysand agrees with the basic premise of the fundamental rule and allows a free associative process to be "borne back ceaselessly into the past" the analyst is able to "predict" the past sometimes even before the analysand can. This is because the analyst is a seasoned witness and custodian of the sequential nature of the free associative unconscious "argument", and has learnt to make sense out of the seeming nonsense of a great torrent of words and fantasies and dreams as they spill into the container of the analytic situation. I have always cherished Hartmann and Kris's felicitous phrase "to predict the past" since its irony is so arresting. On first hearing this paradoxical phrase the mind wants to object: prediction is aimed at the future, its target the unknown future, not the stale news of the past. But, given that an infantile amnesia at age six (approximately) "relocates" the files of consciousness into a wordless state of unconscious "thing presentations" rather than "word presentations", the forgotten past (except for a handful of screen memories—see Chapter Seven) is as unknown to most of us as the mysterious future. (In *The Mind of a Mnemonist* (1968), Luria described a man who could forget nothing, a state of affairs that was more burden than gift, since the average expectable amnesia at age six may be an absolute necessity for civilized adulthood, as most of us know it). It is the existence of a profound infantile amnesia in most human minds that keeps us relatively sane, just as it is the existence of such amnesia that makes prediction of the past not just a felicitous phrase but a common clinical experience for many analyst–analysand relationships. If the prediction of the past is a kind of "uncanny" skill of "reading" unconscious tea leaves, so to speak, most of the exposure of the past that occurs in analytic process is less "magical". It is an ongoing process of piecing mental things together, a collaboration of two psychic historians who sift through affects, memories, symptoms, dreams, fantasies, character traits, transferences and countertransferences, the better to paint a portrait of a neurotic maladaptive illness, whose purpose is to block the whole portrait of adaptive mental-health from emerging and being seen. As analysis proceeds and approaches termination, two portraits are being painted simultaneously: the analysand is given a choice as to which portrait represents him/her better.

I have introduced several concepts in this chapter. I have defined transference and described how the ego must learn to differentiate distinct object representations from each other in the internal representational world, before transference, which essentially confuses one representation with another, can be identified at all. I have also introduced the concept of a genetic hypothesis in psychoanalysis. If the free associative process can not only "predict the past" but expose it well enough for its flaws and errors and magical assumptions and convictions to emerge from repression, and then be re-pressed into a new more adaptive utilitarian working image of itself, the genetic hypothesis suggests that exposed errors of affective, cognitive reasoning can be corrected and redressed in the therapeutic alchemy of psychoanalysis. I would like to illustrate all of these ideas with a clinical case so that theory can be tested out in the living crucible of analytic experience. Throughout this clinical exegesis and discussion I will be attempting to demonstrate how difficult it can be at times to distinguish the concepts of genetics, transference and differentiation from each other in the tumult of actual hour by hour clinical process, as the past projects itself into the present, and the present tries to inform the past with its current viewpoint.

Clinical case

My purpose in this brief clinical vignette is to compress years of clinical process into a single session or two. I want to focus on the topics of this chapter: transference, differentiation and the genetic hypothesis in psychoanalysis.

Peter was forty-eight years old when he sought analysis. His father had died of a mining accident in South Africa when he was six years old. He "survived" his father's accident, so to speak, but not the psychological sequelae. The father's trauma led to a protracted illness that cast a shadow not only over the child's formative years but over all subsequent years as well. Initially Peter claimed that the loss of his father was insignificant compared to all the other problems of his life, but it became increasingly clear, as the analysis proceeded, that the so-called subsequent problems were indeed all derivatives of the primal tragedy. The strategies that the child had come up with to deal with his devastating loss were mostly magical: his father was not really dead; Peter could resurrect him at will. He had killed his father with his death wishes, which were magical; to avoid killing his father, Peter himself must die. Better still, both would die together and always be united. Peter had grown up in South Africa and eventually would call this lack of differentiation between himself and his father the opposite of apartheid. The self had no identity: if apartheid seeks exclusion of the hated/loved object, Peter's defense was over inclusive in a self-annihilating manner. The self was a collection of scraps of itself, trying to become one integrated whole, but afraid to do so, since as an individuated self it would have to deal with anger, guilt, frustration, anxiety, love, dependency, all of which it sought to abandon in the disguised conflicted ferocity of its merger with the dying man.

Peter had a wife and child, both of whom he often confused with his father. In a way he had married his father and sired his father, his wife and son mere clones of the original ambivalent relationship. This lack of differentiation extended to the analysis itself. The analyst was not his analyst but yet another version of the relationship with his father. Peter was not psychotic at all and knew very well on another level that his wife and son and analyst were distinct differentiated people in their own right with whom he had profound, if conflicted relationships. As analysis excavated the unconscious determinants of his current philosophy, he came to know that it was a legacy of unconscious fantasies that distorted his reality testing in the service of defense.

When he enters the consulting room each day he imagines as he crosses the threshold that his analyst is a dying man that he must take care of. When he greets his wife in the morning he imagines that she is angry with him. When she reminds him that she is her own person with her own unique thoughts, and that his anger is a mere projection, he is quite surprised. This insight liberates him momentarily from the lack of differentiation that seems so essential for him to maintain, for complex, dynamic reasons. Here is a typical session: in the previous hour Peter has dreamt that he is working in a hotel. There is a man serving wines who is very officious and busy and yet not doing a very good job. Peter wants to tell him everything that is wrong with his hotel management but "forgets" what he had in mind to tell him. In the next session he has forgotten his appointment time and comes very late. We discuss how the parapraxis that was represented in dream-time (see Chapter Six: a parapraxis in a dream) invaded the actual time of the subsequent session, making him significantly late for an appointment he was eager to keep. This conflict about the wish to tell me everything and tell me nothing has been the basic topic for weeks, if not in fact throughout the whole analysis. In the next session, which is the one I want to focus on in more detail, Peter hands me a cheque, says "Ahah", and tells me he feels very efficient this morning. Even with his wife away (which usually destabilizes him, since any separation is analogous to the tragic separation from his father) he conducted some business and went to the gym. I ask what the "Ahah" referred to. He ignores the question. I comment on this. He responds that he was commenting on the feeling of efficiency; and yet he feels inefficient in analysis. He feels inefficient because we go over and over the analytic information again and again, but something is missing, since what we have explored does not lead to change. I say: "There must be some information we still do not have." He responds: "I do not want to hear what you have to say: too much *skrik* (fear), too much *vrek* (dying animal)." This was South African for "too much fear. Too much dying animal." This is a theme the analytic process has explored often, except in this instance Peter has thrown in some South African slang. The slang was an expression of intimacy and distance all at once. He was trying to include the analyst in the dialect of his childhood. But he is also trying to exclude the analyst, in the sense that the dialect excludes the analyst initially until the analysand translates. This wish to include the analyst intimately, also excludes him linguistically at least briefly. Through the invocation of slang he clings to the transference resistance that depicts the analyst as a dead man, a living ironic replica of a father who "betrayed" him, a living symbol of *skrik* and *vrek* all at once. This transference is not all resistance of course. Initially Peter believed that his father's demise had little significance. He was happy the man was dead. Death afforded him the opportunity of having his mother all to himself. This fantasied Oedipal triumph was a cover-up of the real loss Peter had experienced. Transference was the analytic achievement that allowed us to expose the primitive denial of the immensity of the tragic loss. It was memory reclaiming what was initially too painful to acknowledge. Eventually however, this repetitive transference enactment became a resistance. It was a wedge Peter drove between himself and the development of intimacy with me. This phase of analysis was most poignant and most fruitful. His dilemma was tormenting: if he allowed me to be a real person in his life, then the real loss of me, the eventual termination of our work together, would be unbearable. If we were differentiated people, who actually had individuated real relationships with each other in a finite world, then his fantasy of undifferentiated existence, in which he and his father were forever one in the intimacy of death, would be untenable.

What was it that we did not know despite years of "research" on these topics? Why was it so necessary for him to view me as a corpse, rather than as a living analyst who could be useful to him? It came as a major surprise to him once on the couch when a free association liberated itself from the hegemony of resistance and blurted out: "You have a lot of insights about me that could be most useful to me if I could let them in." This insight was analogous to the one experienced with his wife when she once challenged his many inappropriate projections onto her, saying "Peter, I have my own thoughts and feelings that are completely different from the imaginings you pin on me." Transference and lack of differentiation seemed almost impossible to distinguish from each other in this confused state that Peter needed to inhabit. But in this session he wanted to explore this dynamic confusion more deeply. He was aware that he projected his own anger onto a bust of Freud, a statue that always condemned him as he entered my office. In childhood it was not statues, but wild dogs, that he projected onto. Their menacing eyes could see through him. As we examined this need to constantly project his anger, Peter began to realize that the natural spontaneous possession of his anger created enormous anxiety in him. This anxiety was never experienced as an affective signal that might be considered and reconsidered. It was immediately experienced as somatic pain, usually located in the regions of the body where he imagined the father's mine injuries had been. As Peter began to repossess the initial anger that he felt towards his father, a remarkable free association emerged from the depths of his pain: "I feel so angry I must throw myself away." When the irrational pseudo-logic of this utterance was confronted Peter realized sadly that it was impossible for him to formulate the sentence in an active voice: "I feel so angry with my father I want to throw him away." It was at such moments that Peter's clarity of insight seemed too transgressive to bear (see Chapter Three) and he retreated defensively to the seemingly much safer disenfranchisement of the self.

However, when he returned for the next session he could acknowledge that in yesterday's session we were really working together trying to unravel the confounding neurotic knots the child had woven with his protective, perverse magic, a childhood magic that persisted into adulthood with profound consequences. He returned to the pseudo-logic of his formulation: "I am so angry I must throw myself away." Anger was a forbidden affect. I commented that the moral part of the mind that runs off with his anger and uses it against him is in fact a psychological construct that he concocted. His response was most insightful, expressed in an arresting metaphor: "I bent the metal of reality terribly. And now I cannot unbend it."

"You're afraid to show your strength," I suggest.

"Today these are mere words. I cannot use them to effect a change," he said, and began to complain of pain in his side. "Your body speaks when your mind is afraid to open its mouth," I suggest. Peter had often referred to these somatic expressions as "windows" into the workings of his mind, a place where words dared not go.

A dream highlighted these issue dramatically. One image of a dream stands out and as he relates it, a deeper, earlier dream emerges:

> There is a woman in an opera that seems to be taking place at the edge of the ocean. She is preparing herself to reach the culminating high note of her aria but she seems to hesitate too long, misses her cue and never sings the note at all. The dramatic action of the opera continues and perhaps the audience has not noticed the missed cue. The woman however smiles knowingly. This seems to be a silent recognition of her failed entrance.

As this dream is being remembered another longer dream from earlier in the night emerges from a repression that had almost banished it forever, and makes a sudden entrance:

> I am in a car with my wife. We are being driven by a chauffeur who reminds us that we have not fastened our safety belts. The car stops. I get out to pee. When I return a third passenger has entered the car. We make room for him but I am angry with our chauffeur for allowing such an intrusion. The stranger is an interesting cultured man however and we enter into a lively conversation. The

car stops again. We all get out. I instruct people about the location
of the bathrooms since I have peed there earlier already. I put on
the shoes of the stranger mistakenly. I say to my wife: these shoes
fit perfectly. The chauffeur points out that they seem too small for
me, but nonetheless they fit very well.

The associations to these dreams seemed insightful and passionate.
Disowning his own voice at times was a frequent theme in the analytic process and Peter could readily identify with the operatic woman.
Identification seemed to be the main theme in the second dream
also. The threesome in the back seat of the car seemed to be an obvious Oedipal reference. Initially annoyed about the stranger's intrusion Peter's solution to the Oedipal conflict was to wear the shoes of
the rival even if they seemed too small for him. He was aware of the
regressive tendency to wear and settle for infantile shoes rather than
embrace the full size of his own impressive wingspread. One association was particularly revealing in light of the theme being explored in
this chapter. Peter would occasionally get tipsy on wine in the evenings.
"When under the affluence of incohol" he chortled, reversing "'under
the influence of alcohol'" playfully, "I sometimes imagine that there is
an influence of my father entering my body", a fantasy of union with
the idealized parent of childhood before the mining accident. The word
influence seemed to capture the transactional nature of his relationship
with his father, as if he sensed that he was trying to solve an internal
crisis of consciousness and unconsciousness by imbibing a magical
influence, as if the temporary, transient inebriation was a regressive
defensive undifferentiated union with an object he had much more
complex affects to work out with in the theatre of reality. It was as if
he were trying to work out what Harold Bloom has called the anxiety
of influence, which when considered psychoanalytically (as opposed
to its strict sense as a profound commentary on the nature of creativity
and literary criticism) would mean processing the conflicted affects and
instincts of the Oedipus complex, but without conflict. In other words if
an author imbibes the influence of all previous authors slavishly he or
she would avoid conflict but at the expense of their own unique voice
or style, like the operatic woman in the dream who never releases the
final triumphant note at all. A chameleon may escape notice through
clever co-option of the attributes of others, but some sacrifice of identity
seems inevitable in the process. Peter was aware that a similar tendency
in analytic process would sacrifice self-identity and never develop the

analysand's unique personal voice. Peter felt excited about the insights he had extracted from these dreams especially the idea that influence did not need to be a magical infusion like alcohol but could be an ongoing active evaluation of the process of identification itself, its defensive and seemingly obligatory quality in childhood as opposed to the selective, discriminating assessments one could subject it to in analytic process.

Are we in a better position to discuss the genetic hypothesis, as well as the role of transference and the concept of differentiation at this point? Has the clinical provided enough of a window into the theoretical as unconscious fantasy and genetic distortions of reality are exposed in the analytic process? Peter seems more aware than ever that he is working to correct "theories" concocted by the magical thinking of a child who felt overwhelmed by the traumatic circumstances of his childhood, and all the "information" he was bombarded with as his father's medical condition worsened month by month. Reflecting on his precarious existence as a child Peter would often claim that he was afraid to be present in the past, by which he meant that the affects of anger, sadness, and guilt that he must have felt so acutely as a child could not be processed then by the developing sense of self. Peter "swallowed" the affects and regressed to a state of pain, the somatic becoming more "vocal", the psychological more "silenced". To understand the violence Peter had done to his own selfhood required Peter to allow himself to be present in a past he believed not to be as safe as he had experienced it initially. Reviewing that past through the ministry of free associative analytic process did not feel safe either. Nor did the transference of these childhood affects onto the person of the analyst. Peter could not be present in the present, experience transference in the here and now, and by experiencing it, deconstruct it. Transference resistance seemed to be the only form of transference that was safe. The analyst as a "dead man" could be managed. The self of the analysand could "play dead". The two corpses, united in an eternal embrace, could not "damage" each other. This collusion of the two "dead" parties seemed to be the only way to contain the aggression that might destroy the living analyst. This transference enactment seemed "obligatory". When challenged, the self felt the need to regress, run away, stop listening, somatize, or pretend it was an undifferentiated entity that couldn't be expected to know what was going on. There were moments, of course, when Peter allowed himself to be present in the present, to challenge the magical appeal of this transferential deadening of himself. At such moments Peter would feel liberated from pain and would feel that the scraps of his disintegrated self had pulled themselves together and become momentarily whole. The "ahahs" of such moments were often quite short-lived, their sudden demise a crucial "bending of the metal" against himself that the analytic partnership would attempt to understand more and more doggedly and deeply, each time the clinical process confronted the regressive repetition. Peter's lack of a sense of differentiation seemed highly defensive. It was not a constitutional ego defect that hampered his emotional acuities. "I am but mad North/ Northwest," as Hamlet puts it. "When the wind blows from the South I can tell a hawk from a hand saw."

Brenner objected to the concept of working through as a distinct phase of analysis since he believed analytic process from its inception to be an organic, integrated exploration, with elements of working through being one of its integral components from the very beginning. The past is contained in the present as surely as the present is the only conflicted witness of a past it avoids and embraces all at once. As Eliot suggested in the Four Quartets, the past and the present are both contained in the future, and the future is paradoxically present in the past. Dickens anticipated Eliot no doubt with his spirits of past, present and future. In that context, analysis is an attempt to use the ever present, and the transferences from the past that forever seek to distort it, as an instrument of therapeutic leverage. To be present in the present is required so that the transferences that complicate the present, augmenting it and diminishing it all at once, can be understood in all their complexity. To be present in the past is a metaphor that attempts to envision the genetic hypothesis of psychoanalysis at work. When the work of analysis exposes a genetic theory such as "I was so angry I had to throw myself away," both parties to the analytic labor have to roll up their sleeves and get to the deeper hidden sentence "I was so angry with my father I wanted to throw him away." To get there, the self that has "scrapped" itself out of fear needs to find the courage to return to the scene of the imagined crime, and be present in the distorted past it is trying to straighten out. It must forgo its wish to claim that it is not a differentiated entity. In other words it must not regress permanently. As a differentiated self it can adjudicate the truth of reality and not keep settling for magical distortion. As a differentiated self it will be able to process memory as transference and therefore be able to claim memory as part of its own historical record as it traces transferences back to the original sources that set them in motion. As a differentiated, cohesive self it will be able to say what Peter said recently: "If I can allow myself to be present in the present, and present in the past as well, the future will be a safe place to visit."

In this chapter I have attempted to distinguish between transference, differentiation and the genetic hypothesis, concepts that every practitioner uses all the time. I have suggested that if the analyst understands their subtle differences his interpretations of clinical data will be more developmentally informed as well as more empathic. Up to now our focus has been on the past as it informs the present of adults in analysis. But there is a world from which the past originally sprang. And it is time for the odyssey to approach the shores of childhood with trepidation and wonder, and explore how psychoanalysis which began with such timidity in the face of a direct approach to children, gradually learned to embrace the brave new world and learn from it. In the next chapter I will be focusing on play. There is an important link between the port of call we are leaving (transference) and the contours of the new port of call (play) that we are approaching. Freud defined play as the equivalent of fantasy except for one essential distinguishing feature: play needs to link fantasy to concrete playthings to get its act in motion. But transference, as we have just experienced, could be viewed as unconscious genetic fantasy displaced onto the concrete representation of the analyst in the emotional turmoil of the consulting room. In that way the past gets a chance to look at itself anew even though it will not recognize itself at first given the compelling illusion of the displacement. Later, in a chapter on dreams, I will focus on the cunning artistry of dream work but I believe I have shown how transference itself is not devoid of cunning as it reveals the past, and conceals it, all at once, with the sleight of hand of a magician.

CHAPTER FIVE

Play in child analysis and adult analysis

Man is most nearly himself when he achieves the seriousness of a child at play.

—*Heraclitus*

The direct observation of children has the disadvantage of working upon data which are easily misunderstandable; psychoanalysis is made difficult by the fact that it can only reach its data, as well as its conclusions, after long detours. But by cooperation the two methods can attain a satisfactory degree of certainty in their findings.

—*Freud*, Standard Edition Vol. 7, p. 20

In this chapter I not only introduce child analysis and one of its unique features, play, but also try to show how significant the capacity to play is, not only in childhood and child analysis, but in adult analysis as well and indeed throughout life. For instance play is essential in parenthood. A parent who cannot remember the crucial role of play in his/ her own childhood will have trouble invoking it and employing it in the service of an empathic understanding of what is perhaps a child's premier method of communicating very important issues to those peers

61

and guardians that matter to the child so much. Parental creativity, so crucial an aspect of resourceful child rearing, is an art form that has never been celebrated appropriately despite its critical role as the social glue that keeps the fabric of society cohesive and stable. It deserves a chapter in and of itself (Mahon, 1993). Play in the Holocaust is another topic of crucial importance. A Polish diplomat visiting the Warsaw ghetto and seeing doomed children playing amidst the stench and degradation of their milieu commented with wrenching spontaneity: "They only make believe it is play." It too deserves its own book or chapter (Brenner, 2011). But what I want to focus on primarily at first is the role of play in child analysis.

The "who painted him?" of Chapter One is a question that suggests that already by age three, two childhoods are occurring simultaneously in the mind of a young child. (It brings to mind that tragic comment of Nathalie Sarraute "already when I was very young it was too late"). Who painted him, as we have discussed earlier, addressed the "loss" of the old pet and his "return" as a painted replica of himself. While we can acknowledge that a three-year-old does not process death as a biological final entity (that cold-blooded assessment of reality requires more cognitive experiential affective understanding than the three-year-old mind is capable of) it is clear that the "disappearance" of their pet had an effect on the children. On one level the children knew about their loss and the emotional reaction they had to it; on another level they seemed to need to deny their cognitive affective "reality". The division of the mind into consciousness and unconsciousness is what characterizes adult psychological conflict, but even by age three we can appreciate how an unconscious portion of psychological existence has already been established.

As we discussed in the early chapters children are able to repress. As just mentioned, the concept of a painted guinea pig illustrates it well. Some of the affects have been repressed, painted over. At age six, when the infantile amnesia descends like an intrapsychic Iron Curtain, most of the early record of childhood is repressed. As the years go by only a handful of screen memories (to be discussed in detail in Chapter Six) represent that most emotional era. We have discussed transference earlier, suggesting that once object representations and self-representations are differentiated in the developing mind, transference becomes at least theoretically possible. The expectations a child has of its internalized caregivers can be transferred onto others: in the analytic situation the significant object of transference is of course the analyst. If children can deploy defense and transference as they struggle with psychological conflict why is the child analytic situation different from its adult counterpart? The most crucial difference becomes obvious when we consider the fundamental rule of adult analysis. That rule invites the adult analysand to free associate, an invitation that the analysand accepts even if he/she is not always able to comply with its demands. In adult analysis the resistances that challenge the spontaneities of the fundamental rule provide as much information as the associations themselves, given that spontaneity and desire are not the whole analytic enterprise. The study of resistance, defense, character etc. is equally important. But the fundamental rule itself, as a desirable therapeutic attitude, is embraced philosophically by the adult analysand. This is not the case with children. To ask a child, who has only quite recently begun to master sphincters and instincts, to abandon his newly acquired linguistic skills, through which much of his mastery has been accomplished, would be inappropriate. A child would feel threatened by the idea that language itself could be rendered unstable by imaginative linguistic horseplay. One couldn't expect any sensible child to go along with it. The analyst might be accused of corrupting the morals of a minor with such a licentious invitation. This was in fact one of the early concerns of Sigmund Freud who therefore decided to work with Little Hans via the father. That was 1909 and the technique of child analysis had not been "invented" yet. When the early child analysts (Hug Hellmuth, Anna Freud, Melanie Klein, Berta Bornstein) began to realize that play could be exploited as a substitute for the free associative process used in adult analysis, individual analyses of children became possible. It is important to note that the significant role of play in child analysis, which is now taken for granted as a crucial window into the psychodynamics of a child's interiority, was not obvious from the beginning. Freud, who made some of the most insightful comments on play ever penned, did not see its value as a therapeutic instrument initially. As astute a clinician as Ferenczi, in his evaluation of Arpad, the little Chanticleer, decided in the midst of his evaluation, when the child stopped conversing and began to play, that the evaluation had to cease at that point. It didn't occur to him to follow his patient into the corner and continue the evaluation in a new ludic mode. This was 1912 and the technique of child analysis and the central role of play in it had not been established. What is this important modality? How would we define it?

Towards a definition of play:

Whereas the modern definition of play as "games, diversion" captures the ludic nature of the activity, the word derives from the Old English *plega*, which implied a less sportive intent—to strike a blow (*asc-plega* means playing with spears, that is, fighting with spears; or *sword-plega* means fighting with swords) (Skeat, 1910). The progression from play, meaning to strike a blow, to play meaning a game or a diversion, brings to mind Freud's comment "the man who threw the first insult as opposed to a spear was the founder of civilization." Freud's idea that thought is trial action captures the essence of thought's capacity and play's capacity to rein in the immediacy of instinctual action and make it reflect on itself before it acts. One other insight of Freud's is crucial: he believed that fantasy and play were practically synonymous, the essential differential being that play needed to represent itself in action with external inanimate props such as toys and hobby horses and even with some animate objects such as pets. Freud did not stress the action component of play as much as I intend to and therein lies the additional theoretical addendum I am suggesting.

My working definition of play therefore would suggest that play in humans or animals is action that does not seek immediate gratification of desire or aggression but seems rather to explore alternate or multiple possibilities of experience. Freud argued that the aim is the factor in instinctual life that acts to bring about satisfaction: I am suggesting that play is the vehicle that allows the mind the opportunity to inhibit the immediacy of the aim and explore other options. This is the essence of all defense perhaps, whether we think of sublimation or reaction formation or all the other defensive maneuvers of the mind. Play therefore could be thought of as one of the midwives of defense, a reflective arc so to speak as opposed to the more primitive instinctual reflex arc. One can see how this aesthetic midwife might indeed be crucial in child analysis, a topic I want to turn to now. If play is one of the essential ingredients of child analysis it often makes an entrance on the playroom stage wearing a mask of humor.

Adam: analysis in two phases

Phase One: A four-year-old in the full throes of Oedipal romance leaves his mother in the waiting room and dashes into the analyst's office and sits on the analyst's chair. This is a new game that is a tribute to the several months of analytic process that have preceded it. The four-year-old who began the analytic journey with tentative footsteps is now comfortable enough to "steal" the analyst's chair and even "free associate" somewhat to the theft. He beams when the analyst suggests that he is pretending to take over the whole world and be big like his doctor and maybe even order people around, especially fathers and doctors. In this "humorous" mood he asks the analyst if he would like to hear a joke, and then proceeds to tell what he thinks is a joke, but might not qualify as such to adult ears.

Q: "Why did the chicken steal the bagpipes?"
A: "Because he wanted to have a perfect house."

Since this did not sound like a joke, I tried to get more information about its origins and developmental function for the child. It turns out that this joke began its psychological life as a dream that subsequently became a joke as the dreamer tried to "play" with it in a waking state. I was not sure if my young patient fully understood what bagpipes were. But as clay was manipulated into the shape of the primitive musical instrument, producing an object decidedly like a scrotum with an erect penis, it became clear that he not only knew what bagpipes were, but also sensed their symbolic phallic possibilities. This became clear as "phallus" got chopped from "scrotum" in repetitive attacks on the clay instrument. There was further corroborative associative evidence in drawings in which father's initials were erased and the patient's own initials preserved. A variation on this Oedipal theme in script showed father's name erased with the word "no" after it, and the child's own name preserved with the word "yes" after it. At moments such as these he would leave the office to check on his mother in the waiting room. He readily agreed with the interpretation that he needed to see her to be sure she could still love him, even if he played out murderous wishes against her husband. He even gave me "a star" for this interpretation.

Returning to the function of the joke, it is interesting to note that even if this attempt to turn dream into a joke did not work, the capacity for understanding of comic mechanisms was present, as the following joke he told in the same analytic hour makes clear.

Q: "Why was there a fight in the bakery?"
A: "Because two loaves were fresh!"

In a subsequent session, the child "steals" my chair gleefully and the game of theft begins again. At one point he returns the chair to me, saying, "I don't want your chair. I want your job." When I wonder what I will do without a job, he reassures me that I will get his father's job. The link between stealing father's job and my job seems obvious. The theme returns to the chicken stealing the bagpipes, the joke he had made up out of a dream. Does he make jokes up all by himself? Yes, and he demonstrates: "I'll steal your chair. I'll take your job." This mock-serious threat is presented as a joke. At this stage of development, is pretense synonymous with the comic?

When I "enter into" this joke, saying, "Oh, what will I do without my job and my chair?" he says reassuringly, "Oh, it's only a joke." For a moment he must have felt that I was seriously pleading for the return of my property and status. The line between illusion and reality seems precarious in this animistic world of beliefs and make-believe. The "scene" shifts to the construction of an elephant out of clay, followed by its immediate destruction. After making body, trunk, limbs, tail, the whole construction is torn apart limb from limb. Going behind my chair, he "knocks" on my head. "Oh, you've become a head-knocker. A new job, eh?" I ask playfully. Next minute he is fixing my shoes and saying he has many jobs—destroyer, fixer, head-knocker. The wish to castrate and the wish to undo the castration seem obvious. This is all playful, even comic. At one point he makes spells, writing scribble on paper and chanting gibberish that will make doors open and close magically. "The spells are like jokes or different?" I ask. "They are the same," he says, "but spells don't have any words." I muse, "Jokes and spells are wonderful. What would children do without them?" The child responds, "If the parents took all the jokes away and hid them in a closet, they could get them back by being good." It is fascinating, but also typical of child analytic process with a four-year-old, to watch a child go from action, to play, to spell, to joke, as he struggles with Oedipal conflict. An adult analysand could probably contain all these components of Oedipal conflict in one sequence of verbal associations, a tribute to the adult ego's facility with language, frustration tolerance, renunciation of instinct, sublimatory channels, etc. A child's ego, on the other hand, relatively new to language, new to joking, represents the conflict partly in action, partly in language as it tries to put a comic face on issues that are not necessarily funny.

Let us look at the "joke" again:

Q: "Why did the chicken steal the bagpipes?"
A: "So that he could have a perfect house."

Can we assume that this dream turned joke disguises the Oedipal wish
to steal father's penis and make off with a possession that would give
the anatomically underdeveloped robber the perfect body he feels so
lacking in? The dream-joke disguises the infantile Oedipal intent with
a few displacements (child becomes chicken, penis becomes bagpipes,
body becomes house). The fact that this joke does not meet the criteria
envisioned by older jokesters should not diminish an appreciation of
the four-year-old's impulse to put a comic mask on a dream that may
have revealed too much of its dark intent to the little boy on first waking. (If "Why did the chicken steal the bagpipes" had been answered
"Because he wanted to be a rooster booster or a rooster roaster" the
joke might have begun to resemble the adult examples it was trying to
mimic).

It is unusual perhaps to be able to witness a joke so embedded in the
therapeutic process. Before, during, and after the joke, the stealing of
my chair looms as preamble and postscript to the comedy in action and
word as it unfolds. The "theft" enacted in play is at once day residue
and association to a joke that never quite makes it, given the amount of
anxiety it is attempting to deal with and the developmental equipment
of the comedian. One can only marvel at the developmental courage of
the four-year-old who plots the overthrow of his father with one side
of his mouth and makes a joke out of it with the other. It is clear that
the parents have the power not only to steal his bagpipes but steal his
jokes as well and lock them in the closet. Even infantile omnipotence in
the form of "spells" may not work against such formidable opponents.
In latency when the Oedipus complex has been repressed and the
child's ego comes into contact more and more with the non-incestuous
group life of that developmental phase, and all its heritage of riddles
and games and jokes, it may be easier to joke about the return of the
repressed with classmates than joke about the crime and the act of
repression itself with your father or analyst.

I have focused on Adam's humor but there was much more going
on in his analysis. His language sophistication was remarkably precocious and his play was most creative. He made remarkable and swift
progress and his analysis (the first phase) ended when Adam seemed
to be content at home, content in school, and fully engaged with his

friends and schoolmates. Adam's analysis ended when he was six years old. When Adam returned to analysis five years later an extraordinary perspective on how development changes analytic process became evident. I have already briefly described the first phase of Adam's analysis to which I wish to add only one further piece of genetic material. At age four Adam had developed a symptom that puzzled and alarmed his parents and seemed to bewilder him as well. A personable and playful boy, he would occasionally lash out unexpectedly at children in his vicinity. Precipitating events, either current or genetic, seemed elusive. The parents, sensitive, responsible overseers of the child's development, entered into a cooperative, non-defensive alliance with the analyst in the service of understanding and correcting what had gone awry. The only developmental incident that seemed to have etiological significance was the dismissal of a nanny who may have "accidentally" spilled some tea on Adam's head. The parents were unsure how much significance to assign to this event, and had Adam not developed his "aggressive" symptom at age four, the nanny's behavior might well have been forgotten. The nanny's unusual name, Grasiena (Siena for short), would reveal its significance not in the first installment of analysis but in the second, when Adam was eleven.

One further comment about the outcome of the first phase of treatment. The symptom of impulsive aggression gradually diminished and eventually vanished altogether, its energies undoubtedly rechanneled into the transference and sublimatory manifestations of analytic process. The analysand's intellectual potential, always impressive, was now soaring, given its new freedom from neurotic harassment. The Oedipus complex having bequeathed most of its resources to its heir, the superego, through the usual processes of identification, repression and infantile amnesia had paved the way for a latency of incredible potential and Eriksonian industry. Some practical issues (geographic distance, financial considerations) influenced the mostly developmental psychoanalytic factors that informed the decision to terminate or at least interrupt analysis at this stage. Parents and analysand were completely comfortable with the notion of resumption of analysis should the need arise. The subsequent analysis would suggest that not all of the aggression had been rerouted into channels of ego mastery but that one of the heirs of the Oedipus complex, the superego, may have made off with more resources than it was supposed to and that its embezzlement of developmental funds was not always in the service of adaptation.

Demoralization was being proposed and perpetuated rather than an age-appropriate enlightened sense of morality. It was in this demoralized state that Adam returned to analysis at age eleven, puzzled by the unconscious forces that seemed suddenly to have impinged on his psychological processes.

Phase Two: The five-year interval between the two phases of Adam's analysis, while seemingly "latent," was nonetheless packed with existential incident and psychological achievement and struggle. At the end of the first phase, Adam presented me with a parting gift: a drawing, a child's-eye view of the universe, one could call it perhaps, in which an impressionistic distribution of the world's oceans and land masses was captured with grace and simplicity. It was a psychological as well as a geographic statement, perhaps Adam's view of an expanded internal world as well as its objective correlative in the external world of reality. (In any case, Adam's drawing adorns the shelf of my consulting room, a silent witness to one episode in the never-ending story of analytic process.) Adam wrote to his analyst a few times about his progress and about his missing the analytic relationship. I responded to these communications. When his grandfather died, Adam wrote about his love for the man and the sadness of his loss. Much moved by this letter, I replied in a letter that contained the idea that "love is the great wheel that turns the universe" even when sadness and loss darken its contours for a while.

After that communication, I didn't hear from Adam until his parents, sensing that he needed to return to analysis, called for a consultation. Subsequently I learned that Adam had had a very difficult time with his grief over his grandfather's death but that he wanted to deal with it "on his own." He eventually gave up grieving when a boy, whose father had died, managed to get over his grief quickly and resume his academic progress: Adam, in a seemingly competitive, comparative attitude, decided that if his peer could handle an even greater loss, he should pull himself together and get on with his development. This was the non-empathic "stiff upper lip" state of his psychology when he returned to analysis. He also felt harassed by increasing academic pressures; and the exercise of his unusual intellectual endowment, once a matter of pride and pleasure, was fast becoming a chore.

In the first session he described his sense of academic ennui, which he knew was only the tip of an iceberg of a deeper psychological suffering—i.e., his shattered sense of self-esteem. Recently he had told his parents about his diminished self-worth. The parents felt partially reassured when Adam expressed confidence in his ability to redress that state of affairs with another bout of analysis. The academic ennui was perhaps an easier point of entry into a resumption of analytic collaboration, and that was where we started. Reflecting on his recent academic slump, he complained that his teacher, Mrs. Swift, favored the other children and seemed to be unappreciative of his efforts while praising those of his peers. Not having seen Adam for a few years, I proposed a trial interpretation to test the current developmental state of his psychological mindedness.

"Do you suppose that there might be a Mrs. Swift inside you as well as outside?"

"You mean the problem is inside me but it colors what's outside? But why would that be?"

He clearly had come back prepared to work, and I told him we would figure it out together. He said, "It's not as if we're starting from scratch. We've done a lot of work already." I agreed. As if seeking a genetic answer to his earlier question, he began to talk about his best friend, a boy in early latency who had abandoned him and taken up with a new clique of friends. Adam felt unworthy, betrayed, and hurt, but the anger was not accessible. "Where did it go?" I asked. "You mean it went inside, don't you? I am very mean to myself inside instead of being mean to Jimmy outside."

He went on to describe the interior of his mind as a kind of Supreme Court ruled by a triumvirate—Boss One, Boss Two, Boss Three. Boss One was severe, totalitarian, unrelenting; Boss Two was empathic, decent, fair; Boss Three, instead of being cruel inside like Boss One, was cruel to others. "But Boss One and Boss Three work together," Adam asserted knowingly. He wished he could be rid of both of them and be guided only by Boss Two.

I was very impressed with Adam's capacity to reflect on the workings of his mind; it was clearly a continuation of our earlier work but in a new, more mature developmental key. A major portion of the ensuing analysis would be an elaboration of the pedigree of Boss One and a redistribution of energy between the three psychological power brokers.

Two parapraxes from the early phase of the analysis highlight the way in which conflict was represented and interpreted. Discussing the triumvirate of Boss One, Boss Two, Boss Three, Adam, intending to say, "I want Boss Two to comfort me," actually said, "I want Boss Two to confront me." He could not immediately understand the function of the psychological mischief that turned "comfort" into "confrontation," but when the analyst suggested that Boss One seemed to have usurped Boss Two's agenda—putting words in his mouth, so to speak—Adam was amazed at this notion. "Boss One is sneaky and speedy," he acknowledged soberly. "And he seems to think you shouldn't be comforted," I suggested, trying to make the conflict more obvious.

Another parapraxis began to convince Adam that unconscious influence behind the scenes could upstage the conscious narrative when it was least expected. Meaning to describe the new covenant between him and his teacher, he said "convent," suggesting that he saw the teacher as an authoritarian nun rather than as a human role model with whom he could forge an alliance. Adam saw both of these parapraxes as evidence of the spin Boss One could put on things from his unconscious power base behind the scenes. Adam became more and more fascinated by the concept of who was the real boss in his mind, himself or some hidden aspect of himself. He would often return to Jimmy, the boy who had betrayed him, but he slowly began to realize that he had betrayed himself when instead of standing up to Jimmy he had swallowed his anger and began to berate himself in the privacy of his own imagination. Jimmy "is only a red herring", Adam would say in his most Sherlock Holmesian manner, insight never too far from humor in his quick-witted analytic mind. As he began to talk about his competitive rivalry with his father, the "red herring's" reason to shift the emphasis became more transparent. Playing chess with his father, Adam would bristle when father, instead of playing "for real", would patronize him. "If you were to make this move instead of that, you would gain such and such advantage," was a remark by his father that pushed Oedipal buttons of near-lethal potential in a pre-adolescent whose hormones were plotting the permanent de-stabilization of whatever vestiges of latency remained intact at this transitional stage of development. A dream brought these issues into sharper focus.

> I am in a grungy room. The wall paint is peeling. It's a motel called The Sands of Time. There's a centipede in the bedclothes. I try to smash it. The softness of the mattress seems to shield it. I tip it onto the floor the better to smash it against the hard surface of the floor boards.

His associations at first led backward in time to a centipede on his wall when he was five years of age. He awakened and called his father.

Then the associations led to current events: a friend teasing him with a rubber snake, like a centipede with jaws. He was angry, not with his friend, but at the centipede. "Anti-centipede, anti-Semitism," he mused enjoying his mastery over these "big" words. He knocked the head off his friend's rubber centipede and then began to reflect on Boss One. Could Boss One be anti-centipede, anti-temper? It was temper that first brought him to analysis. He could reflect on the components of that temper more insightfully than ever. Not only had tea been spilled on his head, but the family had moved from a beloved home to one that took time to get used to. The idea that his phallic strivings and the loss of nanny and home might be used against him by Boss One, in one of his many insinuations, was not accessible to interpretation at this point. Centipede penis was flatly rejected, Adam insisting that right now his interest was still much more in teddy bears than in sexual exploration. In less than a few months of analytic process the centipede's obvious sexual symbolism would no longer need to be denied. The analysis of dreams seemed to be stirring up genetic memories. A complex dream led to many new insights.

> A nuclear power plant. About to blow up. Trying to keep the lid on. Hitler, Mussolini dividing up the spoils of Italy. I let them have the country but not Venice, Milan, Siena. In the cabin of the train where negotiations are going on a guard has a gun but it's pointing toward the ground.

This dream was not only analyzed immediately, but was returned to over many months as the associative process reviewed its contents again and again. In the immediate analysis, Hitler and Mussolini seemed like obvious stand-ins for Boss One, the ego, uncomfortable with its explosive power plants and conflicted downward-pointing guns, trying to at least hold onto some psychological territories. In subsequent analyses of this same dream, Adam would associate Siena with the nanny Grasiena, wondering if he had felt guilty that she was fired on his account. Maybe he loved her and wanted her back. Maybe she was a symbol of childhood, a respite from the future with all its aggressive and phallic implications. In this context he remembered another dream from the third grade: "A large number six is chasing me around. I'm running away from large numbers."

Among the many associations he had to this dream, six = sex was the most humorous. But the topic was no longer off limits. He had seen a movie in school of a baby being born ("a bloody thing coming out of a swollen hole"), and he had discussed erections with his father. He had thought they (erections) were signs of disease and that menstruation was "peeing blood." He was quickly relieved. His mind began to wander. He did humorous imitations of a Chinese man and of Ghandi. He realized that he was putting great distance between the sexual topic and himself, as if Boss One were saying, "Don't think these dirty thoughts in the USA." His humor reminded me of the joke he had told me many years ago.

Q: Why did the chicken steal the bagpipes?
A: Because he wanted to have a perfect house.

When I told him the joke, he was amused, saying, "But that joke doesn't have a punch line." He immediately supplied two witty punch lines.

Q: Why did the chicken steal the bagpipes?
A: Because he wanted to sing and be supper!
A: Because he wanted to research his Scottish origins.

The gulf between a five-year-old's understanding of humor and a twelve-year-old's is nicely illustrated here, but more importantly, when I asked Adam if our recent understandings could shed any new light on the five-year-old's joke, he immediately and enthusiastically replied, "Yes, oh yes. If Boss One insists that the dirty sexual stuff has no place in an American mind (a perfect house), then he would have to hire a chicken to steal the dirty stuff (bagpipes = five little pipes sticking out of a big bag, get it?) and make off with it to keep the house picture perfect!" In a sense, Adam had been tricked and bushwhacked by a one and a five and a six but he was beginning to turn the tables on Boss One and retrieve his libidinal and aggressive development from a bad joke certain unconscious numbers had been playing on him.

Adam's aggression, relatively free of Boss One's tyranny, began to make its appearance socially and also in the transference. Adam was shedding some of his timidity with his peers. His aggression would take an intellectual form, of course, his superior intellect being an assault weapon when he felt the need to turn it on his friends. He would sneer at their excessive boasting when they flaunted their knowledge, a sign of inferiority, as Adam well knew with his astute and developing psychological-mindedness. But he was not reluctant to bring the haughty down by exposing their lack of knowledge of a word like "caduceus," whose meaning and etymology he could then explain to his vanquished foe. In the transference he could be sarcastic, witty, and contradictory when the need arose.

A dream, that stumped both of us with its minimalism, he eventually figured out. The dream depicted the color green followed by the color black. The two colors kept replacing each other sequentially through-out the dream. That was the total content. This dream followed a much more elaborate and more accessible dream, and our first interpreta-tion addressed the resistance that gave us so little to work with, as if the mind were sorry it had revealed so much in previous dreams. But Adam stumbled on a clue that made the dream less impregnable. The chair the analyst sits in is green. Perhaps the green represents his alli-ance with the analyst against the dark forces (black) of Boss One. Then Adam turned the tables: "Of course it could be that I'm on the side of blackness, destroying your chair, the seat of power, stealing it like in the old days." On another occasion he felt comfortable enough to ridicule my analytic curiosity. He remembered a dream he had at age seven. "I woke up in a dream. The dream was about the tale of two cities. "It was the worst of times, it was the best of times." I tore out the last pages of the book." The analyst, betraying his own interest in dreams within dreams perhaps more than his responsibility first and foremost to ana-lyze the dreamer, suggested that if the dreamer woke up in the dream, then the rest of the dream must have been a dream within a dream. Adam pounced, ridiculing my philosophical pedantry: "Oh, you mean it could be a dream within a dream and right now what's happening might not be happening? Is reality reality or is existence a dream?" Try-ing to recover, I said: "I guess my leg was asking to be pulled and you couldn't resist it." We both had a good laugh. I had temporarily lost sight of my patient and gotten what I deserved!

Adam's burgeoning capacity to compete academically and socially with his peers led to the recovery of an important memory: a song he had made up when he was three. The words were: "You just can't wake up the sponge." Adam had been talking about how he stumped his classmate Stanley by reciting the Russian alphabet. Stanley had been bragging about his French, and his ignorance of Russian brought him down a peg. Adam's satisfaction was palpable, yet his memory from age three illustrated how quickly aggressive and competitive thoughts could lead to associations that implied the censure of Boss One. It was clear to Adam that the sponge, like the bagpipes, was a reference to the penis. He talked about an expression four-year-olds use when talking about the penis: "Sometimes my eleventh finger points." The analyst offered a tentative formulation. "So could Boss One be the singer of the song 'Don't wake up the sponge'? Would you buy that?" "Yes, I would," Adam declared emphatically and exploded with a salesman's voice in a most humorous riff: "But the real question is: would you buy the knife that can cut through aluminum?"

Adam immediately commented on his humor as his anti-Boss One side. "Boss One is anti-sex. Humor tries to play with it." He became philosophical, talking about light. "We don't see things. We see light bouncing off things. So in the dark there's nothing there." "Where did thoughts about light come from?" I ask. "I was reading that patterns of colors cause epileptic seizures. I was thinking it's light bouncing off colors that cause epileptic seizures."

"These are amazing ideas," I say admiringly. He goes on to talk about rods and cones and color blindness. "Tiny cells in the retina determine what we see," Adam says philosophically. "Now you're able to think philosophically. How do these grand thoughts feel?" I inquire. "Feels good. The average human uses eight per cent of his brain." Adam says, but quickly turns the tables on himself in a delightful piece of self-mockery: "I use nine per cent!" We both laugh. But I underline the positive aggressive forward momentum: "Now you are not afraid to wake up the sponge of your mind." "Funny you should say that. Sponge of the mind reminds me of Bovine Spongioform Encephalitis. I remember my father talking about it when I was little. But I didn't understand the meaning. Just the words. The sponge of my mind was not yet old enough to soak up all the information until I grew up." "So you feel your development was not complete yet?" I remark. "Yes, I remember my father singing, "Multigrain, my little son, makes you grow up big and strong." That was an indicator that I would grow. The idea was planted in my head."

Adam's impressive analytic work on waking up the sponge of his mind exposed more and more of the unconscious superego pathology that second-guessed his developmental progress. Curiously enough, this alone did not lead to immediate academic or other developmental momentum. This puzzled Adam. He had convinced himself that Boss One's control had been diminished and that consequently his academic *joie* had returned. But his grades did not comply with this wishful thinking. Adam was fooling himself, but he was totally unaware of it, a clinical fact that eventually forced him to acknowledge his impressive capacity for denial. This could not be worked through until Adam recognized his identification with Puck in *A Midsummer Night's Dream*. This represented his wish to be infantile and magical forever and to overthrow Boss One in fantasy without having to develop a hard working ego that could replace Boss One's power through the reality of insight rather than through the self-deception of denial. As Adam began to learn that Puck and Boss One colluded in their attempts to hoodwink a hardworking, maturing, but anxious ego, he could observe that the light at the end of the tunnel of neurosis was switch-operated rather than controlled by external random forces. Locating the switch and the complex functioning is the continuing enterprise of a work in progress. The analysis is obviously not over, but Adam, with his new "formal" cognitive potential and his free-associative skills, has learned how to put sexuality, aggression, censorship, and humor on the analytic table, the better to free his mind from neurotic shackles and to reap the benefits as well as weather the impending storms of adolescence.

Further vicissitudes of play

So far in this chapter the emphasis has been on child analysis and the critical role of play in it. I believe, that in the sample of child analysis cited, one can see the great changes that emotional and cognitive development orchestrate as the mind goes from the concrete operations of latency to the hypothetico-deductive formal cognitive properties that Piaget has described as he outlines the stages of his genetic epistemology. Adam is quite a different analysand not only as his sense of humor develops, but as his free associative skills in general make him more and more thoughtful, insightful and playful in a new sophisticated manner. The momentum of this impressive expansion of playful possibilities does not stop at adolescence obviously and I now want to introduce a new area in which play has a role in adult analytic process.

Playing and working through

I want to propose an analogy between certain features of playing and aspects of working through. Conceptualizing psychoanalysis as the process whereby unconscious fantasy is uncovered and then subjected to rigorous scrutiny, and building on Freud's (1908) insight that play is the same as fantasy—with the essential difference that fantasy links itself to real objects in play, such as toys and playthings—I propose that play can be thought of as not merely symbolic, as a fantasy bearer, so to speak, but as a fantasy tester as well. In the process of working through, some analysands attach their unconscious fantasies not only to a trans-ference object, a primary libidinal object, or a significant loved one, but also to actual props within the analytic setting (a Kleenex box, for exam-ple, or a handbag), making the analogy with play even more obvious and palpable.

A comparison exists between playing and working through that is not immediately obvious. While both deal with fantasy and reality, the connective tissue that links the two concepts is elusive, and the analogy I am proposing has therefore been neglected.

Playing

A child at play is involved in an investigation of the interface between his or her internal world, which is at once magical and "gothic", and an external world that has a mind of its own, so to speak. This is frustrat-ing, to say the least, but of course, it is also the great meeting place of the two principles of mental functioning: pleasure and reality, facing off on a psychological turf that will determine the nature of compro-mise throughout development, a compromise that will have a bearing on the mental health of the player for a lifetime. Play, despite its repeti-tive nature, is the opposite of repetition compulsions of the id, which stubbornly try to maintain psychic inertia. Play is a persistent trying on of the garments of the phenomenal world, until the right fit is selected. This metaphor of trying on (Neubauer, 1987) is apt only if we imagine the wardrobe of the phenomenal world as so extensive that the trying on and fitting could represent a lifetime's enterprise.

Working through refers to the psychoanalytic work that must be done side by side with interpretation in order to ensure that insight becomes practical and leads to change, thus having a real impact on the quality and character of life. If transference and interpretation capture genetic insights from the past and make them palpable in the analytic situation, working through puts the insights through their paces in the actual experiences of daily living.

Both play and working through have been written about extensively. (I have introduced my own definition of play earlier.) I will not review all the literature here, but will instead emphasize an analogy between play and working through that I will then try to explicate, with the aim of shedding light on both topics in the process. The analogy that recently occurred to me was undoubtedly triggered by the interface between child analytic process and adult analytic process, which has informed my professional life for many years. Freud had many groundbreaking, insightful things to say about play, but my analogy deals with only one. He wrote:

> The opposite of play is not what is serious but what is real. In spite of all the emotion with which he cathects his world of play, the child distinguishes it quite well from reality; and he likes to link his imagined objects and situations to the tangible and visible things of the real world. This linking is all that differentiates the child's "play" from fantasizing. (1908, p. 144)

This linkage between internal fantasy life and real objects in the play space (made up of toys, stuffed animals, and so on) is the hallmark of childhood play, as Freud's emphasis suggests.

If play is internal fantasy life trying to find a foothold in the practical world of external life, using playthings to represent itself to itself, so to speak (the better to get to know itself!), isn't working through unconscious fantasy come to life through the ministry of transference and transference neurosis, with the aim of finding a foothold in the new experience of living out the rest of one's life according to a new contract? In this new covenant, (not to be confused with convent as Adam's parapraxis insisted!) fantasy repudiates certain features of itself while retaining others, the repetition compulsions of the id surrendering their energies to the new dynamism of working through. In other words, if play is fantasy seeking a practical expression for itself with props and playthings, does working through in analysis and the uncovering of unconscious fantasy not also seek an expressive culmination in the revised experience of everyday life? If insightful analysis can "predict the past" as Hartmann and Kris (1945, p. 21) so felicitously expressed it, the working-through aspects of analysis refuse to sentimentalize the past, but instead insist on reclaiming it by reworking it so that genuine affect can prevail, the past contained in the character of the future as historical witness rather than neurotic caricature.

Working through

The Hollywood silver-screen caricature of psychoanalysis suggests that the free-associative process invites an interpretation that releases a hidden childhood memory, and in one eureka of insight, the constipated mind is enematically relieved and cured! The concept of working through is reality's dismissal of this magical and simplistic distortion of analytic fact. The psychological inertia that makes this caricature so laughable and unrealistic would preoccupy Freud for most of his scientific life. And speaking of psychical inertia, we might recall Freud's comment that:

> If we search for the starting-point of this special inertia, we discover that it is the manifestation of very early linkages—linkages which it is hard to resolve—between instincts and impressions and the objects involved in these impressions. These linkages have the effect of bringing the development of the instincts concerned to a standstill. (1915, p. 272)

The work of analysis could be characterized as the study of all linkages, conscious and unconscious, and their relation to each other. I am stressing the linkage between fantasy and a child's playthings that is the hallmark of play, and I am also stressing the linkage between unconscious fantasy made conscious in the analytic situation and the influence of such unconscious fantasy on the activities and details of behaviour in everyday life—the derivatives of the unconscious in day-to-day details of the human condition, if you will. I believe that the analogy between playing and working through represents a linkage that not only brings child psychology and adult psychology into an alignment that it would be shortsighted to ignore; in addition, it suggests that the deepest linkages of the mind (such as death wishes, for example) are linked to the details of living through neurosis. The two-way traffic between the two is a linkage that interpretation and its down-to-earth ally, working through, doggedly maintain in analysis, session after session. As Freud (1914) put it, "we must treat ... illness not as an event of the past, but as a present-day force" (p. 151).

If the transference as a playground (Freud, 1914) was Freud's laboratory, working through was an experimental launching pad where hypotheses had to be tested in order to develop wings and to contribute to the flight patterns of the future. Freud (1914) insisted that reclaiming the past must influence the future:

> The analysand must find the courage to direct his attention to the phenomenon of his illness. His illness must no longer seem to him contemptible but must become an enemy worthy of his mettle, a piece of his personality which has solid ground for its existence and out of which things of value for his future life have to be derived. (p. 152)

Specifically addressing the topic of working through resistances, Freud (1914) wrote:

> One must allow the patient time to become more conversant with this resistance with which he has now become acquainted, to work through it, to overcome it, by continuing, in defiance of it, the analytic work according to the fundamental rule of analysis. Only when the resistance is at its height can the analyst, working in common with his patient, discover the repressed instinctual impulses which are feeding the resistance; and it is this kind of experience which convinces the patient of the existence and power of such impulses. (p. 155)

Twelve years later, Freud (1926), returning to the topic of working through, would be even more specific about the origin of the psychic inertia that working through was up against:

> After the ego has decided to relinquish its resistances, it still has difficulty in undoing the repressions; and we have called the period of strenuous effort which follows its praiseworthy decision the phase of "working through"... After the ego's resistance has been removed, the power of the compulsion to repeat—the attraction exerted by the unconscious prototype upon the repressed instinctual process—has still to be overcome. There is nothing to be said against describing this factor as the resistance of the unconscious. (pp. 159–160)

In 1937, Freud would return again to this deepest stratum of resistance (the attraction exerted by the unconscious prototype upon the repressed instinctual process), defining it variously as adhesiveness of the libido or, in a darker mood, as a psychical inertia that must represent the workings of the death instinct. In that context, I believe it is cogent to argue that working through therefore represents the agency of the life instincts, a refusal to "go gentle into that good night" (Thomas, 1952, p. 942) or to succumb to the seductive attraction that the id's compulsions seem to offer. In working through, the ego insists that it will doggedly pursue the return of the repressed in every linkage possible, and that, in the tiniest details of everyday life, it will seek linkages to the vast unconscious tracery that got them started.

If Freud seemed willing to embrace the death instinct conceptually as bedrock mental inertia and entropy, his own concept of working through suggests the contrary, and the latter is the emphasis and implication I want to stress. I am suggesting, for instance, that an analysand's embrace of the death instinct can be played with or worked through as aspects of a dialogue between the ego and the attraction exerted by the unconscious prototype. In other words, if transference works the genetic past into the analytic relationship, where it can be insightfully studied, it needs to be worked out and worked through also in the here and now of life lived, so that it becomes genetic in a new way, no longer shaping neurosis but instead modifying the future before it happens. Working through could be conceptualized as not only work with resistance in the transference, but also as work with resistance to the actualization of change in the analysand's day-to-day life. That these are not mutually exclusive enterprises is obvious to any practitioner who tracks transference not only as it appears in the immediacy of the consulting room, but also in its subtle displacements in the traffic of everyday life. Much as the unexamined life is not worth living, the unlived analytic life is not worth examining unless working through can crack the mould of neurosis and create new paths of adaptation.

My topic is linkage of various kinds: the linkage a child at play makes between inner fantasy and the reality of props and playthings, the linkage between insight and unconscious fantasy made conscious in the adult analytic situation, and the linkage between play and working through itself, which I would like to first explicate clinically by describing two case examples (one from child analysis and one from adult analysis), and then more theoretically by way of discussion.

Play and working through in a child analysis

Luke, a four-year-old boy, who "lost" his mother to malignant melanoma, depicts his dilemma in an analytic session. An airplane constructed of toothpicks and masking tape, about to make its maiden voyage, is grounded to the runway by layers and layers of tape adhering to its surface, making lift-off impossible. Child and analyst have applied a voluminous amount of tape in an orgy of flight control, while questions expressing the airplane's desire for lift-off have been met with applications of even more tape. Eventually, another plane is built of toothpicks and masking tape, and a long piece of wire that connects the grounded plane with the unbridled plane makes lift-off possible. The exuberance that follows is extraordinary. Both planes, interconnected, manned by the boy who once seemed passive, take flight in a Kitty Hawk of emotion analogous to what the Wright brothers must have felt on that fateful day in 1903. The analyst, who thought that the grounded plane represented Luke's state of passivity, was surprised many months of analytic process later when the child referred to the "masked" (masking-taped) plane as the cancer-ridden mother who could not fly.

Play straddles these disparate interpretations, one could say, and countertransference forms the bridge between two meanings as one human in distress leans on another. That the adult other in this communicative experience understands that the child is working through the childhood expression of grief—hiding his teeth behind the masking tape of play, so to speak—is surely crucial, if the insights of understanding are to render the masks of distortion unnecessary in the long run. I have used working through here in the same sense as play in order to capture the activity of the child's mind as it engages in analytic process and addresses the problem of grief.

That the airplane can represent either the cancer-ridden mother who cannot "fly", or Luke's own sense of paralysis as he addresses his loss of her, is a tribute to the ability of play to convey multiple aspects of the conflict that the child is attempting to represent and master. In his play, Luke is at his most adaptive. At other times, he holds onto his bowel motions, reluctant to think of himself as a big boy who could flush them away. Death is perceived on one magical level as a force that sucked his mother into the toilet bowl and destroyed her.

Freud believed, as noted earlier, that play and fantasy are equivalent, except that in play the child links his or her fantasy to concrete objects in the real world. This linkage is what makes child analysis possible, one could argue, since analyst and child use the floor and playthings, rather than the analytic couch, to set in motion the regressive and progressive dramas of play. Having played with airplanes for many weeks, Luke was able at times to reflect on his play. A plane that flew out of control again and again was characterized as a plane whose mother did not teach it how to fly. The stark reality of the mother's neglect of her son as cancer claimed more and more of her maternal competence, not to mention the ultimate abandonment signified by death, entered the playroom at such moments. The plane's anger and sadness at not being taught how to fly could be addressed—not all at once, but as much as could be tolerated, as the child displaced his affects onto the inanimate object to better understand his loss of the animate one.

Resistance is the great force that working through tries to overcome, but the act of overcoming is an act of sympathy for the resistance, since resistance, after all, is not merely adhesiveness of the libido, but also the factor that constitutes half the human soul—the half that is ashamed, afraid, unable to muster the courage to be self-assertive, that turns away from power and dignity and instead embraces self-pity and masochism, that believes safety can be achieved only through self-hatred and renunciation. After months of analytic work with Luke, he was able to watch his aunt feeding her young child without turning away and sulking, saying simply, "I wish *my* mother were not in heaven"—indicating that affects of yearning and envy could now be expressed rather than acted out regressively. Something had been worked through, using airplanes as the linkage between displacement and insight, between play and reality.

A similar piece of working through appeared more directly in the transference in this case: at the end of the hour, Luke would bar the door, forbidding the analyst from bringing the session to an end. The mother may have made an exit beyond his control, but the mother of transference could be controlled in a playful endgame in which the area in front of the playroom door was strewn with playthings, a barricade that made exit impossible. Furthermore, the physical weight of the child against the door would impede the analyst's efforts to open it, and negotiation was necessary in order to bring the hour to an end, often quite a few minutes behind schedule. The barricade was interpreted as an act of love and hate, like the other communication about the grounded plane and the neglectful mother, and eventually the script underwent a significant change: When the analyst went to open the door at the end of the session, the barricade was cleared by the child. "Let me clear the way for you," he said. The analyst was surprised and impressed that Luke had reclaimed a new sense of self-confidence, in which one person's leaving another was no longer experienced as the equivalent of death.

This piece of child analytic process would be hard to make sense of without utilizing the concept of working through. Grief, sadness, anger, and love, instead of being acted out in regression, had been played out and worked through in the progressive enactments of play.

Play and working through in an adult analysis

Yvette, aged thirty-eight, in the middle of a productive but very painful analysis, tried to "play" with the idea that her sense of self had always been compromised by her habit of swallowing aggression, rather than spitting it out in adaptive, communicative expressiveness. Married, with a gifted child (who exuded all the self-confidence her mother lacked), accomplished professionally and interpersonally, she nevertheless felt confounded, perplexed, and unfulfilled at the core of her being. She felt like "coral attached to a reef." Safety resided in clinging, not branching out on her own into uncharted waters.

She had dreamed of coral as a child and imagined it not as an inert secretion, but as a living creature—beautiful, magical, but nevertheless afraid to leave the reef. Aggression in her psychic philosophy was not a commodity to be processed and used adaptively in the service of assertive living. The projection of it seemed so essential that any insight into the act of projection itself was an alarming prospect, not an imaginable achievement. "I could never even imagine it," she declared, totally unaware of the implied aggressive internal assault on the machinery of imagination. After a long period of interpretation and reinterpretation, transference and enactment began to tell an alternative story. One day, Yvette entered the office smiling, and on her way to the couch, pulled a Kleenex from the tissue box. The analyst offered to place the whole box of Kleenex closer to her as she lay on the couch. The analysand chided the analyst for his excessive politeness, experiencing it as an act of hostility. The coral was leaving the reef, finally—developing some teeth of its own and snapping sarcastically with them. An opportunity for play and working through had presented itself.

The "Kleenex box incident," as it came to be tagged over time, was only one such analytic instance of something palpable, some detail that transference neurosis could "exaggerate" in the service of investigation and working through. "But there are so many details, so many incidents, thousands of them!" Yvette observed, with a mixture of exasperation and wonder. One essential point I am stressing is that indeed there are, and since such details and incidents are the external accompaniments of internal intrapsychic events, these details in the living of everyday life highlight the same conflicts and new attempts at resolution dealt with in the analytic situation. Insight needs to be tested against these incidents in real time, for insight develops its teeth as it engages these real-life events. If "God and the devil are in the details," human compromise that attempts to integrate and humanize these supernatural imagoes is in the details, too.

Working through ensures that insight is not shelved, as Valenstein (1983) reported, but is instead put to use in the flesh-and-blood "incidentals" of actual living. The word incidental has an additional significance in this case; it was a favorite word of Yvette's to describe what she believed was totally lacking in the analytic situation: spontaneous affect on both sides; unrehearsed, "incidental" experience—not the contrived, manufactured affects the free-associative process dared to call "real."

"It's *mechanistic*," she would explain, another favorite word for "artificial" Freudian discourse. Interpretations reduced the mind to merely mechanisms. Resistance was the only recourse of a belittled, exasperated, mistreated mind. And resistance there was—formidable at times. It was worked through over time, as analyst and analysand came to appreciate the elemental anger housed in it, a genetic rage at mother and father that was never adequately expressed. Yvette had grown up in France. Her father, a maquisard (member of the French resistance) had vanished under mysterious circumstances. This was a void that seemed at first to have aroused little or no curiosity. This total lack of curiosity, which represented hatred and dismissal, as well as defensive disavowal, was interpreted and worked through over time.

A crucial aspect of Yvette's lack of curiosity about her father was a protective wish not to overtax her already burdened mother. This protective fantasy turned the young child into a responsible overseer of mother's needs, a total reversal of what the child needed for her own development. These aspects of interpretation and working through with Yvette during long periods of resistance are very germane to my topic, and could be described in greater detail, but I want to return to the word incidental and to report a phase of working through that I believe will illustrate my points even more clearly.

The concept of a biting superego as the repository of much rerouted genetic anger had been developed and interpreted with Yvette mostly through transference. The analyst would surely turn away from her, abandon her, never love her, even retaliate against her if sexuality or rage were expressed openly. Her husband's forceful character and ambitious nature corroborated these internal convictions. But she knew it was her own character that was the issue, not his, even though collusion often blurred the psychological goals she set for herself. She had no teeth, never did, never would. But irony was about to play a trick on her: another analytic "incident" was about to happen. She had placed her handbag beside the head of the couch when she lay down. When she got up to leave, one of the clasps on the handle of the bag had attached itself to the fabric of the couch. Her bag had "bitten" my couch, the clasp having sunken its teeth firmly into the fabric, and it took what seemed like ages to disengage.

In the next several sessions, and indeed at intervals throughout the subsequent analysis, the incident in which Yvette's bag "bit" my couch became a symbol of all she would like to work through, but was in despair about being able to accomplish. Criticizing me about the Kleenex incident had been almost unbearable for her. If she asked where I would be on vacation in summer and I did not answer her, rage and hurt sent her into despair. She knew it was exaggerated; her hypersensitivity astonished her at times. Could it really be all about childhood, her absent father, her overburdened mother?

The analysand's lack of curiosity about her father was an identification with, and idealization of, a mother who seemed to need no man in her life and who implied that her daughter would do well to follow suit. Yvette, despite her marriage, had tried to maintain this fantasy of union with an all-sufficient woman as her unconscious goal. It was a kind of symbiosis, and it could only be imagined or achieved through utter existential happenstance. This was the fantasy that lay behind the word incidental: a casual, spontaneous, affective union with the other, not set up by desire or agency. This was the baby before teeth pushed their way through gums, a pre-Kleinian baby—blissful, symbiotic, conflict free, like coral in its reef, safe, undifferentiated. The irony that forced itself upon this most literate woman was that the word incidental, while not etymologically related to teeth (the root is cadere, to fall, not dent, for teeth) did lend itself by sound association to dental, describing the very aggressive orality that her fantasy had fought so hard to conceal!

She was aware now that her passivity and sense of psychic illegitimacy were based on an unconscious fantasy that pictured her without agency, a self without teeth. But what to do about it? She sensed that she must play, an activity she could not remember as part of her childhood repertoire. But playing meant engaging with the analyst and others, and engagement meant danger, since in her definition of object relations, the other was the repository of all the sexuality and aggression the self felt impelled to disown. The other could therefore co-opt the self—harass, enslave, seduce, and engulf it, and the self, without any sense of I, could not lift a finger or use any teeth to save itself.

An interpretation from the analyst suggesting that Yvette's conscience had run off with her teeth, and that the self was now afraid to retrieve them, sent a shudder through her as if the very thought of teeth was alarming. But she began to stand up for herself, to practice having teeth, to play. When her husband chided her for drinking a glass of port, implying she was alcoholic (she certainly was not), she immediately quipped, "Don't confuse me with your colleagues. I'm just enjoying my port." This felt to her like putting her head in a lion's mouth, but she knew her life, her new analytic life, depended on it. Her husband apologized. Maybe teeth were useful after all.

In the transference, Yvette became more competitive. She complained that many of my other patients seemed old. Was this a measure of how long I held on to them, unable to cure them, given my incompetence? This was unusual; next to mother, I had been enshrined, untouchable. Since some of the other analysands were not as old as this misperception seemed to insist, Yvette became aware that she was killing them off, claiming me all for herself. These new teeth she was experimenting with came with new insights that were disturbing and liberating all at once. She described the changes she was trying to integrate into her character as "mundane", but the word had a positive meaning for her, since she so often felt like a disembodied spirit; to be mundane or incidental—that is, of this world—was a significant goal for her. She thought of the work we were doing as an attempt to "reform" her, and this word, too, meant something positive to her: to reshape, restructure, reconfigure the whole armature of the psyche. But she was aware of the irony embedded in the word: that reform also meant changing a criminal sense of self into a new, less guilt—ridden vision of psychological reality.

Transference and genetic recall were intimately connected at this stage. The analytic process, productive as it was, could seem like a mandate to produce, the anal imagery making the analysand wince visibly on the couch. She was bitter that precocity and a Protestant work ethic "came with mother's milk", as she put it. In such a developmental whirlwind, there was no time, no room for play. Learning to play now "will take some work", she quipped, with playful, sardonic humor.

A dream description from this phase of the analysis was extremely productive: "I am swimming in a heart-shaped swimming pool. But I am dropping cement as I swim and soon my swimming space becomes smaller and smaller." Yvette had awakened from this dream angry, for once, at its implications. She felt sure that the dream had been triggered by a recent analytic session in which she imagined stepping out of her swimming pool, showing me her pink toenails, and envisioned my admiration of her, "the equal of your admiration for your wife, perhaps even greater." This daring, spontaneous fantasy had been reported in the previous session with excitement and fear, but also with a sense of analytic achievement. The dream seemed to be an unconscious undoing of her courage; and anger at her own dream work seemed to be her first association.

When all the elements of the dream were analyzed, Yvette realized that she was deeply afraid of the working through upon which she was embarking; but she realized that her fear could be analyzed, too! "I can dream without cramping my style. If I analyze it, I can confine it to dreams and swim better in my waking life." Maybe there is no more fitting metaphor than this to depict the suffering and triumphs of working through.

The retrieval of the unconscious fantasy, "I am coral attached to a reef; it is not safe to individuate and swim on your own terms through life's waters," and a concomitant fantasy, "a woman should not need a man; men are abandoners who are not to be trusted: they have no sense of accountability" became the hard-won insights of an intense analytic process, but we found that making them conscious was not enough. They had to be examined within the transference and within the incidental details of life outside the consulting room.

When Yvette asked the analyst, "Where do you find the patience for all this?" (referring to endless repetitions of conflicts and attempted resolutions), she was not only marveling at the idealized analyst/mother; she was also identifying her own impatience with herself, an identification with the father who had impatiently abandoned ship, "never to be seen or heard from again." The identification was defensive, of course, and Yvette came to realize that it protected her from a furious dialogue with her absent father. Her total lack of curiosity about his whereabouts was not only an identification with the mother who forbade curiosity, but also a disavowal of the object of her love and hatred in the service of avoiding a stormy dialogue.

As she arrived at such recognitions, Yvette often said to the analyst, "You are crucial. My relationship to you is essential if this is to work." Sometimes she wept as she said this. Through her tears, she was angry, hopeful, and loving, all at once. The analyst acknowledged an understanding of how crucial he was, since the analysand was picturing him as both the sustaining coral reef and as the abandoner. It was hard for her to picture him as a reliable human being who worked hard with her to understand the nature of the traps she had set for herself, eventually releasing her from them through analysis.

If we view Yvette's question of "where do you find the patience for all this" as a pun—"where do you find the patients for all this"—an additional irony is revealed, an irony of intense abandonment that yearns to be "found" in the transference and elsewhere. Yvette knew that she must work all this out with the analyst, but she also had to work it out with her husband, child, her aging mother, her colleagues, and friends. At this stage of the analysis, one could say that the coral had left the reef, swimming mostly in individuated waters, but carrying cement with her just in case!

Working through is the yardstick that assesses the swimmer's progress (not to mention the many meanings of cement!). In fact, I believe it was the working through in Yvette's analysis that allowed a new metaphor to emerge, a metaphor that went completely beyond the coral-reef conceptualization. She imagined the analytic relationship as a space in which she would have a voice equal to the analyst's, a space of mutual respect that would promote a new dialogue in which no emotion would have to be disavowed. When this new metaphor of the analytic space or analytic dialogue dawned on her, she came to her session with an affect of analytic achievement and triumph, a newfound sense of courage and presence. As all the components of this state were examined from the here-and-now angle, as well as from the perspective of the genetic past, Yvette suddenly accused the analyst of changing the subject. What she meant was that focusing on genetic aspects meant a flight from the intimacy of the here and now, that I was the victim of my own countertransference, and that changing the subject in that way hurt her feelings deeply.

I am making this interaction seem simpler than it actually was. In fact, it took a good bit of interpretation and working through to get things out on the analytic table, so to speak, but the point I am stressing is that the whole discussion embodied the nuts and bolts of the analytic activity that goes into the labor of working through. In other words, when coral that seems to need to cement itself silently and desperately to a reef begins to develop autonomy and to indignantly declare that one party to the analytic dialogue has changed the subject, the previously passive discourse has taken an active, assertive tack that highlights the complexity of working through, which is the painstaking work of identifying the subject, not only its genetic origins and their representation in the here and now of transference, but throughout all the vicissitudes of displacement as well.

When an analyst, connecting the immediacy of transference with its pedigree in the past, is chided by the analysand for changing the subject, one could argue that the great topic of change itself is being addressed, is being worked through, as the analysand dares to criticize authority in a way that would have once been unthinkable. Yvette never felt safe playing as a child; in fact, the concept of it made her shudder on the couch, as if its precarious premises could shatter the small island of static stability she needed to cling to. Even though working through has been called suffering through by Waelder (1932), and one can certainly agree that some aspects of working through are painful enough to warrant that description, there is also a playful quality to working through as new ideas are experimented with and "tried on", as Neubauer (1987), using a sartorial metaphor, has so felicitously characterized it. I suggest that Yvette, a child who never played, learned how to play as an adult in the analytic playground of transference, fantasy retrieval, and working through.

To be more than an intellectual exercise, an analogy should throw new practical as well as theoretical light on the topics being compared. I believe that, in bringing together play and working through, comparison and contrast can highlight unique features of both. Ironically, the etymology of analogy and neglect exposes a common verbal root (*legere*, legend), which essentially means to gather together in the case of analogy, or not to gather together in the case of neglect (*neglegere*). By bringing together what had not been appreciated earlier (playing and working through), neglect is redressed and a heuristic pathway of intellectual and clinical associations is advanced.

By conceptualizing psychoanalysis as the process of uncovering unconscious fantasy and subjecting it to rigorous interpretation, by emphasizing play as fantasy tester as much as it has been extolled as fantasy bearer, and by focusing on a particular active ingredient in working through, I have undoubtedly narrowed the focus of all three of these elements, in order to peer through the particular lens of analogy that I propose. Ironically, my thesis gains additional support from a similar analogy that Freud used in a totally different context. In 1915, in a letter to Ferenczi, he concisely and memorably described the "mechanism" of his scientific creativity as the "succession of daringly playful fantasy and relentlessly realistic criticism" (Falzeder and Brabant, 1996, p. 55). Somewhat irreverently, I would like to suggest that the extraordinary mechanism of Freud's creative genius can be compared to the ordinary mechanism of neurosis and working through, in the sense that neurosis can be compared to a compendium of internal fantasies that compromise the wingspan of psychological life, whereas working through is comparable to a process of persistent, realistic assessment that paradoxically grounds fantasy in reality, thereby setting it free. In a sense, play is the working through of childhood, and working through is the newfound play of adulthood, both informed by fantasy and "relentless, realistic criticism," as adaptation and compromise try to wean themselves from self-deception, Luke, Adam and Yvette examples of what play and work can accomplish together.

CHAPTER SIX

Manifestly misleading: the cunning artistry of dream

Bottom: I have had a dream, past the wit of man to say what dream it was .... it shall be called Bottom's dream, because it hath no bottom.

—*A Midsummer Night's Dream*, Act Four, Scene One
William Shakespeare

The last chapter dealt with play, that extraordinary mixture of fantasy and action without which child analysis would be difficult to conduct; and adulthood, as I have implied, would be impoverished also. I have suggested earlier that play could be thought of as fantasy that needs to link itself to external concrete objects such as toys and other playthings to give expression to its own interiority. I also suggested that transference could be thought of as unconscious, genetic fantasy displaced onto, and thereby distorting the current person and reality of the analyst. It could be argued that dreams too are latent fantastic infantile wishes displaced onto a manifest grid or tableau, the better to disguise their original intent. In fact the displacement of disguised meaning from a latent sphere to a manifest sphere is essentially the whole argument of this chapter. What I emphasize over and over is that the manifest content of a dream can be ingeniously infiltrated with puns and parapraxes, jokes and even a dream itself embedded within the envelope of another dream, in an elaborate façade of disguise. In other words, dreams can be playful in the most confounding ways, as if the unconscious mind was a perverse tease that believed in depositing communications of the utmost importance on the doorstep of awakened consciousness, but in such a disguised code that the awakener would be mostly bewildered and exasperated rather than enlightened or enchanted with his strange nocturnal gift. To Freud, dreams were the royal road to the unconscious, but finding that road and traveling on it successfully was a labor that only genius could have pulled off. Of his greatest masterpiece *The Interpretation of Dreams* Freud said: "insights such as these befall the lot of a man only once in a lifetime." They have befallen the lot of all of us thanks to Freud's ground breaking, immortal book. Any contribution to the theory of dreams is unimaginable without Freud's *The Interpretation of Dreams* as its springboard. What I plan to attempt in this chapter is an in-depth study of certain unusual "inclusions" in dream content and then to end with an examination of the dreaming process from a longitudinal developmental perspective. Basically I will be illustrating the cunning artistry of dream work and its manifestly misleading ministry of disguise that ensures that the latent remains hidden while a host of manifest red herrings steals the oneiric limelight in the most ingenious manner. In this way I hope to augment Freud's theory in places where his own comments were not so exhaustive.

1. For example, Freud touches on the importance of dreams within dreams but there is only half a page on this curious phenomenon in *The Interpretation of Dreams*. So I therefore describe the phenomenon in greater detail with a substantive clinical example and commentary.

2. By way of another example, Freud suggested that jokes in dreams were not really funny. I describe a dream wherein an embedded joke is quite funny, and I investigate its unusual, rare presence in a dream. Basically I ask and investigate what these usually diurnal phenomena are doing in dreams and why they have been co-opted into the collage of the dream text in the first place.

3. Continuing the theme of unusual inclusions in the manifest content of dreams I investigate a parapraxis and a pun in a dream.

4. If dreams are uncanny in toto, I examine one particular inclusion of the uncanny in a dream and its defensive, disguising function.

5. Freud was enchanted with children's dreams: they so elegantly and with such transparency confirmed his major thesis about the infantile wish and its central agency in all dreams. I take this a little further by following a sequence of dreams in one person at age five, thirteen and twenty. A developmental and longitudinal perspective can be outlined in this manner.

Dreams within dreams

The concept of a dream within a dream is fascinating. If dreams are uncanny by definition when they seem to employ a kind of oneiric mitosis to bamboozle the dream censor even further, then the weird experience of a dream within a dream is born! The illusion created by the dream work portrays one portion of the dream enacted within the envelope of the other. Freud (1900) emphasized that the function of placing a piece of reality in a dream within a dream is an attempt to rob it of its significance and obliterate it. However, he seemed curiously disinterested in the fact that segmentation of a dream text into two seemingly discrete fragments does offer a dream investigator the opportunity to explore the dynamic relationship between the two fragments and the multiple meanings of the illusion created during sleep. In this study, the linkage between the two parts of the dream sequence is highlighted. While Freud's intuition is corroborated, his lack of interest in the duality of the dream events is puzzling, as if he believed that only the dream within the other dream was meaningful and the other "containing" dream could be ignored. In this section of this chapter I suggest that both portions of a dream within a dream are significant, the one helping to explicate the other as the free-associative process of dream interpretation gives equal democratic time to both.

I pose the following question: why would a dreamer immersed in the illusion of dream imagine that he has awakened, but in fact go on dreaming a "new dream" so that on actual awakening his experience will seem to have been that he has had a dream within a dream? If one pictures a dream within a dream cinematically and if it is possible to retrieve the unconscious moment that signals the end of reel one and the activation of reel two, so to speak, what unique unconscious psychology could account for this cinematographic decision?

The topic was first introduced by Sigmund Freud in 1900 and since then has received surprisingly scant attention, Berman and Silber being notable exceptions. Whether this means that the phenomenon is rare or simply under-reported is not clear.

Freud in 1900 insisted that a dream within a dream was a sure sign that something that had actually happened was being disavowed vehemently. "If a particular event is inserted into a dream ... by the dream work itself, this implies the most decided confirmation of the reality of the event" (1900). To place a dream within the envelope of another dream suggested that a reality was being hidden with such precision that an astute awakener would raise his eyebrows at the elaborate mechanism of disguise.

My goal in this chapter is not only to re-examine Freud's thesis but also to address his neglect of the envelope as he focused solely on its contents. In other words, I will argue that a dream within a dream has two dream portions, one seemingly housed in the other, that both portions are part of one elaborate illusion, and that both can be studied profitably.

One assumption of this segment of our dream exploration is that a "formal" re-textualization of the unfolding screenplay of a dream must be in response to the emergence in the dream state of affect that cannot be disguised with the "usual" primary processes (condensation, displacement, symbolism) but requires a fundamental relocation of the drama to resolve or at least manage the conflict and keep the dreamer asleep. That is, reels are switched dramatically for urgent dynamic reasons.

The dream within a dream that is scrutinized here occurred in the eighth year of an analysis, a clinical context that allowed the topic to be viewed through the lens of a complex transference neurosis. Genetics, dynamics, transference, and countertransference had been explicated again and again so that termination was now the focus and perhaps one of the main triggers of the dream.

The dreamer is fifty-six years old, French by birth, an ex-priest, professor of philosophy, recently married, with one child. The analysis could be portrayed as the deconstruction of a conscience so Jesuitical in its brilliant mixture of menace, mischief, and multiple ambiguities as to be almost unreachable, its mental quicksilver visible, touchable, but hard to pick up or hold onto.

The dream was reported as follows:

I awake at the sound of a car pulling into the driveway of our Connecticut house. It is pitch dark but a child is being dropped off as if our home were a nursery school. All this seemed natural in dream experience even though the time, the darkness, would have been highly unusual for such a drop-off in real time. The scene shifts. I am now outside my house but lost, trying to find my bearings. A child on a bicycle guides me home. Then I walk from my house in Connecticut to Greenwich Village, which in dream geography seems no more than a hundred yards. I am so surprised by the spatial novelty of Connecticut's being a stone's throw from Greenwich Village that I wake up, an illusion, as I will discover on actual awakening. In Greenwich Village I walk into a wood-lined office in a townhouse. A bearded man, not unlike the young Freud in the Freud-Fliess era, greets me. I start to tell him the unusual dream I've just had about being lost and how it was a child who guided me home.

When the dreamer awakens he begins to tell his wife the dream immediately and while recounting the dream has a déjà phenomenon, as if he had told her the dream already. He is aware that the dream-within-a-dream phenomenon of telling the dream to the bearded man in Greenwich Village is what gives the déjà experience with his wife such an uncanny feeling. (A dream followed by a déjà feeling is noteworthy, in and of itself: it suggests that the magical thinking of dream time spilled over into immediate post dream experience, night refusing to accept, too readily, the terms daylight insists on imposing). The associations were genetic, dynamic, freely flowing, and far ranging. New insights were generated as dreams, and dreams within dreams were examined for several weeks. The theme of a lost childhood as well as an actual experience of being lost at age five had been analyzed from various angles over the years. But the dream-within-a-dream treatment of it seemed to generate new affects, more intense memory. The analysand, whose reading of Freud was deep and well integrated into his overall philosophical knowledge, (a factor that could be a resistance at times but often was a promoter of insight), was not unaware of Freud's contributions to the topic. "One hides in a dream within a dream an actual event," he commented, paraphrasing Freud. "In that case, depending on which of the dreams is within the other, being lost could be the disavowed actuality, or is it "telling" about it that is the significant reality that is being relegated to dream life, doubly displaced and captioned as non-real in its dream-within-dream status?" Several questions had been raised that would take time to address. If there was no new "topic" at this stage of analysis, the same could not be said of affect. Memory and history were not files in an unconscious library but sudden revelations of the self in a living mirror that could surprise and astonish no matter how clever the defensive anticipations. Which part of the dream was within the other? If the totality of the dream is looked upon as one text, the illusion of waking up and telling the dream to a bearded man in Greenwich Village would seem to be the part of the dream that is within the other, larger, earlier part. However, looking at the dream as a total text, one could argue that the first part is being told again in the later dream and is therefore "within" it, making the analysand's question not as "intellectual" as it seemed at first blush. This raises the question as to whether the two dream pieces can be studied in isolation or separately, a task Silber (1983) set himself in his brilliant paper on the topic, no doubt to keep his focus scientific and uncluttered.

Which actuality was being disguised, the experience of being lost or the telling about it? This led to a series of intriguing sessions, but some genetic context must be described to make the narrative intelligible.

Mr. Perdu (a fictitious name for the analysand) had recounted early in his analysis how once as a child in the south of France he had been playing with older boys who suddenly went about their own business, forgetting the younger one who had been entrusted to their care. He imagines that he was five or six in the memory. A kind gentleman on a bicycle rode him home to his house. In later years, whenever this incident was recalled, his mother would rail against the boy to whom she had entrusted her son, taking little responsibility for her own negligence. "Quel salot" she would scream blaming the boy for her own delinquency. Mr. Perdu was aware that in the dream "a child on a bicycle who guided him home" was a reversal of the actual roles of child and adult fifty years before the dream. This childhood memory had been analyzed intensely, but the reversal and the elaborate dream work that dream-within-dream implied suggested, as Freud would have argued, that this was the reality whose disavowal in dream-within-dream was in fact a powerful affirmation of its significance.

Mr. Perdu, an only child, had for years insisted that a great closeness had existed between him and his mother—an assertion that memory and dream seemed to challenge. His father's alcoholism and fiscal irresponsibility left the family in dire straits often, until the mother started her own business and essentially became the breadwinner. He idealized the mother's resourcefulness and courage and could not remember ever feeling any anger toward her. The anger he felt toward his father could not be expressed either, except in pity and shame. A vicious superego became the heir of these unspeakable hatreds for years, quite ego syntonic with the vicious Catholic god Mr. Perdu had enshrined in the Vatican of his mind throughout his pre-analytic existence. But an unconscious rebel was there too, as mentioned earlier, longing to break the shackles. The shackles, like most psychological shackles, were "mind-forged manacles," as Blake suggested, and the forge had a complex artistry that displayed its symptoms but not the mould, which remained well hidden. Mr. Perdu was aware that the dream-within-a-dream had exposed the mould more than ever and that the revelation should be pounced on and exploited. "There's loss in one piece of the dream and telling about it in the other," he exclaimed. This eureka of insight provoked a re-examination of all the previously stoked genetic embers. The concepts of "loss" and "telling", themes that were sounded often, were about to lend themselves to variations that surprised the analysand with their novelty, despite their ancient origins. Loss had been a theme that both antedated and postdated the actual childhood loss that occurred, when his older playmates abandoned him. The Oedipal years were characterized by incestuous closeness to a mother who had distanced herself from a negligent husband, "seducing" her son, figuratively speaking, with confidences and intimacies that belonged more appropriately in the relationship with her husband.

"There's no telling what I was told," the analysand would quip ironically and cynically as he tried to invoke the childhood atmosphere of loneliness and closeness, a paradox that made more and more sense to him as he explored the absence of his father from his life and the undifferentiated presence of his mother. The "loss" of his father had been passively experienced in the sense that Mr. Perdu never questioned his father's self-destructive character nor his mother's compliance with it. He never "told" his father off for his chronic neglect, and he never told his mother off for her abandonment of her dialogue with his father and "seduction" of her son. Instead he assumed that his "loss" was coming to him, something he deserved for secretly hating both of them. The actual incident of loss at age five, traumatic and real in itself, was also a screen for deeper losses. Religion was "telling" in the ironic sense that the analysand felt he was telling very private intimacies to the wrong people, priests who in hindsight often seemed unworthy of his revelations. Minor childhood symptoms of latency stealing were adjudicated as major crimes in the confession box, a kind of childhood supreme court that would eventually, of course, take up permanent residence in his superego, through processes of introjection and identification. In retrospect he realized that he hated his mother for supporting a primitive institution that exploited a child's guilt rather than explaining it and exploring it empathically, as analysis would do many years later. "I should have told the priest off. Instead I swallowed my guts and became a priest myself, identification with the aggressor and victim all at once I suppose." The bitterness of this reconstruction was palpable as insight savored anew the old love, the old hatred, and the relentless conflict.

That his life was about being lost and telling people about it had become more central in the analysis than ever before, thanks to the double vision of the dream and the insight it afforded about the meaning of loss and the meaning of communication (telling) and how both could be corrupted by a defensive psychology that would attempt to keep them apart. "It will be important for me to tell you how much I hate you as termination reprises this sense of loss for yet another time," the analysand said, stepping into the reality of the analytic journey's end with very genuine affect.

The many meanings of the dream-within-dream psychology were uncovered in this rich free-associative process. Telling intimacies to parent, priest, analyst seemed to be one psychological seed of the dream process; loss as experience, loss as unconscious punishment or fear, the other.

The dream thoughts beneath the manifest content of both segments of the dream sequence could be summarized as follows:

> The child "delivered" to the house at an "odd" hour is the wish to have a child in the primal scene. The primal crime of the first part of the dream is punished by loss of bearings, loss of home. This stirs up the reality of the actual traumatic loss in childhood, which is reversed in the representation of "a child guided me home." This reversal seems not adequate to the task; "reel switching" becomes necessary. In the "new" dream portion, after the illusion

of awakening there is confession to a bearded man who represents father and analyst (neither one bearded in reality). "Beard" represents undoing of the wish to castrate father and analyst for "forcing" him to confess, for not having a baby with him, for not allowing him to be a permanent analytic baby, for forcing him out as termination approaches. The distance between Connecticut ("connect" as opposite to the "disconnection" of loss) and Greenwich Village is "destroyed", time space altered magically in the new "Greenwich Mean Time" of unconscious timelessness.

This summary does not address the central question I am pursuing even though it is an essential preamble. The analysand's intellectual doggedness about the dream-within-a-dream mechanism was the engine that generated more and more free-associative information about what he playfully referred to as this "unconscious curiosity". The possibility of reaching a compromise between the wish to tell the dream to someone and the wish to stay asleep was entertained as one potential motivation, but there were deeper currents also, he felt sure.

Mr. Perdu was puzzled that the reality of being lost as a child, which had received much scrutiny in the analysis, could still show up in a dream within a dream, as if to insist that it still needed to be disavowed intensely! We had reconstructed pretty well. Which stone had been left unturned? As Mr. Perdu pursued this issue associatively, overwhelming "new" affects appeared genetically and transferentially. Deep-seated anger toward mother emerged. How could she have entrusted a five-year-old to careless older boys? What did that reveal about the whole ramshackle structure of early care he must have received from a harried young mother starting her own business on the ruins of her husband's psychological and fiscal collapse? Who was this makeshift father; what made him tick? This genetic current of intense affect could turn transferential from hour to hour. What kind of an analyst could have reconstructed so intellectually, leaving the deepest affects untouched? Was the analyst lost in some dream-within-a-dream of his own to have overlooked the most significant meanings? This analytic volatility, genetic and transferential all at once, led to the revelation that the reality of childhood loss had not been fully analyzed, if it ever could be. It was clear that affect would always remain. Sorrow, pain, anger, memory could be understood in analysis but not eliminated, not exorcised. The confessional offered absolution, the wipeout of sin. The couch could offer only understanding, the sober dignity of truth rather than the appeal of illusion!

Communication itself was corrupted in childhood, he believed, when "telling" to a priest became mandatory. Even when he was no longer a priest, the inquisitional dialogue continued within, in the internal confessional. Much of the analytic work in the transference neurosis was an attempt to rehabilitate communication itself, to rescue it from its inquisitional origins. By putting trauma in one dream and "telling" in a dream within it, the analysand was declaring that "telling" was as great a trauma as trauma itself, and that the two should not be confused. If he had been able to "tell" his mother off for entrusting him carelessly to the older boys, the original trauma might not have retained its "actual" significance or its symbolic significance as a screen for all the other "tellings" that had been left unsaid. Considering the first part of the dream as the dream within the larger dream (the dream in its totality), the analysand argued that the child guiding him home could be viewed as a fulfillment of the wish that the older boy had not betrayed him or, better still, that he had been able to tell the boy off and demand that the boy not betray him but guide him home. The capacity to talk straight to one's peers in childhood (or adulthood, for that matter) is a measure of how "straight" one felt one could be in the dialogue with father or mother. Developmental achievement cannot be sustained without some early object constancy. If the breast is the first curriculum, baby talk is the first dialogue that leads eventually, developmentally to all later dialogues. Essentially 'telling' and "loving" go hand in hand unless the system breaks down for defensive reasons.

If one undoes the division between the two dream parts and treats the text as a seamless document, one reading of the text could be articulated as follows: "I want a baby delivered to me in darkness, a primal-scene reversal in which I am not excluded. For this the punishment is loss of the object or loss of the love of the object (castration fear disavowed perhaps as 'regressive' object loss screens the more Oedipal punishment). 'A child guided me home' redresses this. Finally, the wish to tell all to a bearded man represents the undoing of the father's castration and a man-to-man dialogue between son and parent in which aggression and sexuality need not be denied in the new space analysis has cleared for straight talk."

If that was the seamless vision of the dream, why was the illusion of dream within dream necessary at all? To all the defensive reasons alluded to earlier, the analysand added that a dream-within-a-dream is like one dream spawning another. The wish to have the Oedipal baby with the analyst, with the mother, with the father, could be represented through the formal disguise of one dream giving birth to another, one dream invaginated in the other in an act of oneiric copulation. One dream was the dream child of the other, so to speak. When the analysis ended, the patient remarked with characteristic irony, "There's no telling what the future holds." While this was obviously true, it seemed clear that the future would hold a more enlightened vision of the past and that a dream within a dream could claim some of the credit for it.

A joke in a dream

If a dream can "pretend" to embed another dream within the artistry of its own disguise, confounding the awakener with the virtuosity of its sleeping sleight-of-handedness, we now pursue this irony of a sleeping ego that seems to be wide awake in the middle of the night, weaving layers and layers of manifest imagery, with the purpose of completely hiding latent meanings. This time an embedded joke rather than a dream is our topic. Freud believed that jokes in dreams were not really "formally" successful, the dream work exploiting them, with "defensive" rather than "comic" intent. Adam's joke in Chapter Five comes to mind again. Adam may have plagiarized his own dream to construct the diurnal joke he told his analyst. Adam's dream, as Freud argued, has no interest in comic correctness, given its wish to disguise rather than entertain. In any case, Adam's cognitive equipment at age five seemed unable to pilfer a joke from a dream and make it conform to the aesthetic principles of adult joke telling. Now I want to present the content of a dream in which the embedded joke was actually "funny" by aesthetic standards. It did conform to the usually acceptable standards of joke telling in real as opposed to oneiric time. We now turn our attention to why the dream work employed this unusual technique and the dynamic reasons for such an extra flourish of disguise in the midst of what is, after all, a pretty elaborate concoction of disguises already.

> I go to a restaurant. You (the analyst) are there too with your wife. Suddenly I bite my tongue. You (the analyst) say, "Oh, at least one

of us will have a good meal." Paul Newman is in the restaurant
also, and I comment, "Oh, he comes here too."

The analyst was immediately struck not only by the sarcastic piece of
comic humor that had been assigned to his persona in the dream but
also by how genuinely funny the structure of the dream joke seemed.
It was not a dream joke that "leaves us cold" and "does not make us
laugh" as Freud had suggested. This is true of most dreams: if the comic
appears in a dream it is merely part of the whole *mise en scène*. Its function is not to amuse but to further disguise like all the other manifest
components. But there are exceptions, as the dream I have just described
illustrates. It seemed to be an example of a true joke, exploited no doubt
by the dream work in the service of disguise, a piece of dream text
that would not reveal its meanings until the free-associative processes
of dream interpretation made sense out of its opacities as well as of
what seemed to be its transparencies. While the analyst was genuinely
amused by the perverse laughter the joke seemed to elicit, he was also
aware of the analytic challenge of a piece of humor that seemed to celebrate sadism's comic triumph over misery's self-inflicted wounds. The
"good meal" the dream joke celebrates was after all a swallowing of
one's own flesh, the self its own totem meal in a piece of savage canni-
balistic self-sacrifice. Was masochism ever better captured symbolically
than in this caricature of nourishment, horror masquerading as humor
as the self makes a meal of the self?

    The dreamer's analytic context must be cited in an attempt to bring
coherence to a piece of clinical material that has been presented so pre-
cipitously without associative or genetic background. The dreamer is
a forty-five-year-old architect who had recently received a significant
commission, which would prove to be a turning point in his career,
financially and artistically. He was the younger of two siblings in a
highly successful artistic family (mother a successful novelist, brother
a renowned musician). His own success seemed more conflicted given
his identification with a depressed father whose career as a writer never
amounted to what early promise seemed to have assured. This identification and a sadistic superego that seemed to accompany it became
the main focus of an analysis that was most productive and nearing
termination when the dream under discussion jolted the dreamer with
its wry sarcasm and arresting ironies.

    In the next several sessions, the main themes beneath the manifest
content of the dream slowly revealed themselves. The analysand was

a nail biter for the first twenty years of his life. Oral issues were often prominent as free-associative process and genetic recall gave shape to his childhood conflicts. The biting of the tongue in the dream was a reprise of an ancient oral sadomasochistic assault on his own flesh, self-punishment a defense against a complex dialogue of love and hate with mother, father, and brother. Identification with a successful mother and a castrated father created a dual internal conflicted imagery that was confounding when Oedipal issues were being processed. Regression to masochistic oral imagery of auto castration (biting his own tongue) seemed safer than competitive displays of castration wishes toward a father who might not be able to "take it," given the already dilapidated state of his self-esteem. This old genetic theme was very much alive in the transference neurosis, as the dream imagery suggests. The dream arena is a restaurant which Newman, a "new man", frequents. The patient's new identity as successful architect and successful analysand occupies one pole of the dream, while auto castration dominates the other pole, the analyst's endorsement of the neurotic resolution cloaked in humor. For many sessions, in fact, the analyst's sarcasm in the dream was experienced as if the dream were factual rather than a product of dream work. The idea that the analysand's success could "finish off" the father or "finish off" the analyst (one meaning of the termination phase) needed the massive reversal implied by the biting of the tongue. The dream joke, in other words, was a would-be collusion between a hoped-for countertransferential analyst who would "celebrate" the analysand's self-destructive neurosis rather than analyze it. The "collusion" had genetic roots, of course, in the childhood fantasy that the patient and his mother had successfully "finished off" the father, a piece of unconscious mental imagery that was exciting and terrifying all at once. It would be "fun" to get away with "murder", neurosis seems to suggest, but the joke is on the neurotic in the sense that one doesn't get away with the imaginary crime at all but suffers forever as if one had! Neurosis is a bad joke against the self that the neurotic acts out without realizing the tragicomic drama in which he is trapped. As these issues became even more obvious in the analytic process, the "function" of the joke in the dream became more accessible. The analysand, well informed by this stage of analysis about the basic components and strategies of dream disguise, was able to ponder the unusual appearance in a dream of a joke that would have seemed funny even in waking life.

A pun in a dream

From humor in a dream we turn to yet another example of dream work virtuosity: the appearance of a pun in a dream, a pun that concealed half of its meaning from the dreamer but revealed it to the astonished awakener, who eventually made very good use of the insight. In this section of a chapter that deals with dreams from a variety of novel view points, I am trying to emphasize again the cunning of the dream work as it selects what it needs to fulfill infantile wishes, using the most beguiling disguises.

Mr. J, a professor of English literature, in analysis for many years, recently reported the following dream:

> I am at the closing of a real estate transaction. All the parties are assembled around an official looking table in a typical room of a bank or some such institution. The lawyers are present, but the deal cannot go through because the didn'ter isn't present.

The strange word didn'ter seemed to make sense in the dream, as if the didn'ter were as expectable a presence as the lawyers or bank officials who attend closings. Didn'ter was pronounced in the dream like didn't (the contracted form of did not) with an "er" attached to it, turning the verb into a noun. Initially, Mr. J did not recognize the pun that didn'ter concealed. When he did, he was jolted: didn'ter, with a slight change in pronunciation, became did inter, meaning did bury the body.

The verb inter had been on the analysand's mind for two very significant reasons: (1) He had just reread Shakespeare's The Tragedy of Julius Caesar (1599), and the lines "The evil that men do lives after them;/ The good is oft interred with their bones" (Act Three, Scene Two, 75–76) had jolted him as if he had just read them for the first time. (2) A friend had just died and was buried the day before Mr. J had this dream.

Further associations eventually made it possible to reconstruct the latent dream thoughts that the dream work had disguised in the manifest content. Mr. J's friend was buried in his hometown, a village called New Place. The analysand knew that New Place was also the name of the house Shakespeare had acquired in Stratford-upon-Avon after he became famous and prosperous. Mr. J began to sense that the coincidental irony of two New Places had been coopted by the dream work while the unconscious scaffolding of the dream was being constructed. In playing free-associatively with the manifest content, it became clear that, not only was a closing being stalled because the didn'ter was not present, but also the alternative meaning, did inter, was being concealed lest the reality of the burial of his friend be exposed.

On deeper reflection, it became clear that it was not just the reality of the burial that was being denied: the psychological reality of Mr. J's death wishes toward his friend was even more objectionable. The analysand had visited his friend in the hospital just prior to his death, when he was semi-comatose and close to the end. Mr. J left the hospital with a great sense of sadness and a great sense of his own mortality and how tenuous the human lease of life seemed upon reflection on occasions such as these. He was not aware of how angry he was with his friend for reminding him to "ask not for whom the bell tolls," since "it tolls for thee." Nor was he aware of how happy he was to be alive, and how happy he was that it was his friend who was dying and not he.

When his friend did die a day later, Mr. J became aware of his sense of paralysis and deadness—as if he, too, had died, or at least would do so very soon. This "identification" with his friend reminded him of how deeply he had been identified with his own father since childhood. Like Mr. J himself, his father had been a professor of English literature, but alcoholism had destroyed his academic career as well as his social life. His wife finally left him after trying for years to put up with his exasperating behavior, but the analysand was aware that he himself had never left him, so profound was the ambivalent identification with him. The death of Mr. J's friend stirred up all these issues, which had been the daily subject matter of analysis for many years.

As mentioned, when he learned that his friend was to be buried in his childhood village of New Place, Mr. J was reminded of Shakespeare's ownership of a house of the same name. What would not become conscious until the analysis of the dream was more complete, however, was the wish to usurp the place of his friend and the place of his father (not to mention the usurpation of the literary status of the father of all playwrights, William Shakespeare!), and to make his Oedipal conquest permanent by carving his name only on the new place.

Ironically, the word assassination makes its first entrance as a verbal entity in the English language in Julius Caesar, a play that had recently captured Mr. J's attention, as noted—especially the line "the good is oft interred with their bones." The analysand was all too aware that the evil men do or feel not only "lives after them", but also lives with them, no matter how desperately they attempt to conceal it. These kinds of ruminations, self-accusations, and free associations led eventually to an understanding of the latent dream thoughts and how the pun had become a useful sop for the dream work to employ in keeping an unwitting Cerberus (the dream censor) beguiled.

Many sessions of analytic process made it clear that the latent dream thoughts were stark, Oedipal, acquisitive designs to plunder "the old man's" estate once death had "closed" his eyes permanently! The dreamer, after years of analysis, was quite familiar with the "professorial" ego style that shaped the manifest content not only of his character, but of his dreams as well. The "gift" of a "literary" dream with which to seduce the "intellectual" analyst is a transference-countertransference issue of no small importance, but I want to focus almost exclusively on one aspect of dream work, which Mr. J came to appreciate over time. As compressed and polished as his impressive character traits and defenses were, he came to realize that the unconscious compression of his own dream work was a marvel of condensed meanings as well, meanings that had eluded him earlier.

In the dream under discussion, for instance, as Mr. J's free associations opened his eyes to the many meanings of closing, the analytic process edged its way toward the hidden meaning embedded in "didn'ter." What began as bemused puzzlement upon awakening, as the dream and its strange new word left the nocturnal realm to enter consciousness, was transformed into the insight that removed the mask from "didn'ter" to reveal "did inter" instead. This could not have been accomplished had Mr. J's ego not become more and more comfortable, over years of analytic process, with the recognition of its own murderous wishes—a revelation that transference, and its ongoing interpretation, had largely made possible. It was the gains of analysis, and the attendant expansion of the ego, that allowed the analysand to deconstruct the dream work's compressions and put the unconscious energies to alternative, adaptive uses.

After an awakener has analyzed such a dream and fully appreciated the complexity of its wordplay, he perhaps cannot help feeling like Alice in her puzzling conversation with Humpty Dumpty about the words "glory" and "impenetrability." In this celebrated passage (Carroll, 1872, pp. 238–239), when Alice challenges Humpty Dumpty's definition of glory, Humpty Dumpty says, "When I use a word, it means just what I choose it to mean—neither more nor less." Later, when Humpty Dumpty explains the word "impenetrability" to her in a complicated way, Alice says, "That's a great deal to make one word mean." Humpty Dumpty explains: "When I make a word do a lot of work like that, I always pay it extra."

If the dream work behind the dream described here can be compared to the inscrutable Humpty Dumpty, perhaps we can assume that it paid the word "didn'ter" quite a bit extra for all the work it made it do.

A parapraxis in a dream

Now we turn from humor and puns in dreams to study a parapraxis in a dream. When a parapraxis is put on display in a dream, one can only wonder what service the willful mistake is rendering to resourceful dream work. Freud taught us that anything that appears in the manifest content of a dream may well be a disguise or a distortion of a subject that originally made an anxiety-provoking, and hence short-lived, first appearance in latent dream thoughts. Dreams within dreams and jokes in dreams have been examined from this perspective and now we focus on the appearance and meaning of a parapraxis in a dream, with the argument that seemingly casual "mistakes" are highlighted in the manifest display to cover up some latent, much more deliberate subject matter.

One of Freud's (1900) comments on parapraxes in dreams is sweepingly reductionistic, yet powerful. In addressing déjà phenomena in dreams, he writes:

> In some dreams of landscapes or other localities, emphasis is laid in the dream itself on a convinced feeling of having been there once before. These places are invariably the genitals of the dreamer's mother; there is indeed no other place about which one can assert with such conviction that one has been there once before. (p. 399)

If Freud's assessment of parapraxes in dreams sounds like a recklessly intuitive generalization about the meaning of déjà vu, in another instance, he follows the clinical material in a less sweeping, more focused manner. He reports one of his own dreams:

> I was going to the hospital with P., through a district in which there were houses and gardens. At the same time I had a notion that I had

often seen this district before in dreams. I did not know my way about very well. He showed me a road that led round the corner to a restaurant (indoors, not a garden). There I asked for Frau Doni and was told that she lived at the back in a small room with three children. I went toward it, but before I got there met an indistinct figure with my two little girls; I took them with me after I had stood with them for a little while. Some sort of reproach against my wife, for having left them there.

When I woke up I had a feeling of great satisfaction, the reason for which I explained to myself as being that I was going to discover from this analysis the meaning of "I've dreamt of that before." In fact, however, the analysis taught me nothing of the kind; what it did show me was that the satisfaction belonged to the latent content of the dream and not to any judgment upon it. My satisfaction was with the fact that my marriage had brought me children. P. was a person whose course in life lay for some time alongside mine, who then outdistanced me both socially and materially, but whose marriage was childless. (Freud, 1900, pp. 446–447, italics in original)

Freud sweeps the anagogic interpretation of his own dream aside as too facile to engage him beyond the first waking moments, and reaches deeper for the psychoanalytic meaning: a wish to topple a rival, on the most sexual turf ("my flesh is procreative, and yours isn't!"). Freud, initially seduced by the manifest satisfaction of discovering the meaning of "I've dreamt that before," is not satisfied (ironically enough) until he traces the sense of satisfaction to its deeper, darker core of meaning in the realm of competitive, sexual latent imagery. But, by focusing on the affect of satisfaction, Freud neglects the formal structure of parapraxis itself and its functional defensive armature, and to this neglected aspect of the topic I would like to bring emphasis. It is Freud's revolutionary insight that allows us to understand that intellectual assessment made in the manifest content of a dream should be seen as a disguised derivative of a latent issue: in other words, it is subordinate to the main agenda of the dream, which is dream work, even though its manifest content usurps the limelight in its overt display.

Whereas Freud suggests that déjà vu is a reference to the universal spawning ground of the mother's genital, a place about which everyone could assert, "I have been here before," I would like to argue that a parapraxis that claims "to have been here before" is making a rightful claim from another vantage point: since it has been displaced from its original latent context to its more high-profile, manifest role of disguise, it has made a prior appearance in dream space and is therefore right to claim that "I've been here before." The same could be said of all parapraxes: they are mistakes, which is to say that they reflect a facet of unconscious meaning whose "out-of-place" quality is, after all, what gives them their essential, uncanny identity. The mind is aware, on some level, that the unconscious engines seem to have misfired: there is a subjective sense of mistaken identity, of false perception or expression, even if one is not able to correct it immediately.

A sixty-year-old lawyer in the eighth year of a very productive analysis had a dream in which a parapraxis appeared, the first ever as far as he could remember. A man of keen intelligence and rigorous curiosity, he found that the appearance of unusual fauna in a dream landscape aroused as much interest as a new sighting in an astronomer's telescope. "I've heard of day's residue," he joked, "but this is not residual—it's functional," and he set to work to decode its meaning. Here is the dream as he reported it.

> I'm walking down a city street—New York, probably. Skyscrapers all around. I am walking with Nelson Mandela, but I am calling him Tomás Magadin in error.

In the dream, the error does not seem to generate any anxiety, but on waking, the dreamer is struck by the parapraxis and puzzled by its meaning. The analysand noted that Lord Nelson was an admiral who won a famous sea battle by placing a telescope to his blind eye, therefore not seeing how outnumbered he was, and his ultimate victory proved that blind courage is sometimes more effective than cold-blooded visual reality. "An ambiguous ideal, to say the least," chortled the analysand, impressed by the double-edged wish embodied in the condensation of Nelson the blind and Nelson the victorious. Mandela seemed to pick up the same theme almost in the same breath. Mandela was man with the feminine appendage Della (as in Della Hopkins, a childhood sweetheart of the analysand). Hopkins led to an association to Gerard Manley Hopkins, the innovative poet who introduced the concepts of sprung rhythm and inscape into modern poetry. And the poet's name seemed to condense the manly and the feminine (the analysand thought of poetry as an expression of feminine aspects of the psyche).

The dreamer's genetic context needs to be summarized before the dream can be discussed further. As mentioned earlier, the analysand was a sixty-year-old lawyer nearing the end of analysis; he was the product of a white, Anglo-Saxon, Protestant family, in which a powerful mother had steered the family's "ship of state" throughout a lifelong illness of the father, with her son (the analysand) beside her at the wheel. His considerable career and social successes were thus forever tinged with Oedipal guilt. In fact, the analysis in large part was an attempt to rescue him from the wreck of success, given his unconscious tendency to undermine himself upon reaching his goals.

Returning to the dream with these bare bones of a genetic sketch, let us attempt further deconstruction, while not losing sight of the parapraxis and its function in the dream. Tomás Magadin was the substitute name for Nelson Mandela in the dream. Why Tomás Magadin? The analysand's older brother, Tommy, had cardiac failure at a relatively early age. The analysand was angry and disappointed that his father and brother were not made of sturdier stuff. Magadin was not too dissimilar from the analyst's name, and thus, illness was being wished upon the analyst via transference. "Better you than them," he quipped. "Blood is thicker than water." Magadin elicited the further associations of "maggots in" (symbolic of death), and of the Magi (three wise kings bringing gifts to his royal highness, the baby)—the latter a regressive, compensatory wish in the face of so much death and castration.

Following these associative leads, the analysand had enough information to probe deeper. The eight years of prior analytic work were, of course, the most profound day's residue for this analysand, whose memory was quite remarkable: "Long day's residue into night" was an expression he often applied to the analysis, with characteristic sarcasm. The analysis of bisexual conflicts, for instance, had undergone profound revisions from the first year of the analysis to the eighth: whereas the early years of analysis had been full of heterosexual protest, bisexuality in the eighth year was a topic that aroused curiosity and interest rather than anxiety.

The concept of resolving a conflict with its negative Oedipal or pre-Oedipal solutions made the analysand marvel at the variety of his options, rather than doubt the solidity of his sexual identity. Given this newfound comfort with the multiple determinants of heterosexual and homosexual tendencies, the play of ambiguities in the dream puzzled him. If he wanted to be castrated and heroic all at once, like the black phoenix Nelson Mandela, who had leaped from the flames of apartheid and incarceration to be born again as the leader of his people, why could the name Nelson Mandela not stand on its own terms in his dream—as a multiply condensed compromise between defeat and victory, between the blindness of Lord Nelson and the unrelenting vision of Mandela? Why confuse the issue with Tomás Magadin? Why drag in a slip of the tongue to a well-orchestrated dream landscape?

At this point, the analysand had the intriguing insight that Tomás Magadin/Nelson Mandela was not a slip of the tongue in the sense that parapraxes of everyday life are examples of faulty functioning (Fehlleistung). On the contrary, excellence of functioning was being demonstrated as the dream work pulled out all the stops in the service of disguise. The dreamer's bemusement on awakening that a slip had appeared in his dream was a measure of the success of this red herring in throwing him off the scent of the dream's latent meaning.

Tomás Magadin was not a slip, an error, but a profound association in its own right, as the dreamer's association to Tomás revealed: Tomás sounded like no más, the infamous words of Roberto Duran in his boxing match with Sugar Ray Leonard. Duran refused to continue the fight, throwing in the towel with the words "no más"—no more—a great humiliation for the legendary boxer. Tomás Magadin and its associative siblings, "no más" and "maggots in", were protests against the death of the analysand's brother or the death of the analyst, but behind the protests lay a death wish against both. "I'm glad I'm alive" was the dream's major message. "I'm glad others are dying, not I—make no mistake about it." The bold starkness of the wish had to be concealed in ambiguities and compromises, as if the guilty dreamer could only be heroic in his defiance of death and his wishing it on others when he embraced death and life together in a bisexual compromise! He could not be simply Nelson Mandela in the dream; he needed to cover up this heroic, phallic identity with a more castrated alter ego, Tomás Magadin. And he needed to pretend it had all been a mistake!

When James Joyce (1922) said, "A man of genius makes no mistakes. His errors are volitional and are the portals of discovery" (p. 190), he was talking about Shakespeare and, none too modestly, perhaps, about himself, but he could have been referring to the mind in general: its mistakes, as I have demonstrated in regard to parapraxes in dreams, can be recycled by the dream work, their form and content pushed into defensive service, as the mind loses no opportunity to enhance the complexity of its disguises. The dream interpreter armed with these insights has an additional strategy at hand with which to keep pace with the magical sleight of hand of dream work!

The uncanny in a dream

So far in this chapter I have focused on particular types of inclusions in dreams (A Joke in a Dream; Dreams within Dreams; A Parapraxis in a Dream; A Pun in a Dream). I have tried to explore, in each instance, the dream work's unconscious dynamic motivation for employing such extra flourishes in the service of dream disguise and defense. In this section I focus on an instance of the uncanny in a dream, and speculate on the particular function such an inclusion might have served. A patient dreamt about the proper name of an author (Thomas B. Costain), which he believed at first to be a fictitious dream concoction. In fact all of his initial associations dealt with the dream inclusion as if it had no connection to reality. When he later googled the name "for the hell of it" he was surprised to uncannily discover that what he was referring to as "that strange dream name" was in fact the proper name of a moderately well known twentieth-century author! His subsequent discovery, that one of the author's books, The Silver Chalice, re-minded him of silver paper chalices his father used to make for him as a child, jolted him further. This revived repression, not only of an author's name, but of its significant connection to repressed genetic memories, filled him with a sense of awe as if he had suddenly been awakened from a hypnotic spell. If dream experience in general can be considered uncanny, I argue that the dream work deployed this particular inclusion of an uncanny 'fictitious' representation of reality for complex dynamic reasons.

The whole dreaming process could be considered uncanny of course but I want to draw attention to a particular isolated instance within the total fabric of a single dream. Having associated to all the elements in the dream, including what he believed to be the fictitious name (Thomas B. Costain) he googled the name, expecting to find that the fictitious name was indeed a concoction of the dream work. He was amazed to discover that the "fictitious" name did in fact correspond to the letter, even the middle initial, to the real name of a rather famous author! Thomas B. Costain, born in Canada in 1885 was at first a journalist, but he began to write historical novels in his fifties, one of them (The Silver Chalice) being a best-seller that spawned a famous movie that Paul Newman starred in. The Silver Chalice refers to a fictional chalice that was made to house the wooden goblet Christ used at The Last Supper. What was truly uncanny for the analysand was that as a child his father used to make him silver chalices out of the silver paper his cigarettes came wrapped in. The uncanny, in this particular instance, seemed to have retrieved at least two significant repressed components from the past: silver chalices offered as playthings by the father; a fictitious name that turned out to be real. There was a transference context of course: all sorts of artifacts from the past had already appeared over a lengthy process of excavation. Initially the analyst believed the name Thomas B. Costain to be a concoction of the dream work also. The analyst's ignorance could be attributed to the fact that he had arrived as a young physician in New York in the sixties, and many aspects of the culture had not been incorporated by him. He had never heard of Costain or the Paul Newman film *The Silver Chalice*. The analysand's initial ignorance did seem however to be a dynamic issue of great significance.

The dream should be presented at this point so that the reader can appreciate the uncanny in statu nascendi just as the dreamer did.

> I am at a conference. A journalist is being interviewed. His name is Thomas. B. Costain. The interviewer inappropriately asks the journalist if his chronic depression had compromised his professional life in any way. I cringe at the interviewer's crassness and would have undone the insult if I could.

Before I present the collaborative analytic work on this dream a few words about the uncanny in general are in order. Freud's paper *The Uncanny* was published in 1919. He refers to "this modest contribution of mine" as having been affected by "the times in which we live," a reference to the war Europe and the rest of the world was trying to recover from. In his paper Freud concluded that uncanny experiences occur "when infantile complexes which have been repressed are once more revived by some impression, or when primitive beliefs which have been surmounted seem once more to be confirmed." Freud, like most of the intellectuals of the time, believed that the First World War would restructure the world in some romantic idealistic manner. Looking back with hindsight on the folly of such romantic idealism one can only assume that some uncanny "infantile complexes" or primitive un-surmounted beliefs had indeed usurped the common sense of a whole generation of thinkers.

Freud was fascinated with the antithetical meaning of primal words in general and with the etymology of the word uncanny (*unheimlich* in German) in particular. In German the *heimlich* and the *unheimlich* can be equally disquieting in connotation. The same is true for canny and uncanny in English. Freud suggests that when the "familiar" (infantile complexes) is repressed, and then revived by "some impression," an uncanny affect occurs. Since it is the "familiar" parent that the child wants to engage in incest or murder, no wonder the child invokes amnesia as the ultimate resolution. But amnesia is always relative: "some impression" can, when least expected, trigger a return of the repressed. Having very briefly reprised Freud's ideas on the uncanny I will now return to the discussion of the dream and describe the impression in consciousness (the days' residue) that got the whole manifest and latent choreography started.

The analysand, intrigued with the *mise en scène* of the dream, began to free associate immediately to the fictional name, as if it were a fabrication of days' residues and ancient artifacts. On a recent short trip to Italy he had heard a politician named Costa pitching his case for election to an audience in the town square. He had been at a mercatino (a small Italian outdoor market) earlier that day and one of the vendors was inviting people to sample his wares, proclaiming: "Cedere, cedere, costa niente" which in translation means "yield, yield, my products cost nothing." Associating to "cost" in "costain" the analysand became aware that the cost of analysis seemed to be on his mind. He was convinced that the issue of a product that cost nothing had insinuated itself into the dream. (It seemed clear that "cost" and "costa" were the impressions in consciousness that had awakened disturbing, unconscious affects.) "I wish analysis cost nothing" was the obvious implication and that analytic love was unconditional as opposed to market driven. Continuing to take each phoneme of the dream apart, he associated to the "stain" in Costain. "We are all stained with mortality" he reflected, his anger at the analyst's "conditional" love deflected onto a more defensive, philosophical plane. He associated to "Thomas" as the name of his dead brother and to the middle initial "B" as "to be or not to be" from Hamlet's soliloquy. He associated the whole name "Thomas B. Costain" as not too dissimilar from the analyst's, which also had the middle initial "J". When the transference was at its most ambivalent the analysand had often joked that "J" stood for Jesus or Judas, a piece of irony I will return to later.

Up to this point the analysand had been free associating to Thomas B. Costain as a fictitious name, a proper name concocted solely by the dream work's artistry. It came as a shock to him when he googled and discovered that Thomas B. Costain was in fact the name of a real journalist/novelist. This uncanny experience was rendered even more disquieting as he began to reflect on the strange coincidence of his father's gifts of the childhood chalices and the completely repressed name of a novelist who had written a famous book called *The Silver Chalice*! For it was beginning to dawn on him that a significant act of "repression" was the only way to explain the seemingly total ignorance of an author whose name and novels had been stored with such accuracy in the forgotten files of memory. The correct assignation of the dream "Thomas B. Costain" as not only a novelist, but a journalist as well, seemed yet another instance of the uncanny. If the dream in toto was uncanny, these precise particulars seemed to out-uncanny the uncanny.

The eventual interpretation of the dream that emerged from the collaborative analytic process could be summarized as follows: the analysand acknowledged to himself that he is not only the cringing embarrassed observer in the dream but the brash reporter also who embarrasses Thomas B. Costain with the question about his chronic depression. The analysand was able to admit to himself that he would have liked to have had the courage to challenge his father directly rather than transforming his anger always into masochism, guilt, defensive identification, reaction formations. In a sense the gift of the silver chalices was a screen for all the developmental gifts the father had deprived him of. The father was indeed a writer (not as famous as Thomas B. Costain) and a university lecturer. But he had a chronic manic-depressive illness, which was reflected in frequent unemployment issues. The father had moved his family from city to city many times in pursuit of more and more elusive employment. The analysand could hardly keep track of all the different grade schools he had frequented, but he believed it might have been as many as eleven or twelve in five or six years.

The analysand was of course intrigued by the uncanny structure of the dream. At first he believed he had never heard of Thomas B. Costain before in his life and that the strange appearance of the name had to be a magical confluence of accidentals, similar to a monkey writing the script of Hamlet by chance if the monkey had forever to work on it. But then, as alluded to earlier, a more probable explanation dawned on him: he must at some point in his life have heard of Thomas B. Costain.

What's more, he must have known Costain wrote *The Silver Chalice*. He must have repressed the information at a period in his life when the ambivalence about his father (the traumatic neglect as well as the poignant compensatory childhood gifts) was too painful to acknowledge and had to be removed completely from consciousness. Years must have passed before the repressed was able to represent itself again in the free-associative climate of analysis in an uncanny manner in a dream. The initial repression was most impressive: the return of the repressed in the dream brought no affect of recognition in its wake, unless one argues that the decision to Google the name Thomas B. Costain had some premonitory trace of recognition in it in the first place.

Some genetic material is essential at this point to illuminate the appearance of the uncanny. The analysand had an older brother Thomas who was retarded. This brother had died recently and Thomas B. Costain was in part a reference to this tragedy. Though retarded his brother was nevertheless an accomplished swimmer. When he died in a freak accident in the ocean the analysand was plunged into an extraordinary episode of grief that he believed was two-fold: it represented grief for the brother to be sure, but also an unrelenting grief about the loss of his father, not only through death itself but through the even greater loss of life lived to the fullest that chronic depression entails. He became aware that Thomas B. Costain wove together so many over-determined threads in the fabric of his unconscious. Intense analytic process on these issues unearthed a most significant unconscious fantasy: "My father, my brother and I are costained forever with the undifferentiated magic of genetic life." The middle initial B refers to "to be or not to be", a declaration of symbiotic suicidal co-dependence that tries to erase guilt from the wake of robust individuation through regressive non-individuation. "If only I could be costained forever with father and brother I would never have to recognize my unique differentiation from both of them." (I have summarized months of analytic process in the service of aligning the uncanny nature of the analytic process with the uncanny nature of genetic psychology.)

Let us consider the dream in statu nascendi. The initial dream thoughts ("I hate my father for neglecting me. I'd like to interview him and embarrass him with the truth and expose his irresponsibility for all the world to see") need to be disguised. This direct vehement exposure and critique of the father needs to be sanitized. The dream work "decides" to displace the direct critique onto the "interviewer" while the personification of the dreamer "cringes" in embarrassment at the interviewer's crassness. If the dream conflict divided up in this manner is not enough of a defensive disguise to keep the manifest level from revealing too much latent content, the dream work can call up the reserves so to speak. Enter Thomas B. Costain, a fictitious sounding name if ever there was one. The supreme irony is of course that only the dream work (assuming that all repressed content is available to it, and it can, like a painter, choose any unconscious pigment it likes to produce its effects) knows at this point that Thomas B. Costain is indeed a real writer! In fact if the dreamer had by chance been reading about Thomas B. Costain a few days before this particular dream was "assembled" and the repressed had thereby been returned to him, surely the dream work could not have used reality masquerading as fiction in such a manner. The dream does seem to flirt with exposure by employing Thomas B. Costain as a decoy, not unlike a cheater in a card game revealing a protruding sliver of the hidden ace up his sleeve. All defense seems to ride on such irony as if the wish to reveal and the wish to conceal thrived on such ambivalence (Shafer, 1968). In the case of Thomas B. Costain the dream work seems to rely on the solidity and stability of repression as if the awakener's eventual decision to google can be discounted as a most unlikely possibility. In a sense the awakener's reaction is Sophoclean: Oedipus insists on pursuing the truth even when he knows it will spell his own doom. The dramatic irony of Sophocles' play rests after all on the idea that the audience knows everything before Oedipus stumbles on it, just as the dream work knew what it was concealing from the dreamer before the oracular google spilt the beans, and just as the awakener on some level knew what he had repressed so dramatically many years ago. *The Silver Chalice*, Thomas B. Costain, Paul Newman, as well as the much earlier memory of silver paper chalices made by a tragically depressed man who wanted to offer his son more than his constitutional endowment would allow him, all played their part in the construction of the dream. As analytic insights over time allowed the analysand to reflect deeply on the nature of his father's chronic mental illness, the silver paper chalices became a great symbol of love and hate, satisfaction and deprivation, instinct and repression, tragic loss and resilient resignation. "You can't give what you don't have" he would wryly say when sympathy for his father's illness outweighed his resentment. There was bitterness in such wry commentary and sober reflection also. To become the '"new man" analysis projected, his guilt about his death wishes toward his father and brother and "incestuous possession" of his mother would have to be revised and reclaimed from the tragic neurotic conviction that he was as tragically "costained" with depression, death and failure as his father and brother were. As the analysis nears termination the analysand has come to realize among other things that though all men are "costained" with mortality, neurotic defensive unanalyzed identifications with the dead, or the living for that matter, need not "costain" us all in some kind of symbiotic blindness that would make independent individuated ambitious exuberant pre-Oedipal and Oedipal life impossible.

Freud argued that the uncanny had several components. He made a distinction between the inheritance of those component "animistic" elements that are "surmounted" in the course of civilized development and the repressed components that have more to do with psychodynamic infantile life and its conflicts. When either the "surmounted" or the "repressed" returns the analysand feels an uncanny affect. Freud agreed that both the surmounted and the repressed could operate in conjunction. The uncanny affect would seem to be that moment of surprise when complacent repression assumes that the objectionable has been censored, only to discover that the dream interviewer for instance, like a child in a Hans Christian Anderson story, is bound to confront the emperor's self deception with its full frontal nakedness. When the dreamer awakens into the uncanny nakedness of himself, or when the free associative transferential process awakens into the surprise of its own forgotten genetics, the emperor is willing to relinquish his defensive omnipotence and reclaim the little kingdom of reality where there are no kings at all. At that moment the seemingly fictitious Thomas B. Costain and the very real writer of the same name will recognize each other in the aesthetics of dream analysis as the repressed returns and is no longer afraid of itself.

If dream is a compromise between instinct and repression, a compromise that teasingly manifests a portion of itself while rigorously hiding the most significant aspects of itself, this drama of exhibition and disguise is always on the verge of aesthetic exhaustion and collapse. When the aesthetic "suspension of disbelief" begins to falter and the dreamer suspects and fears a sudden descent into nightmare or into rude awakening and panic, the dream work exploits all of its resources to keep more and more balls of disguise in the air. I have argued that when a dream, which is after all a pretty uncanny disguise in toto, highlights one particular instance of the uncanny, the alert dream interpreter will recognize the introduction of the uncanny as a desperate cover-up manoeuvre designed to disguise a major fault line in the overall structure of the dream. Such an alert dream interpreter will recognize the uncanny red herring and not be fooled by the dream work's impressive sleight of hand.

Dreams: a longitudinal, developmental perspective

I would like to end this chapter with a developmental and longitudinal perspective. I am reintroducing Alex whose "person terminal" comment has already been alluded to: I will describe three different phases of his dream life by comparing and contrasting his dreams from age five, thirteen and twenty. I will pose the following question: what can a five-year-old's dream, a thirteen-year-old's dream, and a twenty-year-old's dream tell us about developmental aspects of mental life, if the dreamer in all three instances is the same person? This question came to mind recently when an "old" patient who had been a child analysand from age five to ten returned at thirteen and twenty for brief consultations about academic and other matters.

If a dream is the disguised fulfillment of an infantile wish, would dreams from different developmental phases give us an evolutionary perspective of desire and disguise that would deepen our understanding of the adult dreaming process? Such questions, easier to pose than to address, will nevertheless provide a focus as I examine the many currents of analytic data involved in any longitudinal investigation. I will begin by presenting the anamnesis of the young analysand, his three dreams, and will then try to describe the analytic and post-analytic contexts that the three dreams emerged from.

The three dreams

The three dreams, manifest content only, are presented first, with anamnestic, psychoanalytic, and developmental contexts to follow.

The first dream (age five)

There was an octopus. As big as the Empire State building. I had a stick. It (the octopus) swallowed me. I was fighting it. It spat me out.

The second dream (age thirteen)

> I am running in the woods. Snakes appear. They come close to my face. I run and run. There are other children younger than me playing nearby. I try to make the snakes go in their direction.

The third dream (age twenty)

> I am in a Batmobile. Batman is driving. I'm in the back seat. The Batmobile is not all it's cracked up to be. We are trying to chase some bad guys. We are slow to pull out of the garage in pursuit because we have to make several broken "U" turns just to get out of the driveway. Finally we get going. I take the wheel. Eventually we catch up with the bad guys. We follow them over a desert and give chase round and round an oval.

Clinical material

The anamnesis

Alexander's parents sought help for their four-and-a-half-year-old for a variety of symptoms, some of which they had noticed, some brought to their attention by the nursery school. The parents were alarmed by his boastfulness, boisterousness, lying, provocativeness; the school was alarmed by his unruliness and hyperactivity: he seemed to wear his castration anxiety on his sleeve, grabbing at the penises of other children as if to acquire more of what he feared to lose. At naptime, while others slept or at least rested, he needed to be on the go, activity his only resource it seemed against the pressure of anxiety.

In the playroom for the initial consultations, his words, deeds, drawings, and play began to reveal the seething unconscious energies that lay behind all of his symptomatic acts. He could be provocative, scatological, one minute, presenting his anus in mock submission to the "baboon" that was "interviewing" him; another minute he could be telling a story and illustrating it coherently and co-operatively. If there was a desire to shock and provoke, there was also a clear wish to communicate, which made the prospects of induction into analysis slightly less daunting. His initial stories and illustrations describe small animals that leave home and have lots of adventures with huge adversaries. They usually have two psychological escape routes—the oral or the phallic. They eat up the universe or they try to become as big as it. Poignantly the ant hero will make his way to the top of the Empire State building, a preposterous King Kong mask bravely covering the terror of the little endangered face.

The first dream

The first dream was reported in the seventh analytic session. In the preceding sessions Alex had talked and played, presenting himself basically as brash and defensive on the one hand and open and communicative on the other. Digging to the bottom of the sandbox, he commented, "I want to get to the bottom of things." He also hoped that the analyst would give him "the greatest memory in the world." All the meanings of this request would slowly emerge later in the analysis. He would build tall structures out of blocks of wood, reveling in the spatial majesty and in the destructive glee of toppling and dismantling. He would write his name on the blackboard and chalk in the number of times he had seen me, a somewhat arrogant "pupil" seizing as much control as possible from the "teacher" analyst.

I will present session seven in its entirety so that the dream and its context are fully exposed:

Alex entered the playroom, noticed that the block design from the previous session was not exactly as he had left it, and complained, "Why didn't you leave them up?"

ANALYST: You're angry that things are not exactly as you left them? (Pause) Could we make it again?

ALEX: No.

ANALYST: Oh?

ALEX: I can't remember. The mouse that takes things from the back of my head to the front ... I can't get him to work now.

ANALYST: He's angry, too! He'd like things to stay in their place forever.

ALEX: Not forever. For one day!

ANALYST: (Touché—not voiced.)

ALEX: I'll make a bed. Pee Pee Doo Doo Wee Wee.

ANALYST: That's the way you talked when you were ... how old?

ALEX: Three. I did peepee in bed last night.

ANALYST: Oh? How come?

ALEX: I wanted to.

ANALYST: Oh?

ALEX: To get Mommy to clean the sheet.

ANALYST: Oh, you get back at Mom that way?

ALEX: Yeah.

ANALYST: How did she get to you?

ALEX: She spanked me.

Alex suddenly climbed on the block shelves. I moved instinctively to protect him should he fall (the shelves were "tall" given the size of the child).

ALEX: Why did you move?

ANALYST: To make sure you were safely up.

ALEX: (Independently) I'm up now.

From his perch on the shelf he erased his name and the number of sessions he had seen me from the blackboard, saying good-bye Alex to his name as it disappeared and began to draw. "I want to draw a dog," he said, but instead he drew a dinosaur, a brontosaurus, and the bird dinosaur, saying, "The bird can eat the brontosaurus but not the tyrannosaurus." Then he drew a lady snake and snake eggs and then a star, saying a star was a part of the night, "I don't like night."

ANALYST: Why not? Is it the dreams?

ALEX: Yes.

ANALYST: Last night?

ALEX: Yes.

ANALYST: What about?

Alex tells the following dream:

"There was an octopus. As big as the Empire State building. I had a stick. It swallowed me. I was fighting it. It spat me out."

ANALYST: It sounds scary.

ALEX: I had another dream about an octopus in a spook house.

ANALYST: What's a spook house?

ALEX: I don't know.

ANALYST: Sounds scary, too. Was it?

ALEX: Yeah.

ANALYST: Where do you think those dreams came from? Were you worried about something maybe?

ALEX: Yeah, an accident.

ANALYST: Oh?

ALEX: Grandfather died. (This turns out to be a lie, but I am unaware of this at the time.)

ANALYST: Oh, I'm sorry to hear that. You miss him?

ALEX: Yeah and my uncle Abe.

Alex went to a drawer, extracted a hammer, and started to make a plane, cars, and a motorbike tinkering away like a mechanic.

ANALYST: It feels good and strong to make things, especially when talking about scary dreams.

ALEX: (Went to the sandbox.) Let's bury grandfather.

He spilled a lot of sand in the process and I asked him to try not to, even if he was showing his feelings that way.

ALEX: I like to spill the sand.

ANALYST: Yes, you told me you like to mess and have someone else clean it up. Like a baby, I guess?

ALEX: I'd like to be a baby.

ANALYST: Oh? How come?

ALEX: I wouldn't have to eat roast beef and squash.

ANALYST: Oh? What would you prefer?

ALEX: "Sol."

ANALYST: What's that?

ALEX: Soft baby food. I still like it.
(It's time to stop.)

ANALYST: Let's stop here.

ALEX: Oh, I'll take the airplane.

ANALYST: Can you leave it so we can use it again when we need to?

ALEX: Oh, but I want to paint it. (And he runs off with it.)

I shall postpone commentary on the first dream at this point and attempt instead to give a synopsis of the subsequent psychoanalysis and developmental progressions so that the second and third dreams will also have a context.

A synopsis of the psychoanalysis

The analysis brings to mind Ernest Jones's conviction that pathology of the phallic phase of development is intimately related to earlier disappointments at the breast. In other words, a phallus that "protests too much about its captivating seductiveness" is really a mouth in disguise, a mouth that did not possess the nipple adequately and, feeling dispossessed in one erotogenic zone, tries to make up for it in another. Too much phallic pride, in other words, is a sign of oral incompetence. What has just been stated in libidinal, zonal language could be restated in structural or object relational terminology, but shorthand in a synopsis is permissible, if not mandatory.

Using the first dream as a guide to the initial transference communications, I believe Alex implied that his needs were urgent and even octopoid and that the little stick of his defenses might not be up to the task of taming so primitive an instinctual source unless an ally could be found in the analytic situation. There were many other "meanings" of the first dream, one could argue, but this particular transferential meaning highlighted the opening phase of analytic work and was being accentuated for that reason.

Two themes from the first year of analytic work seemed to grow like offshoots not only of the first dream but also of the story outlined in the anamnesis above. One theme developed into a play sequence where the analyst was Dr. Doolittle, the block-shelf, which had wheels and could therefore "voyage" around the playroom, becoming a ship for Alexander and Dr. Doolittle to explore wild territories and "tame" all the wild animals. The other "theme" was closely related to this analytic investigation of Alexander's instincts and his struggles with control and compromise, adaptive expression, and symptomatic action. In this theme, as reported earlier, the ship was actually compared to the analytic situation itself in a remarkable piece of insight for such a young child. When a ship was lost at sea and buffeted by storms but still managed to make it home safely to port, Alex interrupted the play for a moment and compared the work of analysis and the relationship he had with me to a voyage and a return trip to the safety and security of the analytic "port," or "terminal" as he called it. (As explained earlier my concept of analysis as odyssey is indebted to Alex's imagery of storm and terminal and his "invention" of the concept of a person terminal to describe the analytic relationship). If Alex wished to fly and spit and swallow, he also hoped that there was a "vessel" somewhere that could contain him, hold him. In the final analysis, an analysand learned that the vessel was, of course, nothing other than one's own mind and its structures and instincts operating in that ironic harmony called conflict and compromise. In the course of the analytic journey one did not always feel that the mind was one's own as it leaned so desperately and so dependently into the deep paradox of transference that regressed it the better to strengthen it. At times the vessel seemed hopelessly lost at sea, and contact with another "human" vessel was mandatory if safe harbor was ever to be reached. A psychoanalytic odyssey without an Ithaca to compass it home would flounder at sea forever.

These two images of "taming" and "vessel" are not the only generative metaphors of a lengthy analysis, but they have an organizational focus that can be exploited in the interest of making a long analytic story short.

If Alex was frightened as well as exhilarated by forces that could dispatch analytic grandfathers—not to mention extra-analytic ones even closer to home—his skills at taming and vessel building were beginning to give him the confidence needed to pursue his analytic voyages no matter where they led to. In child analysis, vessel building is not merely a metaphoric image: Alex actually carved boats out of wood, their meanings as variable as their contexts. For instance, a boat that he carved early in the analysis had quite a different meaning from the boat he carved at the end of the analysis. The first boat was carved in a context of exploration, which was complex and painful. The termination boat was more of a statement about journey's end than an exploration of any new unconscious territories. The first boat was called "The Catch Up" and the termination boat could have been called "The Letting Go" but was, as will be disclosed later, given a more personal hieroglyphic code name as befits latency and all its developmental intrigue. "The Catch Up" was carved while Alexander was reviewing some complicated affects about a substitute caretaker Rosa, who left abruptly when Alexander was three, promising to return but never keeping the promise. In a poignant moment when Alexander's phallic shield was lowered a little, he admitted that he took her at her word and counted the days to no avail. The loss of Rosa was made more traumatic by the even earlier emotional loss of mother (the mother had confided in me that it was not in her nature to be close to Alex at bedtime, an emotional legacy that she inherited via the constricted affects of her own mother). If the little bunny left home never to return, it was emotional retaliation, not first strike; or so it seemed in Alexander's talionic morality. But "The Catch Up" seemed to be an attempt to go beyond repetition compulsion and heal developmental wounds, not just rub salt in them. Alex was trying to break a vicious cycle of neurosis in the mutative process of analysis: he was trying to replace neurotic convictions that warned (a) that loss of the object and its love would always cramp his phallic style; (b) that phallic disguise could always hide a broken heart with the new conviction that would assure him that his libidinal expressiveness need not lead to such tragic consequences.

This new conviction was the offspring of several years of psychoanalytic working through. Highlights of this process will give the gist if not the bulk of the analytic work over a few years. The latency years of the analysis were conducted in the typical climate of schoolboy psychology and defensiveness: an obsession with sports and other games hid the unconscious life of the mind with a developmental expertise that was impressive and at times impenetrable. However, in "scientific experiments" that were conducted by mixing "detergents" and other objects from every "primal" crevice of my office, affects were discussed and compared and contrasted according to their "properties" of speed or density. Anger, for instance, was an extremely "fast" affect, whereas sadness was extremely "slow." Out of this alchemy of affects came the admission that the grief in the wake of Rosa's rejection was "slow" to leave him, the sadness lasting many months as he counted the days. Surely this was grief, a child's way of mourning, as discussed earlier in Chapter One. Even the "baseball" resistance would occasionally surrender an unconscious meaning or two. Once in the middle of a baseball game with me, Alex complained that he had to interrupt the game to go to the bathroom, a deprivation that would not be necessary if the bathroom and the playroom were all one room instead of being separated. When I commented how much Alex hated "separations" and "interruptions," Alex said, "When the doodie goes out, the poopie goes up." Analysis of this cryptic comment in the ensuing months and years made it clear that what was said casually had quite deep levels of unconscious meaning. Since doodie was Alex's infantile word for feces, and poopie his word for penis, his comment was a variation on Freud's penis = feces equation. In Alex's psychological calculus, "when the doodie goes out the poopie goes up" meant: when you are faced with loss, you can cover your ass with an erect penis. The phallic boast attempts to hide the anal loss or the more deeply repressed oral loss. Penis = feces = breast, to complete Freud's equation.

As Alex began to make remarkable progress on all fronts (social, academic, domestic, athletic) and as termination began to make an impression on the clinical process, the baseball resistance reluctantly yielded a few important insights. When I interpreted the flurry of baseball resistances with a question, "Why so much baseball now that we're thinking of bringing our work to an end?" Alex replied, "Every baseball game has to end," proving that resistance is often an analyst's word for his own ignorance and that the analysand was in fact working on the termination phase in his play.

One of the final "symbols" of the analysis was the aforementioned boat which might have been called "The Letting Go" but which was actually given a more phase-appropriate title by an industrious ten-year-old. Alex combined his own initials, my initials, and the numbers of our houses and street addresses into an impressive code name. At journey's end the boats were left behind in the playroom to be retrieved perhaps in some future nostalgic catch-up or letting go. In the meantime, they remain among the treasured possessions of a nostalgic analyst.

This "Letting Go" boat was carved out of wood, while many termination themes were being analyzed. Alex attempted to draw "a portrait of the analyst with a broken arm" in which his aggression toward the abandoning object could not be concealed. His anger at Rosa, his parents, his sister, and his analyst were worked over for many weeks. His fear in the face of all this aggression was that his hatred would destroy the object totally or at least the object's love for him. If he met Rosa in the street now, would he recognize her? Could he have a photograph of me to assure himself that his aggression had not destroyed all hope of ever seeing me again? Concerns such as these had to be broken into their genetic components (he felt like killing Rosa and his mother and father and feared that they would attack him or stop loving him or abandon him) before Alex could begin to realize that the past could be kept "in its place" and that the present could hold the promise of a future uncontaminated by the past.

The second dream

At age thirteen Alex returned for a consultation about the boarding school he would be attending soon. Boarding school was at least the manifest content of a visit that had obvious latent agendas as well which could be addressed when he recounted a dream and began to work on it as if the analysis had not ended at all! (This immediacy of transference availability years after an analysis has terminated is well documented elsewhere, particularly in regard to adult analyses) (Pfeffer, 1963).

The Dream:

> "I am running in the woods. Snakes appear. They come close to my face. I run and run. There are other children younger than me play-ing nearby. I try to make the snakes go in their direction."

Alex's associations were of the superficial variety at first: he had watched a television programme on snakes, which explained their pres-ence in the dream. The younger children referred to all the children that would be left in his school after he went off to boarding school. Then Alex went a little deeper: "close to his face" meant there was something dangerous he had to face—leaving home. Perhaps he was imagining the worst about boarding school. Was he seeing it as dangerous? Was he viewing it as punishment, being sent away? Was his "badness" catching up with him? Alex seemed relieved by airing some of these worries, affects, and distortions, but the dream seemed to be "crying out" for deeper exploration. Alex was now thirteen years old, had grown a lot since I had seen him three years earlier. The transformations of puberty seemed to be waging a psychological civil war with the conservative forces of latency, and a developmental nudge in the form of an inter-pretation seemed appropriate. "What if the snakes represent your penis which must have grown a lot like the rest of you?" I asked somewhat humorously. "Why do you suppose you'd be sending them away in the direction of younger children?"

Alex had no trouble getting the point. His immediate response was a confirmation of the interpretation in the form of a complaint: "My sister (two years older) didn't get her period until she was thirteen. I've had wet dreams and erections since eleven. It's not fair." Soon the irony of his own statement began to dawn on him. Here was the most "phallic" of boys suddenly renouncing his penis now that he was old enough to put it to use! This classical dilemma of the thirteen-year-old who finds progression and regression equally problematic was certainly not unique to Alex, but with five years of analysis behind him, it was easier for him to put words to his plight and recognize the deeply ambivalent psychological currents of his dream. Could he face the transformations of puberty, could he acknowledge that his penis (snake) with its wet dreams and erections belonged to him and need not be delegated to others? Or would he invoke the personal myth of the deprived child whose older sibling had it easier. Even biology was kinder to her than to him, granting her a longer childhood, while he was expelled prematurely from the innocence of Eden by his hyperactive, precocious hormones! As Alex began to "play" with these associations, laughing at himself a good deal in the process, it became clear that his conflicts about sexuality, boarding school, and growing up were the "average expectables" of developmental life and not insurmountable obstacles that were about to derail him.

The third dream

Seven years passed before Alex consulted me again. By chance he had seen me on the street and recognized me, giving the lie to one of his termination fears (his anger would destroy the relationship; I would become unrecognizable). He was home from college working as a cameraman's assistant on a movie being made not far from my office when the chance encounter occurred (actually I was unaware of the encounter until Alex told me later).

The manifest reason for his visit was to discuss academic performance in college, which was reflecting his conflicts rather than his potential. But several more "latent" communications quickly came to the fore: (a) He had learned recently that Rosa's whole family had been killed in an auto accident. He was not sure whether Rosa herself had been killed or not. (b) A two-year relationship with a girlfriend had ended six months earlier: new relationships seemed ambivalent, tentative. (c) It was depressing to come home. His old room was now "a storage room." Mother still seemed obsessed with herself and domestic details rather than with the emotional nuances of his development and conflicts.

We ran out of time on the first visit. We agreed to meet again, at which time Alex began the session with the following dream.

> I am in a Batmobile. Batman is driving. I'm in the back seat. The Batmobile is not all it's cracked up to be. We are trying to chase some bad guys. We are slow to pull out of the garage in pursuit because we have to make several broken "U" turns just to get out

of the driveway. Finally we get going. I take the wheel. Eventually
we catch up with the bad guys. We follow them over a desert and
give chase round and round an oval.

Alex had a wealth of associations to this dream. He had come into
my office carrying a bicycle wheel, the rest of the bicycle locked to a
tree outside for safekeeping. The bicycle wheel symbolized his return
home to relative dependency (in college he had a beat-up used car
and much more freedom). He jokingly referred to this bicycle wheel
as the "Batmobile," making it clear that vehicular symbolism was on
his mind. He had a lot of fun with the idea that the Batmobile in the
dream was not the magical vehicle from the recent movie but a much
more down-to-earth version. The "broken U's" were emblematic of
his recent academic progress, which had been anything but "linear" in
direction. Alex had developed a capacity for laughing at himself, quite
a contrast to the sensitivity and defensive bluster of his latency years.
Alex's most emotionally laden associations were reserved for compari-
sons between the new "catch up" vehicle (the Batmobile) and the old
"catch up" of yesteryear. It was in such a nostalgic moment that Alex
referred to the automobile accident that claimed the lives of Rosa's family and maybe even Rosa herself. Alex's uncertainty about the fate of
Rosa seemed highly significant. While she had not been "a presence" in
his life for seventeen years, she had become symbolic of love, treachery,
object constancy, transience—all the contrary motions of outer experience and inner psychology that left him confused at best, neurotic at
worst. Rosa was no longer a disappointing object out of the past: she
had become a symbol of the internalized loving objects at the core of
his self-esteem—one of the lynch pins that would determine the stability of his adolescent consolidations. In this context it was very clear to
Alex that the Batmobile represented himself at the crossroads of his life.
Batman was a reference to the idealized mother and father (Rosa too
perhaps) who had to be diminished psychologically speaking if he was
to assume the responsibility for the wheel of his own life. (At this point
in the hour the bicycle wheel leaning on the radiator beside Alex's chair
assumed its full tragicomic significance!) Chasing the bad guys round
an "oval" led to several associations: the oval referred to the shape of
the baseball field, "a field of dreams" he wished to return to and abdi-
cate all adult ambition and conflict. In fact, in another dream fragment
that Alex reported, he "surrenders" an old girlfriend to a rival while

he, in Oedipal defeat, becomes preoccupied with baseball. The pursuit of the bad guys leads to the most important association of all: Alex's realization that the "bad guys" are no longer "out there", as it seemed in latency times, but "within." Alex reflected on the fact that his academic progress was a very precise barometer of the state of his object relations. On reflection he could "see" that the breakup of a two-year relationship with his girlfriend had affected him academically and emotionally more than he had been willing to admit prior to the consultation.

In discussing three dreams that straddle fifteen years of development, I must avoid the temptation toward synthetic zeal, lest a process that could be compared to "secondary revision" smooths out all the rough edges and tries to portray a polished anagogic theme that covers up all the dynamic unrest, and even chaos, underneath. It is the beauty of the associative process that prevents the clinician from such simple-mindedness and keeps a wild analyst honest. As Alex learned how to free associate, the latent meanings of the second and third dreams could be deciphered. The first dream was another matter. Associations were sparse and the kinetic mind of the child was unable to see any value in the passivities of sleep. I had to be alert to every nuance that preceded the dream and pursue it to capture the elusive meanings of it. The following is a microanalysis of the hour "frame by frame" in an attempt to interpret without the benefit of a mature free-associative process.

If a dream is also "a part of the night", this will be an attempt to light a semiotic candle in the darkness. Every noun and verb in the sketch that language tries to preserve from amnesia could be viewed as a wish. In the first dream "I wish I were an octopus with eight long extensions not merely one endangered protrusion" is one conceivable interpretation of the barely concealed infantile wish. Even the numerical advantage does not satisfy: a size dimension has to be introduced. The octopus has to be as big as the Empire State building! If this is wish fulfillment, why is the next image necessary, the poignant image of the dreamer in the reported "I had a stick." One can assume that the numerical, spatial greed that casts him in a grandiose fearless limelight one moment, casts him in a consequential fearful retaliatory light an unconscious moment later. If repression claimed the latter moment, the next frame in the unconscious sequence is not censored: "I had a stick" is let stand as a defensive posture that gives the dreamer some solace even if it seems poignant to the countertransferential eyes of the much taller analyst. Images of swallowing, fighting, spitting ensue in rapid succession, the assignment of action to octopus or dreamer depending on wish and retaliation and the self-deception that octopus and dreamer are other than the five-year-old unconscious Fellini responsible for the whole nocturnal cinematography in the first place.

My appeal for day residues of rationality that might connect the fantastic and the pedestrian, a piece of day with a piece of the night, so to speak, met with further flights into the fantastic: the lie about grandfather's death, "an accident" as he calls it. Mendacity and accident are of course "associations" that attempt to remove the dreamer, now fully awake and reporting all to his "analytic grandfather" from the scene of the crime. "Not guilty," he seems to be proclaiming, a state of innocence belied by his subsequent play in which he attempts to "bury grandfather." The aesthetics of play seem unable to contain all the affects homicide has generated in the transference—regressions are called for in the spilling of the sand and the open admission of a desire for babyhood and the final piece of acting out, the "theft" of the airplane.

The clinical events that precede the telling of the dream can be viewed as a string of associations: the hour begins with anger at the analyst who did not preserve the decor of the playroom as it had been at the end of the previous session. An appeal to reason (couldn't we make the same block design again?) is dismissed. He can't remember the design since "the mouse who takes things from the back of his head to the front of his head cannot be asked to work right now." One can see rudimentary psychological theory in statu nascendi in such pronouncements. Is insight too transgressive, as argued in Chapter Two, and does Alex have to invoke the laziness of the mouse to explain his own dynamic inertia? The theme of the angry "mouse" is taken up again immediately in play about wetting the bed (pee pee doo doo wee wee) and taking revenge on mother in this manner. He shifts from play to drawing, saying good-bye to himself as he erases his name, which he had chalked on the blackboard in the previous session. (It is all right for him actively to remove things from the playroom as opposed to being passively subjected to my arbitrary actions.) The drawings elaborate the theme even further. He wants to draw a dog but draws a dinosaur, a brontosaur, and the bird saurus, commenting that the bird can eat the brontosaurus but not the tyrannosaurus. He then draws eggs, snake eggs, a lady snake, then a star, saying, "A star is part of the night. I don't like night." Sensing that the analytic material is moving toward the oneiric, I ask, "Why not? Is it the dreams?" The octopus dream follows immediately.

His commentary on his own drawings suggests that the "mouse" has graduated and is trying on the "bird" for size and contemplating his rivals: he can dispatch brontosaurus, but what about tyrannosaurus? And what about the egg-making lady snake? If the mouse roars, will an octopus swallow him? Can his small solitary stick match a rival with numerical and spatial advantage?

This microanalysis, while not devoid of some interpretive imaginings, is not replete with speculative "wildness" either. The description of the subsequent analysis tries to show how this endangered immature psyche with its octopoid instincts and stick-like ego weathered the developmental elements, not merely surviving but prevailing.

The second and third dreams stand at the entrance and exit of adolescence like sentinels of progress. Now the dreamer is equipped with a maturing free-associative process, and dream analysis becomes a joint enterprise rather than a labor of the analyst alone. In fact, if one were to highlight the differences rather than the similarities between the first dream and the later ones, two issues seem obvious but nonetheless crucial: (a) the rapidly expanding free-associative abilities of the developing mind make analysis interpretive rather than wild; (b) the developmental context becomes part of the therapeutic process.

Addressing (b) first, since (a) has been alluded to already, I believe that Alex, at ages thirteen and twenty, is keenly aware of the developmental context that informs his dreams. In fact, if one were told these three dreams without their developmental context, one would be hard pressed to guess the age of the dreamer. As the developmental context triggers the associations in the second and third dreams, it becomes clear that the transformations of puberty (Freud, 1905) and the consolidations of adolescence (Blos, 1979) are the conflicting triggers beneath the manifest architecture of these dreams. This is not to say that the infantile wish does not comprise the deepest layer of meaning in any dream, but simply to add that the infantile has developmental dimensions that give a dream from each developmental phase different shapes and contours, as the infantile wish weaves its way through developmental pathways. In less poetic language, in Alex's second dream the infantile wish to use his snake-penis in an Oedipal context is disguised not only in the service of defense but also in the service of development. In sleep Alex appeals for a developmental respite from the inexorable transformations of puberty to give his ego a chance to catch up with his id. By displacing the sexual in the direction of the younger children,

Alex's economic strategy seems to imply that as a young "imaginative" boy he can get away with murder and incest, but a young "physical" adolescent with a "transformed" pubertal body could actually commit the Oedipal crime and deserve actual punishment. The infantile wish may be the same for the five-year-old or the thirteen-year-old, but the transformations of puberty provide an existential context that is perhaps even more terrifying than the original prelatency context. Similarly, the Batmobile dream could be interpreted as an expression of the infantile wish to have a most impressive penis, to take the wheel from Batman, and to pursue the "incestuous" bad guys, a thinly disguised depiction of his own forbidden wishes. But it is the developmental context that brings specificity to these theoretical speculations. The Oedipal wish of a twenty-year-old is processed by an ego that has integrated or failed to integrate the transformations of puberty into its development. Blos (1979) has described this "adolescent passage" of the mind in great detail as id, ego, superego, and ego ideal clear a space for all the libidinal realignments and structural rearrangements that object removal calls for. It is a dramatic developmental story that can only be referred to rather than described at this juncture. For an additional insight to augment the dynamic understanding of the dream a developmental point of view is mandatory: Alex is not merely taking the wheel-penis from Batman to castrate father and make off with mother, he is contemplating a future free of parental influence, free of infantile dependence in a non-incestuous setting in which he will act out his Oedipal and pre-Oedipal ambitions and longings in a new home of his own as good if not better than his parents'. This is the Oedipus complex in a new developmental key. Its implications are as rewarding and exciting and terrifying as the prelatency version of the conflict. The infantile wish has grown up, so to speak, and Alex's dreams reflect not only the source of the wish but all of its transformations.

We began this investigation of dreams with what could be called "inclusion bodies" cleverly deposited by the dream work in the manifest architecture of a dream in the interest of attracting as much attention as possible to manifest pyrotechnics and no attention at all to latent desire. I began with what could be called the most daring inclusion of all: one dream inserted within, or contained within, another. I have tried to formulate the dynamic raison d'etre of such an elaborate and elegant illusion. Whereas Freud was convinced that if something were placed in a dream within a dream it had to mean that its reality was being vehemently denied, I have emphasized that both reels of the cinematic dream illusion need to be considered. It would be counter-analytic to focus on one element while totally ignoring another. That would be a violation of the "evenly suspended attention" both portions of the dream experience deserve. Freud's initial insight can be doubly confirmed: the reality of what is placed in each portion of the segmented dream is being denied. The dreamer I have described came to realize that being lost as a child was a terrifying reality he wished he could erase from memory once and for all; but he also was surprised to learn that the act of telling his troubles to priest or parent was a conflicted, traumatic experience he wished to deny also. Both experiences were represented in the segments of dream within dream and both were equally important and crucial to analyze.

Parapraxis or joke or pun may seem like minor inclusions compared to the magnitude of the usurpation of what could be called the usurper dream but I have shown how they each have an important dynamic role to play in the defensive architecture the dream work has masterfully crafted in the interest of disguise. Similarly I have suggested that an inclusion of the uncanny in a dream is a major embellishment of the manifest content of a dream, well designed to attract attention almost entirely to itself and leave the latent free to enjoy its unconscious instinctual pleasures almost unnoticed.

Let us reconsider these inclusions more precisely. Let us start with a joke in a dream. The human capacity not only to dream but also to joke is after all the starting point of this deliberation on the complex relationship between the two. Whereas Freud (1905) has argued that the genetic origins of dreams and jokes are fundamentally different, jokes deriving from play, dreams deriving essentially from primary processes that disguise infantile wishes during sleep, I contend that occasionally the two can co-exist in a collusion that makes for unusual disguise. The question I have raised is why the dream work, in this clinical instance, needed to exploit more secondary processes than usual to house a well constructed joke in a locale where sound, solid joke construction is usually not required or even expected. If a dream joke, in Freud's words, usually does not provide "the yield of pleasure of a true joke" in this instance a yield of pleasure was introduced by the dream work into dreamtime. Why? If the awakener and the analyst laugh together at this dream joke the seductive infantile wish would have realized its ambition and the deeper, more latent biting sadistic intent of the dream would have been enacted rather than analyzed.

The dream pun described is even more cunning in its construction. Let us return to the details of the dream. The latent thoughts are stark, Oedipal, ferocious. The task of the dream work is to disguise all this raw ambition. Enter the "didn'ter", an ingenious creation of the dream work. The didn'ter, two verbs (did inter) transformed into one noun, struts its disguised representation of the death wish center stage in prime time, so to speak. Why did the dream work need a clever pun to maintain disguise? Is it possible that the dream without the didn'ter pun was in danger of exposing the infantile wish to an alert censor? There was disguise to be sure: a real estate "killing" is an acceptable form of capitalistic ambition, a capital offense one can get away with, if another pun is permissible. But perhaps the wish to appropriate the earthly belongings of the deceased was insufficiently disguised in this manner. A humorous pun that revealed one meaning in dream time and its other hidden meaning only to an astute analysand upon awakening might be the ideal last minute, manifest flourish to keep the latent content from being exposed. Didn'ter gets pretty close to the infantile wish (did inter) to bury the rival, Oedipal object, and it is impressive how a small shift of accent, a minor modification of pronunciation, can so radically change meaning. Prosody has been enlisted cunningly by the dream work. A dactyl (didn'ter) changed to half an iamb followed by an iamb (did inter) makes a world of semantic difference! Disguise is maintained by this slight modification of pronunciation.

Let us take another look at the parapraxis in the dream cited.

> "I'm walking down a city street—New York, probably. Skyscrapers all around. I am walking with Nelson Mandela, but I am calling him Tomas Magadin in error."

The dream work's first choice of Nelson Mandela seems splendidly adequate on the face of it. A bisexual theme (too unruly perhaps) was represented in a complex knot of puns and condensations: Nel(l), a woman's name, plus "son" attached to it, "son" the male offspring of woman and man, plus Man, the son claiming his full generic stature, perhaps, and Man Del(l)a, the name of a woman attached to a man! These components, full of their own ambivalent energies, resonate with similar, larger themes of the one-eyed Lord Nelson—and, of course, of the actual Nelson Mandela himself, a historic hero who represents the ego's attempt to free itself, as the actual Mandela did after years of incarceration. But it would seem that the dream-contrived "Nelson Mandela", for all its oneiric elegance and allusive sophistication, was not disguise enough, and the dream work did a double take, so to speak, coming up with the idea of a "mistake" in manifest content as just the thing to fool an all too clever and vigilant dream censorship. The dream work's strategy is the hope or even assumption that the censor will accept the lesser plea of a manifest mistake, without paying much attention to the much more latent offstage crime. A great insight did emerge from the analysand's musing about the function of the parapraxis. Tomas Magadin was not a slip, an error, but a profound association in its own right. Tomas sounded like no mas, the infamous words of Roberto Duran in his boxing match with Sugar Ray Leonard. Duran refused to continue the fight, throwing in the towel with the words "no mas"—no more— a great humiliation for the legendary boxer. Tomas Magadin and its associative siblings, "no mas" and "maggots in" were protests against the death of the analysand's brother or the death of the analyst himself, but behind the protests lay a death wish against both. "I'm glad I'm alive" was the dream's major message. "I'm glad others are dying, not I—make no mistake about it." The bold starkness of the wish had to be concealed in ambiguities and compromises, as if the guilty dreamer could only be heroic in his defiance of death and his wishing it on others when he embraced death and life together in a bisexual compromise. He could not be simply Nelson Mandela in the dream; he needed to cover up this heroic, phallic identity with a more castrated alter ego, Tomas Magadin. And he needed to pretend it had all been a mistake!

I have ended this chapter with a longitudinal, developmental perspective using the dreams of one analysand over a considerable span of time, as a way of investigating how the subtleties of disguise reflect the increasing sophistication of dream work artistry as development proceeds. If the very young child's dream seems to make little distinction between latent wish and manifest expression, as in Anna Freud's celebrated dream about wild strawberries, a longitudinal perspective almost makes it possible to see the cunning artistry of dream work in statu nascendi. It is incorrect of course to say that a very young child latently wishing for wild strawberries, and magically imagining the wish realized in the fulfillment of manifest content, is a completely transparent realization of the infantile wish. The pictorial display of the strawberries in the dream is not the same as the reality of the strawberries themselves. The child has been "fooled" so to speak by the dream *mise en scène* and remains asleep, which is one of the cardinal functions of dream as guardian of sleep in the first place. At a very early age the artistry of dream work need not be so cunning to be sure, but the developmental and longitudinal perspective does dramatize how quickly the dream work's artistry of disguise grows up, matures and flourishes.

The manifest content of a dream is designed as a clever cover-up of latent objectionable desire. By free-associating to every element of the manifest content, no matter how trivial or insignificant, the latent dream thoughts are arrived at. An analysand who was at first "taken in" by the cunning artistry of dream work, falling for the bravura of its intricate manifest displays, eventually gets to the latent hidden dream thoughts and comes away with profound insights. What was deemed objectionable, needing to be bowdlerized at first, can be reclaimed, as unconscious truth exposes neurotic thinking and insists on unrepressed maturity. We have been examining, in this chapter, the great lengths a manifestly misleading dream work will go to, to ensure that latent infantile wishes are fulfilled in the most ingenious ways. If an initial manifest display is not disguise enough to evade the censor's objections, all sorts of additional bells and whistles (jokes, puns, parapraxes, dreams within dreams, the uncanny itself) can be enlisted in the service of disguise. One can only marvel at the mind's repertoire as it hides from itself in the night and dares to open its eyes in daylight as it reclaims in analytic process all that it formerly believed to be objectionable and unthinkable.

CHAPTER SEVEN

Screen memories

It may indeed be questioned whether we have any memories at all *from* our childhoods; memories *relating* to our childhoods may be all that we possess.

—*Screen Memories*, Sigmund Freud, 1899

In the last chapter we were examining unusual contents of dreams the better to understand the dream work's strategic intent. If all days' residues are "kidnapped" from daylight, dipped in unconscious paint and then slyly returned to the manifest content as if they were still unpainted, surreal, casual day-trippers, checking out night-town before they return to their desk jobs, jokes, puns, parapraxes and nested dreams (Balter, 2000) are even stranger, more cunning concoctions and co-options of the dream work, masquerading as daylight commonplaces the better to hoodwink the dream censor. Essentially, in the last chapter we have been examining content, not form. There is virtually nothing new to add to Freud's ingenious dissection of the formal properties of dream work and its astonishing translation of dream thoughts into a collage of manifest imagery that acts as the "guardian of sleep" unless untamed affects break through the dream barriers and erupt into nightmare. The content of dreams is another matter. Dream work has inexhaustible supplies of diurnal artifacts and current events in the traffic of everyday life that it can collage into the manifest imagery of a dream. As we have seen in many examples in the previous chapter, one feature of the dream work's artistry is to occasionally concoct a pun, a joke, a parapraxis, and put it on display in the manifest imagery of the dream, as if it were an "innocent" casual intrusion, when as I have argued, it is a most complex, well wrought piece of disguise, that is essential for the dream's maintenance of its complicated system of illusion.

In this chapter we turn to screen memories, which though diurnal in space-time, do bear some similarity to the exclusively sleeping phenomenon called dream. A screen memory is often quite dream-like in appearance. It has a primitive, luminous presence, as if it possessed a "halo" around it. It is dream-like also in the sense that it "uses" memory as opposed to merely recording it. Historical accuracy is not its raison d'etre. Deception and truth are both treated equally in its surreal democracy of disguise. It is a hybrid of actual experience and fabrication, a wish to reveal and conceal all at once, sharing that love of ambiguity with many other psychic products we have been examining (transference, repression, even insight itself as we have seen in previous chapters).

Freud introduced the concept of screen memories in 1899. He was fascinated by the idea that such memories of childhood seemed to be concoctions as opposed to exact historical records of the events. They condensed early historical events into a collage so to speak: no doubt they retained some connection with the historical past but they seemed to treat it in an impressionistic manner, emphasizing one aspect at the expense of others. Like dreams they seemed to have a manifest façade but the bulk of their meaning was hidden. Freud was intrigued with the idea that the important elements of the past were omitted from memory, the trivial retained: "… two psychical forces are concerned in bringing about memories of this sort" Freud wrote. "One of these forces takes the importance of the experience as a motive for seeking to remember it, while the other—a resistance—tries to prevent any such preference from being shown … instead of the mnemic image which would have been justified by the original event, another is produced which has been to some degree associatively displaced from the former one … There is a common saying among us about shams, that they are not made of gold themselves but have lain beside something that is made of gold. The same simile might well be applied to some of the experiences of childhood which have been retained in the memory" (1899).

Earlier, of course, in the letters to Fliess (October 3rd, 4th and 15th, 1897), Freud had discussed his analysis of his own early memories dealing with impressions of his mother, his nurse, his brother Phillip, and an empty cupboard. It was the analysis of these gaps in his infantile amnesia that led Freud to his momentous discovery of the Oedipus complex, a topic I will devote a later chapter to (Mourning and The Discovery of the Oedipus Complex). But now let us look at Freud's description of the first screen memory ever recorded. Freud ascribes it to a "man of university education, aged thirty-eight." But subsequent research has left little doubt that the thirty-eight-year-old man of university education was indeed Sigmund Freud himself.

"The subject of this observation is a man of university education, aged thirty-eight." With this mask in place Freud continues: "I have at my disposal a fair number of early memories of childhood, which I can date with great certainty. For at the age of three I left the small place where I was born and moved to a large town; and all these memories of mine relate to my birthplace and therefore date from my second and third years. They are mostly short scenes, but they are very well preserved and furnished with every detail of sense-perception, in complete contrast to my memories of adult years, which are entirely lacking in the visual element." Freud is stressing what has been confirmed often since this first report: screen memories, like dreams, seem to stress the visual as opposed to the verbal. Freud then describes a scene that has stood out in his memory for many years: "Let me describe it to you. I see a rectangular, rather steeply sloping piece of meadow-land, green and thickly grown; in the green there are a great number of yellow flowers—evidently common dandelions. At the top end of the meadow there is a cottage and in front of the cottage door two women are standing chatting busily, a peasant-woman with a handkerchief on her head and a children's nurse. Three children are playing in the grass. One of them is myself (between the age of two and three); the two others are my boy cousin, who is a year older than me, and his sister, who is almost exactly the same age as I am. We are picking the yellow flowers and each of us is holding a bunch of flowers we have already picked. The little girl has the best bunch; and, as though by mutual agreement, we—the two boys—fall on her and snatch away her flowers. She runs up the meadow in tears and as a consolation the peasant-woman gives her a big piece of black bread. Hardly have we seen this than we throw the flowers away, hurry to the cottage and ask to be given some bread too. And we are in fact given some; the peasant-woman cuts the loaf with a long knife. In my memory the bread tastes quite delicious—and at that point the scene breaks off."

In a great *tour de force* of self analysis Freud shows how this memory, which seems to reflect events of his early childhood when he was two or three years old actually represents events of his adolescence. He shows very convincingly how the ultra-clear color of the flowers of childhood were really displacements of sexual de-flowering wishes of adolescence transported back defensively in time to a scene of relative innocence. At the end of the paper Freud makes a quite revolutionary statement about memory and childhood: "It may indeed be questioned whether we have any memories at all *from* our childhood: memories *relating to* our childhood may be all that we possess. Our childhood memories show us our earliest years not as they were but as they appeared at the later periods when the memories were aroused. In these periods of arousal, the childhood memories did not, as people are accustomed to say, *emerge*; they were *formed* at that time. And a number of motives, with no concern for historical accuracy, had a part in forming them, as well as in the selection of the memories themselves" (1899, italics in the original).

I have reproduced Freud's first description of a screen memory, including a little of the sense of a dialogue between Freud and his imagined alter ego. I have also included Freud's summation at the end of the paper, which is remarkably modern even in 2013! The paper was written in 1899 when his mind was full of the discoveries of the self-analysis he had embarked on in June 1897. Freud was immensely pleased with his 1899 paper, according to Strachey, which he took "as a bad omen for its future fate." Freud's superstitious thinking has not been corroborated by history. The topic has continued to fascinate psychoanalysts ever since; and it continued to fascinate Freud for many years. He returned to the topic in 1900 and again in 1901. The analysis of screen memories plays a highly significant part in his case histories (1909), (1918) and in his study of Goethe (1917) and Leonardo da Vinci (1910). It seems, in fact, that the subject of screen memories was rarely far from his mind. For instance, in a 1920 footnote to *The Three Essays of Sexuality*, he compared a screen memory to a fetish; and in 1937, he tackled the issue again. But it is perhaps in 1914 that he made his most definitive and comprehensive statement on the nature of screen memories: "In some cases I have had an impression that the familiar childhood amnesia, which is theoretically so important to us, is completely counterbalanced by screen memories. Not only some but all of what is essential from childhood has been retained in these memories. It is simply a question of knowing how to extract it out of them by analysis. They represent the forgotten years of childhood as adequately as the manifest content of a dream represents the dream-thoughts" (p. 148). In fact this close affinity between dream and screen memory, that Freud alludes to, will be the exclusive topic of a later section when I describe the case of Leonora.

Interest in screen memories other than Freud's has been less enthusiastic than one might have imagined. Greenacre (1981) has argued that the interest in ego psychology after Freud's death led to relative neglect of the concepts of reconstruction and screen memories, two concepts, which are obviously allied. (Greenacre herself has done much to redress this balance.) A review of the literature before and after Freud's death reveals that this topic was approached from a variety of metapsychological points of view. Simmel (1925) and Kennedy (1950) focused on the formation of screen memories. Fenichel (1927) provided new information on the economic function of screen memories. Ernst Kris (1956a), (1956b) was interested in the development, in fact, the construction of memory in general, not just its screening function. He argued, convincingly, that analysis is not just a nostalgic Proustian attempt to recapture the past and wallow in it, but rather a pursuit of the vicissitudes of "genetics" as they enter the "personal myths" that human beings construct to make some kind of existential sense out of their life histories. Abraham (1913) and Glover (1929) described the screening function of traumatic memories. Helene Deutsch (1932) suggested that hysterical fugues are sometimes reactivated screen memories. The recent tendency to broaden the concept of screening—Lewin's (1950) screen affects, Greenson's (1958) screen identifications, Reider's (1953) screen symptom and screen character—runs the risk of confusing a useful clinical phenomenon with an over-inclusiveness that blurs the distinction of the definition. A useful heuristic phenomenon becomes screened by such ecumenical thinking. It was again Greenacre who brought a developmental point of view to the study of screen memories. Her purpose in a series of papers (1947, 1949, 1979, 1980, 1981), would seem to be twofold: (1) to explain the intensity of the screen memory (what Freud had called its "ultra clear" quality) as a stamp of its genetic origin in the preverbal months of life, when sensory traumas in the visual and auditory spheres are ubiquitous human experiences (Greenacre even suggests that the sharp edges of the screen memory, as contrasted with the vague edges of Lewin's dream screen, can be explained by the latter's less tumultuous sensory birth in the early hours of our oral origins); (2) to highlight the clinical neglect of reconstruction and analysis of screen memories and to renew clinical interest in these areas.

It is interesting, from the viewpoint of development, that there seem to be few studies in which the child's subjective experience of his screen memories becomes available to him. Piaget (1945) did ask children about their understanding of their own dreams, discovering, in his usual genetic epistemological way, that it takes maturity of the mental apparatus to identify the dream as being a product of the mind, very young children experiencing the dream as a foreign body. At what age a human begins to reflect on his screen memories is perhaps an un-researchable topic. But I am inclined to believe that the dissolution of the Oedipus complex and the massive repression that ushers in the infantile amnesia leave islands of memory that must erupt into the seas of latency with some chronological regularity that we can only guess at. Freud (1899) himself, describing his own memory, says: "it is not, I believe, until my sixth or seventh year that the stream of my memories becomes continuous" (p. 309). And Piaget suggests that the child does not possess a sense of time as an orderly sequence, past leading to present, until seven or eight (Flavell, 1963). This suggests that by that age the child may have the capacity to reflect a little on his own history, where his memories have gone to, and why only certain pieces of the mosaic of memory remain available to him.

Case one

The fate of screen memories in analysis became a clinical phenomenon that intrigued me. As patients changed in the process of analysis would their evaluation of their own memorial processes change also? My interest in screen memories was aroused even further when a patient, toward the end of his analysis, began to reflect on the working-through process: he became subjectively aware of his own structural changes, and developed a new sense of the meaning of his screen memories. He realized that whereas most of his screen memories had lost their uncanny luminous fascination, one or two others had retained their intensity. The patient felt convinced that the remaining "ultra clear" screens signified unfinished analytic business. As Freud might have said, the complete meaning had not yet been totally extracted from the memories. On the one hand, the patient's subjective sense of the status of his screen memories was an intellectual defense, but it also held a kernel of truth. His sense that it reflected unfinished business seemed accurate and clinically useful.

The end of an analysis is a complicated, intense series of communications between analyst and analysand, in which a multiplicity of factors have to be judged: the state of the transference neurosis, for instance, the evaluation of the working-through process, assessment of structural changes, to name a few. I am not suggesting that an analysand can review his memories at the end of an analysis, like a historian, and come to some decision as to the date of his termination. This would indeed be a travesty of treatment and a triumph of narcissistic resistances. But basically I am suggesting that less psychological "paint" is necessary at the end of an analysis than was mandatory at the beginning as memory reclaims more and more of what it believed it needed to hide behind at the beginning of the analytic process.

Two screen memories and their vicissitudes in the analysis of the patient mentioned earlier will illustrate my thesis graphically. As analysis progressed and the process deepened, the patient became aware that the work of analysis had removed the "uncanny" charge from one memory, but not from another, an insight that had major clinical implications in terms of psychoanalytic work accomplished and work remaining to be done. The patient was a middle-aged lawyer. A narcissistic character armor could not completely conceal residuals of pre-Oedipal pathology and poorly resolved Oedipal conflicts. He often perceived his "success" as an ambivalent gift to his narcissistic mother or guilt-ridden victory over a castrated father, rather than an achievement of his own growth and development. The screen memories reflected his conflicts and his characteristic approach to them: one memory depicted a childhood scene of separation from the father, but the memory contained a doubt as to whether the father was "coming or going". The "confusion" was a defense, of course, against positive and negative Oedipal feelings toward the father, but on another level it was a depiction of mistrust that originated in a pre-Oedipal rapprochement crisis with both parents. By focusing on the father, the screen obscured the effective repression of a host of feelings about the mother. The analysis of a poem by the analysand revealed how the screen memory had subtly insinuated itself into the patient's sublimations and into the transference where it could be examined in detail. The poem entitled "Cummings and Goings" was addressed to E. E. Cummings and achieved its aesthetic effect through parody, irony, and the obvious play on words ("comings" in the screen memory/ "cummings" in the poem). The offer of the poem to the analyst prior to a summer recess was an attempt to undo the "comings and goings" of the therapist with a magical "gift." Analysis of such issues led to an eventual "revision"of memory in which the "coming and going" screen seemed to have lost its emotional impact for the patient, not to mention its "ultra clear" quality.

But another memory had not lost its "illumination," its function as a screen still being under unconscious obligatory control it would seem. This memory depicted a childhood scene in which a practical joke had been played on the patient: a weekend guest of the family sent him to his room to discover, by surprise, a paper replica of a woman in bed. The patient became aware in the analytic process that the inert replication of memory was a screen for an entirely different set of memories that lay hidden in deeper folds of the unconscious: primal scene fantasies of a dangerous seductive mother and an endangered species, namely, his passive father. When the patient brought this differential version of memory to the attention of his analyst, they both realized they had hit on an insight that could gauge the progress of the analytic process. It seemed clear that the pre-Oedipal issues which had found expression in the "coming and going" metaphor had been sufficiently worked through, whereas sexual Oedipal components of primal scene fantasy had not.

This understanding of the screen memory allowed the patient to reflect on his inhibition in the sexual transference toward the analyst. If the screen memory was a reflection of the patient's fear that the unavailability and instability of the father could not protect him adequately from his own sexual impulses toward the seductive mother, the patient suddenly became aware that the transference neurosis was a complete recapitulation of his early fears: in a sense, he preferred to think of the analyst as a lifeless paper replica rather than let the full implication of the reality of his flesh-and-blood contact with the maternal transference emerge. In other words, the analysis of this screen memory allowed the patient to wean himself from a one-dimensional asexual vision of the analyst and the obvious defensiveness of this transference distortion, and engage in a more multidimensional relationship. This insight allowed Oedipal sexual memories to rub shoulders with pre-Oedipal tender memories and paved the way to a final undoing of his splitting mechanism—an undoing that was essential to ensure that the analysis would reach a most favorable outcome. It is of significance to report that with the analysis of this aspect of the transference, the corresponding screen memory began to lose its cathexis. As Freud might have remarked, the libidinal residues of the infantile amnesia had been extracted.

Case two

Robert was nine and a half-years-old and in the fourth month of his analysis when he related his first screen memory. The memory depicted him at three years old, in the park, with his father and his newly born baby brother, on a very cold day. He was standing by the baby carriage. His father said, "I'm going to take a picture." Robert reacted only to the first half of the sentence "I'm going," unable or unwilling to understand that his father was not abandoning him, but was retreating to a relative distance from which he could take a photograph of his two sons. Robert's misunderstanding of this childhood event left him feeling cold and lonely and wishing he could be safe and warm in the baby carriage.

During the fifteenth month of his analysis, Robert became aware of a remarkable trick his memory had played on him. Looking through childhood photographs, he was startled to discover that his screen memory was a direct contradiction of a photographic fact: in the photograph he was in the carriage with his baby brother. Not only had his father not abandoned him, as the screen memory suggested; he had actually placed him securely in the carriage, before taking the picture. Robert's need to falsify his memory in this manner will become clearer as the genetic roots of his psychopathology and his symptomatic entry into treatment is described.

Robert was the firstborn of a depressive mother and an obsessional, argumentative father. While both parents were well meaning, they were perplexed and confused by an immediate problem that confronted them when Robert was born. The newborn had a large angioma on his neck. Two modes of treatment were suggested to the parents: surgery or parental massage of the skin until the angioma disappeared. The parents chose the latter treatment, which proved highly successful. But the child underwent a three-month treatment that subjected him to considerable discomfort and necessitated some neglect of the totality of his oral needs.

According to the parents, Robert weathered this initial trauma rather well, and another at eleven months when a cyst on his eyelid required an overnight stay in the hospital for surgical removal. However, the parental reports of his resilience and developmental prowess were belied by his reaction to the birth of a sibling when he was two and a half. He threw his pacifier and transitional object (a blanket) into the incinerator, not unlike Goethe who had a childhood memory in which he threw plates out the window, a symbolic ejection of his sibling, according to Freud (1917). In Robert's case, one senses that he was not merely ridding himself of his brother, but he was doing away with his own dependency wishes as well. It seemed clear that he was disavowing dependency while seeking security in his remarkably precocious intellect, but not without significant compromises along the way. After the incineration of his transitional objects, he began to thrust his tongue, for which a corrective brace became necessary. Later, he prided himself in being able to chew his tongue and make it seem as if he was chewing gum. None of these early preschool symptoms attracted too much attention from the environment. But in grade school, when Robert's orality began to explode in symptomatic impulsivity and greedy attention seeking along with an aggressive argumentative pattern of misbehavior, which was clearly a defense against Robert's more passive strivings, psychoanalysis seemed mandatory if his development was to be rescued from permanent maladaptation. This was the opinion of all parties except Robert.

His analysis began, quite expectedly, with belligerent resistance against the very idea of his needing help from an analyst. Every session started and ended with a defiant question, "When can I stop?" as if he had to greet and dismiss the analyst with a slap in the face, to protect himself and his helper from the impact of his needs. (His constant nagging of the analyst also may have reflected the climate of his home where both parents, while remaining married, seemed to need to threaten each other with divorce.) His fear that his insatiable needs could go out of control and overwhelm him and his caretakers forced him to badger the analyst for reassurance that his needs could be controlled: "I don't need you. But if I discover that I do, will there be any end to my greed?" seemed to be the unspoken fantasy.

His screen memory illustrates his defensive posture in the early months of analysis. Compressing the child's account and translating it into adult language, the analyst understood him to be saying: "Since my father is abandoning me, since my brother is the only baby in the carriage, I will stand beside the carriage, develop a personal myth (Kris, 1956b) of myself in which I am deprived but also stoic." A poem that he wrote illustrates the balances of defenses and instincts quite graphically. He called it "Gnore and Bore went to war, etc." Gnore obviously stood for ignore (denial, disavowal, isolation), Bore corresponded to depression, and war represented potential or actual loss of impulse control. Another poem about fog (his favorite) thinly disguised his wish not to see everything so clearly (denial, disavowal with genetic precursors of defense, triggered perhaps by his early eye problem).

The screen memory and the poems were, of course, offered to the analyst in a cautious transference climate in which the patient's trust emerged slowly from the shackles of analyzed resistances, until eventually he was able to rediscover himself not only in the baby carriage of a childhood photograph but also in the newly created psychological baby carriage of the transference neurosis. The memory of the father abandoning the baby carriage was of course a screen that concealed even earlier memories about the angioma and the eye surgery and the cumulative trauma of maternal deprivation.

This case illustrates the ability of a sophisticated nine and a half-year-old to review his own falsification of memory, a review that reflected his ability to change his attitude toward his family and his analyst, and, of course, toward himself. His screen memory was a defensive, self-deceiving internal counterfeit photograph that he could not discard until psychoanalysis made it possible for him to accept a more realistic likeness of himself. The revision of his screen memory was of obvious assistance to both analyst and analysand as a chart of the progress of the analytic voyage of discovery.

Case three

Brendan, a seven-year-old boy with an older sister and divorced parents, began his analysis by saying, "I get angry for no reason." When it was explained to him that there is always a reason for a feeling, even if one cannot remember it, he related a memory in which, as he put it, "at the fourth or third birthday of my sister when I was twos and threes (he had a slight lisp), I was wearing blue." He went on to describe how he was the only boy among many girls at his sister's party. He assured his analyst that this memory, in which he seemed to play a very distant second fiddle to his sister, was corroborated by a photograph which confirmed, among other details, that he indeed had been wearing blue. In subsequent sessions this young analysand was impressed with the analyst's ability to remember the details of the screen memory as it had been told to him. Brendan was not always complimentary, however, and when he noticed screwdrivers out of place in the playroom, he asked how the change had come about. When the analyst confessed that he could not remember how the screwdrivers had arrived in their new habitat, Brendan chided him, "How come you can remember what I told you happened to me years ago, but not what happened today?" The analyst was impressed with this piece of wisdom and began to reflect on the countertransference tendency that placed more emphasis on the past than on current events. With this piece of countertransference out of the way, the analyst could see the point of the patient's inquiry. For Brendan, the appearance of the playroom was an obvious sign of the analyst's attachment to others; would he (therefore) have to play second fiddle to them and hide his own feelings?

This was a very early moment in the analysis, hardly a time for deep interpretation of all the issues raised by this seemingly innocent question, and yet the analytic situation was vibrating with three dynamic currents: a screen memory, a piece of transference, and an equally important piece of countertransference. In the interest of alerting the patient's insight to the multiple determinants of the transaction, the analyst remarked somewhat humorously, "Other children have been here. You must have feelings about it and you are not even wearing blue." Brendan made immediate eye contact with his therapist and laughed. The analyst was implying that the issues hidden by the screen memory would be reenacted in the transference and that the patient might not always have to use defenses to face them. In a sense, he need not only be blue; all the other colors of his prismatic development need not be neglected; guinea pigs and children need not be painted once they learn to see themselves clearly and accept all their feelings.

A few more details of Brendan's life will help us to understand more clearly the pivotal significance of the memory that straddled a gulf between his understanding of himself and what was lost to repression. Brendan's father left his mother when the child was one year of age. After the divorce the father would visit, however, and take Brendan's older sister with him, "the baby" left behind while father and daughter attempted a rapprochement. "Sister gets everything (including visits with father) while I get nothing," he must have mused. "An older sibling of the opposite sex, not to mention the even older object of my incestuous desires (mother) has claimed the inside track in the Oedipal race toward father: negative Oedipal pathways are closed off; with my father out of the way, positive Oedipal pathways are dangerously close to reality. What a predicament! Let me think of myself permanently as a psychological cripple: all my ambitions can be hidden neatly behind a screen. Every day is sister's birthday, not mine: I'm an ignored little boy blue. My birthdays don't count. My depression will extract love, command attention, misery my weapon against all of them." This dramatization of Brendan's adaptation is of course a caricature, but it does represent a condensation of many months of the analytic process. For instance, Brendan developed the habit of collecting stray pens in the office, pretending to steal them. This was an over determined symptomatic act within the context of the analytic process, of course, but one meaning is worthy of emphasis: Brendan would take what he could not retrieve from primary objects; moreover, this should not be noticed, prohibited, or interpreted since that forced many repressed affects out of their hiding places. Brendan was, of course, furious with his father for abandoning him and favoring another, but he was equally furious with his mother's remarriage that forced him to deal with a new "father" and reconsider his relationship with the old. Brendan was also furious with an analyst who was unwilling to settle for his monochromatic estimation of himself. Brendan's drawings depicted his ambivalence toward the working through of these issues. Interpretation of his "blue" defenses led to revisions of memory that no doubt reflected rearrangements of defenses as well as structural realignments. Brendan informed the analyst that his old memory was only one version of the truth: he could now also remember a birthday party which was a celebration of his own birthday, not his sister's, and he remembered wearing blue on that occasion as well. He would draw both versions and prove his point. Neurosis intervened, however: having drawn the old version (his sister's birthday), he could not draw the new revised version, until his hatred of father, mother and sister were analyzed thoroughly and his need to paint himself "blue"was no longer necessary. As analysis proceeded Brendan was able to "draw" many further versions of himself, and at termination he had no need to paint over the repressed affects that once were compromising his development.

Case four

Prelatency children do not walk into an analyst's office recounting their screen memories. Yet, we know from Piaget (1937) that recognition memory is in existence in the first year of life, evocative memory in the second. We also know that symbolism and rudimentary defenses appear in the second year of life (Jones, 1916; Sarnoff, 1970). This suggests that the screening function might exist from the second year of life on. And yet, clinical data from prelatency children describing their screen memories seem sparse. Is the infantile amnesia that begins at five or six with the waning of the Oedipus complex a prerequisite for the existence of screen memories and their recall? Or could we find precursors of the process even in prelatency?

Willie, a four-year-old in the full passion of his Oedipal romance, was seen in consultation for a sleep disorder, a reaction to the recent divorce of his parents. He described his conflicts in a displaced manner that suggested an incipient screening process. In the second session, he related the following memory: "You know, I had a dog when I was a baby. His name was Silver. He could not be with three people. He bit my daddy who was away a lot: so he did not know him well enough." These were the actual words of the child. The trauma of the parents' separation had occurred one year before the consultation, when Willie was three; yet, the child created a displacement from the human object to the animal and the concomitant distortion of time as if he needed to soothe himself by saying this did not happen last year, it happened three years ago; moreover, it was not I who was angry with my father, it was a dog. This displacement of responsibility in regard to time and object is similar to, if not identical with, the screen memory mechanisms Freud described in 1899. The major difference between this screen memory and its adult counterpart may reside in the amount of insight the patient has into its formation.

This child's parents at first accepted, but later rejected, analytic treatment for their son. Consequently, the vicissitudes of this screen memory received no further documentation.

Case five

In the bulk of this chapter I have concentrated on screen memories in children and adults. I was trying to expand on Freud's contributions by emphasizing an issue that he had not addressed: the fate of screen memories as the analytic process effects its structural changes by reclaiming more and more of the once discarded, repressed conflicts of the mind. I wanted to emphasize that a screen memory will reflect the analytic work as it proceeds and even lose its ultra-clear quality (the *uberdeutlich* luminosity Freud had described) as termination of the analysis approaches. To focus almost exclusively on that point, I was treating screen memories as if they were isolated phenomena when of course they are only one feature of a complexity of contiguous mental products, such as dreams, symptoms, character traits, day dreams, fantasies, somatizations etc. But now I want to correct that impression of screen memories acting alone in a vacuum, so to speak, by describing a case in which symptom, screen memory and dream seem to share the same content (a sense of suffocation or drowning breathlessness) and the same defensive function as they work in unison to represent the conflicts of the analysand over a very extended period of time. When this terrifying sense of asphyxiation that the three psychic products seemed to represent and share, (not unlike the complemental series Freud alluded to in a different context), entered the transference as well, the analytic process was well on its way to resolving the mystery all three had struggled with. But I have gotten ahead of myself. Let us introduce the clinical process more sequentially.

Leonora was thirty-one when she sought help for a variety of reasons, some obviously psychological and some physical. As the analysis proceeded, the physical ailments receded dramatically and Leonora became more convinced than ever that mind and body could not be thought of as such separate compartments. The psychological issues that Leonora wanted to address were her passivity, her depressive moods, her sexual "timidity", and a sense that aggression for her was an intellectual concept rather than an affect or an attitude she could embrace wholeheartedly and integrate comfortably into the fabric of her personality.

A screen memory had puzzled her for years, but her intellectual curiosity about it would develop only as the memory took hold of the transference in a most dramatic way as the analysis deepened. In the screen memory Leonora reports: "I'm learning how to swim. I'm breathless, floundering, frightened. My older sister supposedly helping me is actually drowning me." While the memory had the lucidity of delineation, so characteristic of this genre of "record keeping," Leonora had some skepticism about its historical accuracy, an assessment that would prove to be borne out when, toward the end of the analysis she checked her own genetic record with her mother's version of actual childhood events and was surprised by the disparity!

Leonora came to realize that a symptom that had compromised her sense of well being for years was in fact connected in some mysterious way to the screen memory, but more insight than that seemed to elude her. The symptom in question, as already stated, involved bouts of fatigue and shortness of breath: "As if all my energy were suddenly drowned out," Leonora once commented, not aware of the irony her verbal imagery had stumbled on. Leonora at times felt she was being hypochondriacal and at other times that the shortness of breath, fatigue, and sexual dysfunction were leftovers of a bout of childhood rheumatic fever, which cleared up after the initial assault, but perhaps had left these sequelae. The total disappearance of these symptoms as analytic process expanded psychological awareness and diminished somatic expression was striking: timidity, fatigue, and breathlessness were replaced with robust athletic endurance and engagement.

It was the analytic process of transference interpretation and the integration of insight into the reshaping of character that made the achievement possible obviously; and the almost exclusive focus on screen memory, symptom, and dream, is not meant to ignore or neglect the constant matrix of transference and its interpretation that made it possible for discrete products such as these under study to be explicated.

If screen memory and symptom are static mental products, the manifest tips of psychological icebergs that do not always reveal their contiguity and relevance to the latent depth psychology they conceal, analytic process, and especially perhaps dream analysis, focuses on a product that does invite free associative explication. When a dream seems to manifestly echo the "content" of the symptom or screen memory, the latent process that informs all three brings genetics and current "residues" into a focus that is nothing but thrilling for both analyst and analysand. But I am getting ahead of myself. In Leonora's mid analysis, a symptomatic reenactment on the couch was followed by a most significant dream. They both emerged out of a deepening transferential process that will first be described. At that pivotal time, Leonora's sense of intimacy with her analyst was intense. She was allowing herself to be more and more sexual in her associations; more aggressive in response to analytic silence and the whole atmosphere of conflict the neutrality of the analytic situation generates and thrives on. Pre-Oedipal thirst for the seemingly stony breasts of the mother could coexist in transferential time with hatred of the mother's pathological deprivations, not to mention the analyst's. Oedipal desire for the analyst to punish her for the naughty sexuality transference was "extracting" from her, the brazen sexual womanliness analysis was tempting her to reclaim, was daring to bare its flesh more and more in the sanctioned exhibitionism that the couch was fostering. In this climate, in mid session, a most dramatic enactment of Leonora's psychological conflicts occurred: she began to suffocate, to choke on her words, to gasp for breath, to cough repetitively and alarmingly. The analyst commented sympathetically and genuinely: "You are trying to tell me something." Symptomatically, rather than verbally was the implication of the analytic intervention and the analysand "got it" immediately. In one breath (ironic pun intended) she asked herself whether the fatigue and dyspnoea were not transformations of desire and aggression, a respiratory knot that desire and aggression had "choked" her with, rather than promoting her voice, a knot that could now perhaps be opened, a throat that could develop its decibel reach rather than stifling itself. She began to weep, but the tears did not interfere with expression, on the contrary they rather enhanced it. Screen memory and symptom now came together more convincingly than ever, as if they had been waiting for years for transference, like a go-between, to bring them together. "I am drowning, choking, breathless, voiceless in both of them," was the synthetic achievement of her new readiness to integrate psychic elements that needed to be kept apart until transference made it safe to unite them. Bringing them together in this new insightful rendition of memory and symptom did not completely elucidate the dynamic, strategic functional structure of both, but it paved the way for the subsequent analytic work out of which a most significant tripartite dream emerged. If the insight was too transgressive at first, this dream and the collaborative interpretive work that deconstructed it, allowed the insight to become comfortable eventually with the transgressive elements that seemed too hot to handle at first. Here is the dream as she reported it:

> "Awful dream! I was torturing people … leaving them after wiring them so that if they moved, they would experience an electric shock … lots of people I knew … later, I couldn't identify them … (then I did identify some). I felt pleasure doing that … awful! And in another part of the dream I was drowning and people couldn't reach me … their arms weren't long enough … they looked so sad … I felt sad for them … the undertow was throwing me to the bottom of the ocean … I called out … then couldn't anymore … I was like in a pocket of very rough ocean … if people went in there, they would be caught too. There was a third piece to this dream … I was also drowning … the ocean was rough … people were close to me in space but couldn't touch me, couldn't hold me, they didn't care … I felt angry … I was watching children being held by other people in warmer water … where I was, the water was cold … the people next to me were stronger … obviously they could hold out in the ocean, they had no feelings … I felt hopeless, I didn't call out … I couldn't get air, I gave up."

Leonora's first association was that the sequence of the dream parts was not the way she had reported them initially: the last part came first, then the first, and then the second. The telling of the three dream components out of sequence was significant in the sense that the most sadistic elements seemed to rush to the fore, ignoring sequential etiquette so to speak. The dream's tripartite structure seemed to the analyst to represent the original screen memory sliced in two with the sadistic portion about the "wires" sandwiched between the other two. But it was the free associative and collaborative work on the dream over the next weeks and months that "opened up" Leonora's genetic and current sense of herself rather than countertransferential intuitions or poetic leaps (not that the two are mutually exclusive, but in fact are complementary in ideal collaborative process). In the collaborative work over the years Leonora had learned how to neglect no detail of a dream, such neglect always loaded with dynamic defensive significance of course. The conflicted pleasure she allowed herself to feel in wiring the dream protagonists (so that if they moved they would experience a shock) was perhaps, if not the greatest analytic achievement to date, certainly the most dramatic. Leonora was aware of the deep genetic as well as the current transferential meanings: as a child, she felt not only bed ridden by virtue of her rheumatic fever but also bound and wired so tightly by the stifling parental atmosphere that seemed to choke the playful spirit out of her. On the couch, she also felt confined by the analytic etiquette that allowed the analyst the freedom to "sit up" while she was "trussed" like a sacrificial victim, an Iphigenia in some Greek or Freudian play the analyst was writing. As she came to understand more and more that this was her own unconscious script, she began to bristle at the masochistic ink she felt obliged to write with for most of her life. "I was drowning and people couldn't reach me: their arms were not long enough. They looked so sad. I felt sad for them. Why did I set the dream images up that way?" Leonora mused as she examined the dream piece by piece. "I must have wanted to drown them. I disguised it instead. Their arms weren't long enough," she scoffed sarcastically. "Maybe I had cut them down to size, chopped off a few joints. They were sad. I felt sad for them. The hypocrisy is sickening. You know where the word hypocrisy comes from? From Greek, it means a stage actor. That's what I was, that's what they made me, a tragic actor in a play I didn't realize I had written for myself, with plenty of help from them!" she hissed. "No wonder I wanted to finally electrocute them. My anger drove the sadness out for a while, but it returned." Leonora reflected on the dream imagery about the children in warmer water being held by people, whereas she was in cold water and untouchable: "People were close to me in space, but couldn't touch me." The genetics and the current transferential climate were now accessible to Leonora almost simultaneously. "It's like here. You are so close to me, but you won't touch me or hold me. You're not supposed to, but they were. They were so strange, weren't they, yet so familiar? In the dream I gave up on them. I felt hopeless. I couldn't call out. I couldn't get air. I gave up." The anger returned at such moments drowning out the sadness momentarily. "Maybe I didn't want to breathe the same air they were breathing, maybe my breathlessness isn't so passive, maybe I'm holding my breath not to be contaminated by the stench of their stupidity, their incompetence." The tears would return at such moments when Leonora realized that she loved them of course and needed them no matter how incompetent they were, the incompetence increasing the need, rather than meeting it.

Now that the manifest sadism of the dream in which people were wired and shocked no longer made Leonora turn away from its serious implications, her new "genetic" grasp of herself seemed more real. She knew she was deeply hurt and deeply angry for as long as memory kept records (and even beyond that, "further back than that," she could now quip given her understanding of repression). What she was only beginning to recognize was the complexity of psychological disguise that used every "trick" in the unconscious book to make truth seem too dangerous, too transgressive (as I have argued in Chapter Two) for conscious insight to call its own. It was as if truth needed dream, symptom, and memory to screen itself from a psychological reality it couldn't bear to face. Ironically of course it was the analysis of dream, symptom, and memory that finally allowed the hidden truth to emerge! Leonora as torturer in the sadistic dream was an image she no longer needed to be afraid of, since she knew she was simply turning the tables on the puppeteers of childhood who had made her feel wired like a puppet whose actions were controlled beyond, and in flagrant neglect of the wishes of the self. Leonora's vision of herself in the dream sequence in which she was out of her depth, unable to be reached by the arms of the would be rescuers, was of course analyzed as the opposite side of the unconscious coin as if the dream calculus could allow her to be torturer in one instance, but then demanded her to be victim in another. The act of interpretation, by rescuing the hidden affective meanings in either instance, did of course eventually allow her to be emotionally self-possessed in both. In such a newly balanced state of mind, Leonora could reflect from a complex perspective that had eluded her when she was "a mere puppet." Analysis had made her physical symptoms unnecessary and the total absence of fatigue, dyspnoea, and muscular "weakness" made her more convinced than ever that her new found mental "agilities" released energies that made fatigue and shortness of breath "laughable" and dismissible, even though the symbolic meaning could continue to intrigue: Why had she "chosen" the respiratory as the avenue of expression? Why did dream and screen memory depict drowning? Why did all three "products" seem connected by invisible unconscious threads? It was at this point in the analysis that Leonora began to question certain genetic assumptions. Did the screen memory depict an actual event at all? Could the "unreliable" mother be relied on to provide the "actual" historic events that screen memory may have subsequently amended (doctored) for dynamic reasons? The mother's rendition of the historic record did challenge the testimony of the screen memory, calling memory as witness into question, as Freud so ingeniously hypothesized in 1899! The mother's version of the reality exposed the screen memory's cover up tactics rather glaringly: the older sister had tried to playfully/intentionally choke the younger (Leonora) and might have succeeded were it not for adult intervention! This was a bombshell and led to a most productive period of analysis in which the perilous character of certain aspects of Leonora's childhood could no longer be ignored.

Not only was the older sibling's behavior a constant irrational element in Leonora's childhood, the mother's bizarre and unreliable caretaking (she would mysteriously disappear from family life for periods of time, with no explanations offered) came to light as Leonora's less dumbfounded ego became capable of processing it. Nor were the father's contributions any less noxious, which became clear as the ego tried to master the whole historic record. When Leonora was able to let herself recall his declaration to his children that if any one of them got lost, he would not be responsible for finding them, she winced until she came up with her own counter-declaration: "He was an ass, but of course to a child he was my king." The king, like all kings could be aggressive and irrational: Leonora remembered a dispute between her and a housekeeper in which the king sided with the housekeeper against his own daughter. Leonora was spanked, an assault which produced sexual feelings and a childhood memory that colored adult sexual fantasies with her husband until analytic process allowed her a more expansive sexual repertoire: as analysis proceeded, she could allow herself the freedom to be not only a spanked child in sexual fantasy, but a full-blooded woman as well. As Leonora put it, exploiting a double entendre for all it was worth, "If I can just get the past out of my bed, the present will take care of itself!" Ironically it was putting the past on the Freudian bed of the analytic couch that had made this current freedom possible.

Discussion

While Freud and others (e.g., Fenichel, Glover, Greenacre) have discussed screen memories from defensive, economic, and developmental points of view, this chapter has focused on the vicissitudes of screen memories in the analytic situation. I have argued that the working-through process of analysis allows the analyst objectively and the analysand subjectively to become aware of shifts of emphasis in the reconstruction of the analysand's life history. This awareness of structural change, as seen through the shifting prisms of screen memories, can have prognostic significance.

It is interesting to consider what it is about the nature of screen memories that may afford them a unique role as criteria of termination. Couldn't a similar case be made for symptoms, dreams, parapraxes, character traits, and many other mental phenomena?

Symptom removal was considered the goal of early analysis. A psychoanalysis that was interested only in symptom removal could obviously use this criterion in its assessment of readiness for termination.

As analysis became relatively less interested in symptoms and more concerned with structures of the mind, character traits, and defense organization, it became clear that symptom removal alone could not be a reliable indicator of readiness for termination. However, the structures of the mind and character traits do not vanish, as symptoms do, after the conflicts and compromises have been understood. They are permanent psychic baggage that cannot be interpreted and then abandoned like unnecessary luggage. They are the essence of human identity itself. They can be modified, they can be understood, they can undergo massive change, but it is unthinkable that they could be totally abandoned. Consequently, it is hard to use their presence or absence as precise criteria for readiness for termination of psychoanalysis. This is not meant to deny the remarkable changes in character and psychological structure that are the sine qua non of any successful psychoanalysis. However these changes are as subtle as they are essential and they are extremely difficult for the clinician to measure.

Dreams pose an equally intriguing question. Can we in any way as clinicians use dream content or form as an indicator of readiness for termination? While dreams can obviously reflect not only the primary process elements of condensation, displacement, and symbolism that Freud uncovered in 1899, but also structural elements, most clinicians will surely agree that the royal road to the unconscious is not necessarily a useful road to assess readiness for termination.

What then is so special about screen memories? Are they not creatures of instinct, defense, and compromise formation like most other mental products? Obviously they are made of the same mental stuff as dreams, symptoms, parapraxes, but it is their uniquely contrasting features, not their similarities with these other mental products, that allow them to be prognostic indicators of readiness for termination. What are these unique features?

A man may have a thousand dreams, but he usually has only a handful of screen memories. From a purely numerical point of view it may be more heuristic to chart the vicissitudes of screen memories than attempt to tackle the labyrinth of a myriad of dreams.

Let us compare and contrast a screen memory and a symptom. Clearly impulse, defense, and compromise are involved in both. But whereas some symptoms seem to rely on somatic compliance for their avenues of expression, the screen memory seems to rely on memory compliance, to coin a phrase. It is as if energies being displaced were not discharged somatically but rather found expression in some rigid, frozen, distortion of memory. This inner distortion, as opposed to the outer distortion of the symptom, if one can be permitted to talk for a moment about the mind in spatial terms, seems to have a heuristic clinical value: whereas symptoms can fade early in the course of an analysis, the inner distortion of memory seems to have an uncanny resistance, as if these deep secrets corresponded, as Freud suggested, to the totality of the infantile amnesia. They are deeply buried, tightly sealed forgotten letters of the infantile romance that can be opened only in the utter sensitivity of the therapeutic alliance that characterizes an analysis. It is precisely because these letters cannot be opened at the beginning of a new romance with the analyst that they may have to wait for their final exposition when the transference neurosis—which Loewald (1968) called the recapitulation of the love life of a human being—approaches resolution. Because they can only be fully revealed at the end of the analysis they can be used as criteria for termination.

It is tempting to compare screen memories and dream thoughts. Whereas dream thoughts "can take hold of normal thought, carry the latter away and plunge it into the world of the unconscious" (Mannoni, 1971, p. 54), a screen memory is not plunged into the unconscious, but rather stands at a crossroad between the unconscious history of childhood and all future developmental history, like Janus, one face turned to the past, the other to the future. The screen memory is the point of tension between the two histories, and gets contributions from both sides, or, as Freud (1901) put it, it can be retroactive, displaced forward, contemporary, or contiguous in its chronological relation to what is being screened (p. 44). The dream thought runs off with the contemporary thought into the unconscious and does not rest until it reaches the end of the mental apparatus in charge of perception and becomes the hallucination, which is the hallmark of dreams. The screen memory, in contrast, runs off with the contemporary thought and most of the infantile amnesia, but, instead of turning up as a hallucination in a dream, it maintains a quasi-hallucinatory image in our waking life.

One might well ask: why does a screen memory maintain such an iconic relationship with what Alvin Frank (1969) calls the unrememberable and unforgettable? Except for recurring dreams, one would be hard pressed to find a mental product that so stubbornly insists on sameness. It is as if the memory behaves like a child insisting that the bedtime story be told exactly the same way each time. In a sense, a screen memory is a caricature of the parent-child relationship in which infantile omnipotence insists that the magical parent will gratify the child on demand and unconditionally. Or, to state it from a historic viewpoint, human beings with complicated histories like to imagine iconic remnants of their past as organizers of their psyches. In a sense, screen memories are to the mind what primitive gods are to the history of culture.

Further comparing and contrasting screen memories and dreams, we immediately realize that while both use similar mechanisms (displacement, symbolism, condensation), there is an essential difference: dreams are forever handling conflict in a cinematic flux of kaleidoscopic images, whereas screen memories are more comparable to one frame of a cinematic sequence in which all the other frames lie hidden in the infantile amnesia. It is this standstill quality of the screen memory that allows one to measure significant increments of change as the memory gets revised in the process of working through. It is as if one picture had stolen the pigment from all the surrounding pictures: analysis slowly returns this pigment to the originals and the hyperpigmented fake loses most of its color. The paint gets removed from the guinea pig, so to speak, and reality, warts and all, is restored in all its complexity.

Screen memories may have a special place in reconstructive work. According to Greenacre (1981), "Screen memories are especially helpful, but are often disregarded by students and some analysts who have tried unprofitably to treat them as though they were dreams. Because they are less fluid than dreams and more firmly organized in their enduring defensive function, immediate free association cannot be demanded. Their use depends on the alertness of the analyst for detecting their discrepancies, especially in time and in content. If he is in a good therapeutic alliance with the analyst, the patient becomes interested and begins to question them himself, and later finds ways of checking on the reliability of their content" (p. 42f.).

Greenacre suggests that a patient will not associate to a screen memory. Freud, however, maintained that a patient could associate to an old dream. He essentially says that a patient can free-associate to an old mental product and revive its meaning in a heuristic fashion that can assist the progress of a psychoanalysis. If we compare a screen memory to a fossil dream of childhood, we may ask: why is it that a patient cannot free-associate to this ancient relic and revive its meaning? Surely, what comes between the screen memory and our understanding is the infantile amnesia. If we consider the transference neurosis as a complicated, long-winded association that explains the infantile amnesia, it becomes clear that the screen memory cannot be understood until all its associations, which lie hidden in the transference neurosis, are revealed. In a sense, all associations throughout an analysis can be thought of as associations to the screen memory. Obviously the screen memory itself is an association to the total metapsychology of childhood experience. This is not meant to be a redundant circular theory in which the transference neurosis reflects the infantile neurosis, the screen memory having a foot in both camps. A simple, more clinical way of saying this would be that the gap that exists between the screen memory and its total elucidation in the transference neurosis is a measure of the repression that exists between childhood psychology and the mental life of adults. In a sense, the transference neurosis is a newly created screen memory that allows screen memories to speak.

The emphasis I am placing on certain unique features of screen memories is not meant to imply that the analysis of memories is more important than the analysis of a symptom, a dream, or a character trait. Obviously, all may be analyzed in contiguity, depending on the free-associative forces, as the case of Leonora has just illustrated.

From the clinical data I have presented, I hope to have demonstrated that analytic work slowly extracts what the infantile amnesia hides by means of screen memories. The extract pours itself into the transference neurosis until finally the vessel of infantile amnesia is relatively empty and the screen memories, which acted like lids, become redundant. This metaphor, while it accurately portrays the gist of my thesis, is surely an inaccurate exaggeration, since no sensible clinician can believe that the creative wells of infantile amnesia could ever be truly emptied.

The most analysts can wish for, as reasonable prospectors of the mind, would be that those underground springs of unconscious processes, which directly contribute to human neurosis, be traced to their sources, so that their currents can be deflected from symptomatic channels to adaptive ones. If the screen memory is a psychic landmark that not only can lead the prospector toward his destination but also can inform him when certain wells are dry, it is obvious that the prospector can use these signposts to his profit.

By way of conclusion let me just say that in this chapter I have presented five cases in which I have tried to demonstrate how clinically rewarding it can be to consider screen memories not only as they are first reported in the anamnesis but throughout their later analytic vicissitudes and transformations as well. When Nabokov entitled his autobiography *Speak Memory* he may have been insufficiently aware, given his tendency to sneer at Freudian "voyeurism", that memory is not the most reliable witness of its own historical narrative. Freud's 1899 insight seems more compatible with the factual and fictional aspects of our memorial records. I have cited it already but I would like to conclude this chapter with a repetition of it: "It may indeed be questioned whether we have any memories at all *from* our childhood: memories *relating to* our childhood may be all that we possess" (1899).

Having discussed dreams separately in Chapter Six and screen memories separately at first in this chapter and then in relation to symptom and dream in Leonora's case, symptom itself (and a very subtle symptom at that) is the subject matter of the next chapter.

CHAPTER EIGHT

Symptom as irony

You can't study the darkness by flooding it with light.

—*Edward Abbey*, 1984

In one section of the previous chapter, the interplay between symptom, screen memory and dream was emphasized. Earlier, dreams and screen memories had each been dealt with in some detail. In this chapter I want to focus on symptom itself as a complex phenomenon; in the next chapter I will address the concept of character. Symptom and character seem quite differentiated from each other. However, Lustman in 1962 presented intriguing data from child analysis showing how symptom and character emerged from a common instinctual pedigree, so to speak, before they differentiated into two quite different and distinct pathways, so that eventually, as childhood proceeds into adulthood, the two (symptom and character) are usually not considered as analogous at all. In these two ensuing chapters I want to revisit Lustman's ideas, suggesting that a symptom can be so subtle as to seem characterological, and character, despite its seeming controlled sensibility and stability can be symptomatic. At first I will present a woman whose vision was compromised in the subtlest manner; and then, in Chapter Nine, a man whose vision was compromised in the most tragic manner. I will let this mysterious introduction of both clinical examples stand for a moment, as I review a bit of psychoanalytic history.

One could argue that psychoanalysis began with the deconstruction of symptoms. The symptoms of hysteria, out of which psychoanalysis "grew", so to speak, summon up images of nineteenth-century psychiatry that seem quaint to a twenty-first-century sensibility. It is hard to believe that when Charcot was conducting his experiments on hysteria 150 years or so ago Freudian thinking had no place in the cultural zeitgeist. Charcot was eager to demonstrate that hysterical symptoms were not really neurological. There was something theatrical about his making an "alleged" right-handed paralysis assume its new anatomical location on the left side of the torso. The theatricality surely represented a bias: neurological "reality" could be discriminated from psychological fakery by a physician's clever use of a posthypnotic suggestion. The concept of an intrapsychic psychological world of reality that had a validity as real as the neurological world, a brave new world in which hysteria was not a comic masquerade but a genuine expression of a mind in trouble that should be taken seriously, had not yet been established. Freud was the first scientist who would take hysteria seriously from a psychological, psychodynamic point of view. He insisted that psychological conflict and the symptoms it generated in the course of its turbulent development deserved and should command the same scientific interest as cardiac symptoms or neurological symptoms. Only an unenlightened bias against the mind and its unique symptomatology would argue otherwise. This conflict between hard-nosed neurological science and its test tube certainties, and psychology and its elusive unconscious less tangible raw materials has hardly been settled as over a century has passed.

Freud's conception of a symptom as a compromise of conflicting dynamic psychic forces was the initial basic insight that would eventually lead to the deconstruction of many other psychic phenomena such as dreams, parapraxes, jokes, and character traits. It was as if all these phenomena (dreams, etc.) shared a basic code of complexity: a Champollion (Freud) was required of course to see the hidden pattern of the psychic Rosetta stone and set the captive meaning free.

In the previous chapter I argued that screen memory, symptom and dream all seemed to participate in Leonora's struggles with the dynamic forces of her conflicted mind. In this chapter I want to illustrate a very subtle symptom that seemed to act alone and quite surreptitiously as it slyly deployed its repressive agency. It was of course not acting alone but in collusion with all the other psychic phenomena of a mind in conflict. It was analysis that was eventually able to connect all the invisible dots and make this very elusive symptom reveal its complex meanings. The symptom was quite specific and yet not at all easy to recognize. In fact it had gone unnoticed for years as I will explain, which was truly ironic since it involved the perception of light itself. It was as if the patient was in the dark even though it seemed to be light itself that was at the root of her anxiety. She was seeing the light too concretely, which prevented her from seeing the light in a more metaphoric insightful way. Earlier I have been stressing how play, transference, and dream use displacement of psychic meaning from one mental presentation of themselves to another mental re-presentation of themselves for complex dynamic reasons. In the symptom being focused on now, a concept (insight itself) was being disavowed or repressed by being displaced onto an acutely sensitive perception of light. In this caricature of insight, vigilance (light was being stalked, so to speak, so that it could be prevented from disturbing sleep) seemed to upstage normal alertness in almost comic proportions. This will become clearer as the clinical process is narrated.

Let us call the analysand Lucy. The analysis took place many years ago but it is still very vivid in the analyst's mind, probably because the symptom was so elusive and arresting all at once. In Lucy, the symptom of extreme light sensitivity had been present for many years without being noticed because it was only on summer vacations, when she could sleep late, that she became aware that she was very sensitive to light. The least amount of morning light would awaken her, and she could not get back to sleep again, try as she might. Lucy would try to ensure that the windows were "dawn-proof," so to speak, by closing the shutters and sealing the curtains carefully and tightly when she retired for the night, a ritual that took on a somewhat comical meaning to her and her bemused husband. That the symptom was a revenant of some forgotten issue from the past was an insight that must have lain dormant for years. In fact, most of the time, when not on vacation, Lucy awakened early, and the "symptom" was not even worth considering as she prepared herself for her busy professional life as a financial analyst. As insignificant as the symptom seemed when it first came up for analytic scrutiny, it would turn out to be full of meaning as the analysand came to reflect upon it.

When this symptom first appeared in the analysis, Lucy was sixty years old. It was the fifth year of the analysis. Lucy, whose childhood in France had been severely compromised by the shadow of the Second World War, had learned to appreciate that the analytic process itself was a new theatre of love and war that could reprise the past and render its dangers somewhat more manageable—but not always. At times, the transference of the past into the present seemed to disrupt the process rather than enhance its unfolding. It was this clash between the past as reality and the past as transference that seemed to ignite the moment of insight that will be examined.

Lucy's turning sixty had a profound effect on the analytic process. If life had seemed to symbolize light for the first six decades of her life, suddenly, she found herself beginning to reflect on the darkness of death. She was a joyous person; war had disrupted her childhood, but not her spirit. Her reflections at age sixty about death did not take the form of depressive ruminations, but were rather a realistic confrontation of reality. In the countertransference, the analyst's own reflections on mortality could not be avoided. The analyst was startled when Lucy asked: "When there is no light at the end of the tunnel, then what?" The question was rhetorical, but it seemed to clamor for an answer nonetheless. It led to the telling of a dream that in turn led to the dismantling of the symptom being highlighted here.

"In the dream, there is a Venetian blind flapping a little in the wind," the analysand related. "One broken slat is piercing the otherwise darkened room with a single beam of dawn light."

Her immediate association seemed to break no new psychological ground, given that it had been referred to many times in the past: it was a memory of German soldiers who had beamed their flashlights into the faces of the residents of her village as they slept or tried to sleep in 1943. Lucy, then aged seven, hid with her family and others in a farmhouse not far from where she had grown up in privileged circumstances until war broke out; suddenly, the lives of Jews of all socioeconomic classes had become precarious. A child who did not completely understand the necessity of concealing her identity was a threat to the safety of the group, and this fact lived on in the analysand in the form of an abiding conflict about self-expression that survived years after the guns of war were silenced. This conflict had been the subject of analysis for many years, and much had been accomplished as wartime memories were revived and revised somewhat in the reflective laboratory of psychoanalysis.

A subsequent association to the dream did yield something new, however, as it opened up a prewar trove of memories that not only deepened Lucy's understanding of her genetic complexity, but also entirely eradicated the symptom of light sensitivity. (Eventually, she could sleep no matter how much light entered her room as morning peeped through chinks in the curtains.) A significant association was made between the beam of light from the defective Venetian blind and the light on the forehead of the surgeon who had removed her adenoids when she was three years old—without anesthesia. The child had been brought unsuspectingly to the surgeon's office. When she asked her grandmother, "Where are you taking me?" she was told, "You'll see!"

The adenoidectomy was performed quickly. Lucy remembered the beam of light on the surgeon's forehead, and she remembered her fury at the deception that seemed like an even greater trauma than the surgical procedure itself. For years afterward, all doctors were kicked in the shins by this traumatized child until, eventually, she could tolerate "civilized" medical visits again. For the rest of her life, however, she insisted on absolute honesty from her physicians—the passivity of the "good" patient being an "ideal" she detested. This insistence on straight talk and full disclosure of all information from her caregivers stood her well in her analysis.

The beam of light from the Venetian blind illuminated not only the past; it shone a direct light onto the transference as well. The analysand seemed to be saying in dream language, "My Venetian analyst is blind." While the European identity of the analyst had never been discussed, the accent would have been hard to ignore. This projection of the analysand's blindness (denial, disavowal, repression) onto the analyst was experienced in clinical reality as an accusation: how could the analyst have allowed the analysand to be blind to her genetic history for so long? Where was the analyst when Lucy was being neglected in the past? Wasn't analytic neutrality merely a euphemism for cruel indifference? These reactions were significant: like all transferential accusations, they illuminated a developmental dialogue, the words of which were mostly located in the potential realm until they found an actual voice in the transference years after the fact. Although the transference focused on the immediacy of the here and now, it also hungered for an examination of the past. The dream opened up free-associative pathways that led to exploration of affects about the parental and grandparental deception and the surgeon's collusion. Thus, the light from the window that was interrupting Lucy's sleep was truly kaleidoscopic—a Janus-like window into both the past and the present. Associating to it, she realized that her whole idyllic childhood had been interrupted by the madness of wartime and the incomprehensible prejudice that created anti- Semitism.

But there was also a pre-war memory to be dealt with. Well-meaning parents and grandparents, following the conventional wisdom of the time, believed that deceiving the child was preferable to preparing her with the truth about impending surgery. The trauma of this decep-tion, the trauma of the surgery, the traumatic climate of wartime, the denial of the patient's identity during the family's period in hiding, and the furtive movements from village to village and from farmyard to farmyard formed a complemental series of events that had taken their toll.

The associations that led to the memory of the traumatic adenoidec-tomy reached even further back in time to a weaning experience when Lucy was one year of age. Her grandfather, a revered pediatrician, advised her parents to wean the child in a manner that seems sadistic in retrospect: the parents were to leave the child with substitute caretak-ers, and on their return the weaning would be a *fait accompli*! (Inciden-tally, this was the same grandfather pediatrician who had advised the adenoidectomy.) The story was further complicated by the fact that the grandfather then died when the analysand was two years old. The sub-sequent adenoidectomy may have been arranged as part of a grief reac-tion, a wish to posthumously honor the advice of the wise pediatrician. All of this had to be reconstructed in the analysis as these associations led further and further back in psychological time.

Lucy's seemingly irrelevant symptom of exquisite sensitivity to light had unearthed significant developmental issues from the pre-Oedipal period that had been screened, perhaps, by the trauma of war. One trauma can screen another, as Glover (1929) suggested many years ago. The weaning experience at age one was not remembered firsthand, but was reconstructed from later information provided by the par-ents. There were direct memories, however, of a consequence of the abrupt weaning: a subsequent sleep disturbance ensued whenever the parents attempted to leave the child with a babysitter for an evening.

In adulthood, when the analysand expressed criticism of her mother in regard to the abrupt weaning experience, her father would hear nothing of it, insisting that her mother had been ideal in every way. In such a climate, it was obviously not easy for a child—or an adult—to cultivate her own voice and self-expression.

Thus, recognition and deconstruction of the symptom of light sensitivity were brought to the fore and became a central focus of the analysis. Light sensitivity was clearly a screen for far deeper sensitivities, with the focus on light understood as a massive displacement onto an inert substance of all that the analysand could not address on a much more personal level with mother, father, grandfather, grandmother, or analyst.

Lucy's capacity to "see through" the symptom's deception was a product of many months of analytic process that had dealt with her reluctance to use the transference as a window into her emotional life. Ironically, although analyst and analysand were both analysts—to be sure, of very different commodities (the one a psychoanalyst, and the other a Wall Street analyst of financial risk management)—it was as if no conflict could be allowed to arise between the two, so deferential was the analysand to the authority of her psychoanalyst. This was respect carried to an extreme, a displacement onto the analyst of the idealized state that Lucy's mother and father had claimed during her childhood and seemed unwilling to relinquish even when she reached adulthood.

Lucy began to realize that it was her own unwillingness to wean herself from such idealized illusions that prevented her from seeing the light. She became aware that the expression "seeing the light" is metaphoric: it does not really mean the perception of light itself, but rather the complex appreciation of all the components of reality, no one element of the totality upstaging others in the service of self-deception or distortion. Lucy began to recognize her own skill at shifting the emotional emphasis onto an inert element (light), as well as her lack of skill at displacing emotional issues onto her analyst—the better to understand the complexity of her genetic origins. (This analysand brings to mind another patient. The son of an analyst, who, believing that he had been parented too "analytically" in an exclusively Freudian atmosphere, refused to "play the game of transference" with his analyst. The irony, of course, was that this seeming resistance to the transference was in fact a powerful expression of it).

Lucy came to realize that her seemingly sudden insight into her symptom of extreme light sensitivity had been prefigured in the transference throughout a much longer period of analytic process. It is significant in this context that the analyst was of European origin, and that Lucy, French by birth, unconsciously identified with certain aspects of the analyst—some real and some imagined. The identification was defensive in that it did not allow the analysand to speak her mind at times. For instance, she felt that the analyst's office was more European than American, with the obvious love of ancient artifacts and antiques being a clear giveaway, but she did not at first comment on this.

The lighting in the analyst's office was also decidedly European, in Lucy's estimation, since track lights—which would have illuminated efficiently from above and given a modern feel to the office—were conspicuously absent. A small antique chandelier and a desk and table lamp gave adequate illumination, but just barely! Lucy had often thought of remarking on this quaint and muted illumination, even criticizing it, but had thought better of it. "It's a good thing you're not doing surgery in here," she once felt like saying—but she suppressed such subversive humor.

All of this unspoken *politesse oblige*, which compromised Lucy's voice, was eventually fully aired in the analysis. The analyst's interpretations of such obligatory politeness sometimes seemed like repetitive nagging to the patient; at one point, she snapped and said, "That may seem obvious to you, but we can't all be Einsteins!" Suddenly, a deep trove of repressed affect became accessible.

A dream that the analysand had had many months prior to the Venetian blind dream was perhaps pivotal in this context. She dreamed that "a one-eyed man was pointing in dismay at his forehead, and a crowd was laughing at him." Her first association pursued the days' residue: she had gone to Wimbledon with her husband. The electronic referees, called "Cyclops," had made a significant error at a crucial moment. Her husband joked, "Only the English would trust a machine over the umpire's human eyes!" Lucy did not think the joke was very funny, but kept her criticism to herself at the time. She had wanted to challenge his prejudice by saying: "It's not just the English—Cyclops is everywhere now."

The words "even in my dreams" were another of the analysand's immediate associations to the dream. Deeper analysis of the dream led to some disturbing insights. Was she a Cyclops whose own beloved grandmother had deceived? Was she the nobody whom parents and grandparents took her for as a child when they ignored her in the weaning experience, deceived her about the adenoidectomy, and doubted her capacity not to divulge her Jewish identity to the Nazis?

In classical mythology, Ulysses made a fool out of the Cyclops by disguising his identity with the word *Nemo* ("nobody"), and Lucy began to sense that she herself embodied both Ulysses and the Cyclops, and that her transference etiquette reflected this. She began to realize that the self cannot be deceived unless it colludes in its own self-deception. She began to question the analyst's taste in furniture and lighting, even teasing the analyst about the allegiance to the past, as though the analyst had not fully embraced today's world of reality! Wasn't the analyst's fascination with the past a Cyclopean blind spot that tended to ignore the present and the future, a genetic fixation that blinded her to current reality? The joke that Lucy had suppressed earlier ("It's a good thing you're not doing surgery in here") was now voiced, allowing both parties to relish its humor. When the Venetian blind dream was analyzed yet again, Lucy realized that the retrieval of the Cyclopean surgeon of her childhood—"with one glaring eye on his forehead"—had indeed been prefigured by this earlier work in the transference. She was gratified by her analyst's obvious enjoyment of the newfound irreverence that allowed her to poke fun at and de-idealize the "stodgy" analyst— an analyst whom she had "created" along the lines of the father who had forbidden her to tamper with his idealized version of parenthood.

Reflecting on the total disappearance of the symptom that analysis of these insights had effected, Lucy was impressed not only by her sudden, newfound ability to sleep in any room day or night regardless of the amount of ambient light; she could also see a comical thread in the way she had lived with the symptom in the past and its eventual deconstruction. For example, during vacations, her husband used to go to heroic lengths to make sure no beam of light disturbed her sleep, so intent was he on protecting her from the slightest intrusion. There was great love in this, not to mention much shared zany humor. By stitching together additional attachments to windows and curtains and Venetian blinds, her husband ensured—like an obsessed scientist in a darkroom—that no intrusive light whatsoever would penetrate the sleep-enhancing darkness. With the symptom dismantled and set aside, Lucy developed a curious respect for it, in the sense that it was a portal—a bizarre one, to be sure—into a past that she might not have had the courage to explore and reclaim without the enlightenment of analysis.

Discussion: light, insight, relativity, defense

Insight and defense in general (displacement, in this particular clinical instance) must coexist in a complex, dynamic compromise of unconscious, preconscious, and conscious psychic forces and elements. Brenner (1982) pointed out that our concepts of supposed structural stabilities have to be re-conceptualized, with constant dynamic fluidity and compromise being the rule of the psyche rather than any reified certainties or structural absolutes. The clinical case presented here illustrates the complexity of an insightful, intelligent, and resourceful mind that coexisted nonetheless for many years with a seemingly innocuous symptom, which, when fully explored, revealed hidden meanings of marked significance.

Light and relativity have been inextricably bound since Einstein expanded the Newtonian vision of the universe. Modern man takes pride in his sophisticated grasp of such relativities, but fear of the dark antedates such sophistication—born, no doubt, of the twin genetic seeds of childhood immaturity and imagination. Fear or intolerance of light is more unusual, perhaps, but its presence shows that the mind is free to attach distorted meanings to any feature of the phenomenal world in the service of defense.

In the case of Lucy, a beam of light from the forehead of a surgeon had been repressed, but was later re-pressed (see Chapter Two) into a new service that helped the conscious mind maintain its disguise for many years. This phenomenon brings to mind another case in which a child patient, in his play in the analysis, constructed a whip out of string and paper and would beat the lamps in the office—some of the lashes finding an "accidental" target on the analyst's body as well, as the transference invited an alternative expression of the assault. In the analytic process with this young boy, it became clear that the analyst's lamps had become fused with the overhead lights in the operating room where the child had undergone thoracic surgery many years earlier. It was more acceptable to him, given his defensive developmental point of view, to displace his emotional reactions onto inert sources of light than it was to rail against parents or surgeons or his analyst in the new theatre of transference.

If transference relies on displacement to set it in motion, it is a displacement that requires some practice, it would seem, as analytic process reaches beyond resistance and toward the free-associative expansions that allow it to achieve momentum. Here the word practice is shorthand, obviously, for the complex, incremental, and dynamic starts and stops through which the analytic process proceeds as insight and resistance engage each other.

In the clinical case under discussion, the analysand could not reconstruct the precise journey of the light that began in childhood and ended up in a dream many years later, having been detained on a lengthy detour through a symptom that seemed so innocuous at first that little attention was paid to it. The psychopathology of everyday life is peopled with these minor psychic events that never reach the organizational complexity of a symptom, perhaps—and might always have escaped notice had Freud not brought our attention to them a little more than a hundred years ago. It was the analysis of two dreams that made Lucy's symptom of light sensitivity disappear entirely, its sudden absence illuminating its meaning more than its presence had. Ironically, the resistance to the transference itself was the vehicle that allowed hidden affects to become exposed, the analysand becoming irritated at the analyst as she implied that the analysand was avoiding her, so to speak. Analysis of resistance to the displacement of transferential meanings from the past onto the current relationship with the analyst eventually brought attention to the displacement concealed in the sensitivity to light. Interpretations of Lucy's characterological avoidance of personal affects involving the analyst felt like instances of nagging to the analysand, and she eventually "called" the analyst on these. Her comment that "It may seem obvious to you, but we can't all be Einsteins!" was her first acknowledgment of fury toward pompous intellectuals, and she could eventually see that it was leveled at father, mother, grandfather, grandmother, and analyst all at once. "I'm beginning to see the light" became her favorite expression of a new-found capacity to appreciate how the past and the present were not as far apart as she had perhaps wanted them to be.

It was this clinical and metaphorical grasp of the dynamics of transference that allowed Lucy to be less afraid of its emotional spontaneity and its very personal immediacy and intimacy. It was this almost philosophical—but not at all intellectualized—grasp of her own clinical process *in statu nascendi* that fostered the climate out of which the

Venetian blind dream emerged. It was quite an achievement for this reserved woman when she was able to complain that her foreign (Venetian) analyst had been "blind" to much of the analysand's past suffering. Ironically, it was only after Lucy began to "see the light"metaphorically in the analytic process that she could tackle the more concrete way in which she had been seeing light symptomatically for many years without realizing it.

When the analysis of her dreams made the meaning of this symptom so clear that it could not be (nor did it need to be) maintained any longer, Lucy's curiosity turned to the particular element—light—that she had focused so much unwitting attention upon for years. Although her interest in light had begun tragically as it assaulted her from the forehead of a surgeon—not to mention the more ironic and subtle reference to it in her grandmother's words, "you'll see!"—there had been, she could see in retrospect, an attempt to understand light and to integrate it into her understanding of reality, not merely into the peculiar fabric of a symptom. In a very early prewar but post-adenoidectomy memory, Lucy remembered having talked to a chandelier in her room as if to get answers or to break out of her loneliness in its company. This personification of an inanimate source of light is a poignant depiction of a child's search for insight in the midst of self-deception as conflict is being engaged by the immature mind. This memory, which was probably a screen memory and had an intense luminosity in her mind's eye, eventually lost its "haloed" status, no doubt as analysis stole much of its thunder (and lightning!) in the free-associative plunder of analytic process. (This chandelier memory brings to mind again the aforementioned child patient who enacted repressed memories of his surgery in the flagellation of his analyst's lamps.)

Lucy had an aesthetic appreciation of light as it peered through chinks in the forest and projected images of branches and leaves, a landscape of shadow and light spread out all around it like an artist's canvas. She connected her abiding interest in art and art history to these aesthetic attempts to master and coopt an element that had sometimes turned against her. In adolescence, she had written an essay on the artist Tintoretto, which was recognized by her teachers as an astute piece of art criticism. The essence of her essay had to do with Tintoretto's astonishing manipulation of light in his dramatic artworks. Lucy's interest in embroidery was another aesthetic pursuit that she could trace back to the war years, her beloved grandmother having taught her the technique of fastidious tracery as the elaborate stitch-craft was held up to the light—even as bombs could be heard exploding in the distance. In retrospect, she could appreciate the genius of her grandmother—who knew a thing or two, herself, about displacement—in finding the ways and means to distract an impressionable child from the sights and sounds of war. The great theatre of displacement in psychic life is, of course, childhood—play being the activity, par excellence, that thrives on it as fantasy is harnessed to the concreteness of playthings (Freud, 1908). Dramatic play seems essential to a child in the first five years of life, its displacements making the conflicts of pre-Oedipal and Oedipal life manageable in a little theatre of defense and adaptation where disguise can harness the instinctual to the sublimatory and bring relative happiness and stability to the active and imaginative world of childhood. Relative is the crucial word in the foregoing sentence, as the almost ubiquitous nightmares of these early years confirm. The immobility of sleep removes activity and play from the child's defensive repertoire, making well-constructed dreams essential if sleep is not to be disrupted by the kind of dreams that fail to sufficiently modify instinctual life, and hence turn into nightmares.

In the clinical case under review, the patient's displacement of major psychic issues onto the element of light became clear as a defensive manoeuvre only in the course of her analysis. As Lucy's initial difficulties in using the displacement offered by transference (her resistance to the development of transference) were gradually overcome, the whole issue of displacement and insight in general could be explored. As a child, she had been denied a chemistry set when she expressed an interest in understanding how the various elements of the phenomenal world interacted with each other. It is not clear whether war or gender prejudice lay behind this academic withholding, but her curiosity about how psychic elements interacted with each other was not to be denied as the analytic process promoted or resuscitated some of her dormant ego functions.

Focusing with great intensity on her symptom of light sensitivity, Lucy was not satisfied that the disappearance of the symptom meant that it had been completely understood. Analytic process made it clear that the sensitivity to light emerged from a crucial, complementary series of genetic issues, the free-associative flow of ideas now touching on one source, then another. Lucy's wartime experiences seemed pivotal at one moment, but so did the adenoidectomy and the Cyclopean surgeon at another. Her unvoiced anger at grandmother, mother, father, and surgeon (and eventually analyst), was the root of all conflict for her, she came to believe. She depicted her recognition of her anger as the retrieval of her own voice—a reclaiming of it, a celebration of it.

Seeing the light through even the most complex psychoanalytic lens does not change the human condition into a fairy tale, Lucy came to realize. But it can reclaim the privileges of a human voice that can speak its mind even when reality is at its most menacing. When the eye of the mind flinches at such moments and transforms the truth into a mirage for a period of time, psychoanalysis, which recognizes such defensive displacements, can also in time reclaim the hidden truth in them. This chapter has focused on one clinical dimension of a topic at the very core of psychoanalysis. It is ironic, perhaps, that a concept as synthetic in form and as global in content would seem to suggest by its very name—insight—a perceptual preference, as if visual aspects were its main component. On reflection, after this perceptual prejudice is set aside, insight can be viewed as a much more complex integration of all attributes of mind in the service of self-knowledge.

The idea that an exclusive focus on light could obscure the form beneath the light brings to mind the differing perspectives of the artistic movements of impressionism and postimpressionism—the latter insisting that Cezanne's focus on form was as important as, if not more important than, Monet's obsession with light. I am suggesting that there are two analogous points of view in the analytic situation, reality being a complex mixture of perceptual and conceptual qualities of mind, and that insight ignores none of these as it attempts to take the measure of what is real. Seeing the light is a beautiful, metaphorical way of capturing such complexity, and—as long as one does not confuse metaphor and reality—insight, in all its multifaceted glory, is not compromised.

I began this chapter suggesting that symptom and character were not as far apart psychically as diagnostic precision might claim. In fact Lucy's symptom seemed such an ego-syntonic aspect of her character for years as to almost escape notice completely. In the next chapter I present a character that seems contained and noble on the one hand, rash and symptomatic on the other. A psychoanalytic odyssey must embrace such paradoxes and ambiguities or its reach will never exceed its grasp, and its worldview will, by that measure, be impoverished.

CHAPTER NINE

A psychoanalytic conception of character

He was a man, take him for all in all, I shall not look upon his like again.

—*Hamlet*, Act one, Scene two
William Shakespeare

C haracter could be described as a stable amalgam of psychological traits that seem to define the basic identity of each human being. It is not as genetically "fixed" or as unique as a thumbprint perhaps given its incremental, adaptative, experimental and experiential nature. But it is not as evanescent as a mood or a transient symptom either. Like symptom or dream it is a compromise of psychological forces: when instinct clamors for expression and ego tames it, moulding it into a more socially adaptive form of itself, a compromise of forces has been achieved. At its best compromise formation does not compromise the ideals of a human being, it merely forces them into a better alignment with reality. Character could be viewed as a stable, almost automatic deployment of such compromise formations throughout the flow of psychological time, a psychological compass that charts the course of human sensibility and reactivity throughout the psychological odyssey of each unique life. If ego is the abstract concept for such executive management, character is a more experience-near, personal definition of such agency. When Robert Bolt wrote of, and depicted Sir Thomas More as "a man for all seasons" it was the enduring stability of his character that was being referred to. While the enduring stability of its nature is its most unique and crucial feature, character is of course fashioned out of the crooked timber of humanity and its stability can never be thought of as absolute. In childhood, where developmental flux is the norm, as opposed to the relatively stable maturity adulthood is capable of sustaining, a symptom and a character trait seem much closer to the instinctual unruly energies they were designed to contain in the first place. I want to suggest, that even in adulthood, character can be more symptomatic than its definition as a stable psychic entity seems to claim. If symptom can be so subtle and ego-syntonic that Lucy herself hardly noticed it, I want to argue that impressive character can be less stable than the ego that sustains it would like to admit. I have chosen the character of Hamlet to illustrate this thesis. He is all at once the noblest protagonist in the play and yet his nature, can be capricious and symptomatic.

In Hamlet, Shakespeare has created a fictional hero, whose unconscious life is the protagonist, as much as consciousness itself, as complex character seems to develop in front of our eyes on stage as the five acts unfold. Eissler once remarked that we seem to know the fictional Hamlet more than many of the real life people in our actual lives. (Eissler, 1972). Harold Bloom claims that Shakespeare "invented the human" (1998), an exaggeration perhaps, but one can readily identify with such hyperbole, since Shakespeare's characters "feel" real, authentic and palpable. A mirror has been held up to human nature in all its diversity, and we recognize ourselves all too clearly in the reflection. Hamlet, one of Shakespeare's most extraordinary creations, is a kind of everyman, and for this reason, his character is ideally suited for an attempted psychoanalytic "reading" of its universalities and complexities. If we can deconstruct a character that has bewildered and fascinated audiences and scholars for more than 400 years, it may even help us to try and fathom the mystery and pedigree of character in ourselves.

From the moment we meet Hamlet he seems to make a distinction between genuine internal depth of feeling and external displays that may not reflect depth of character at all. He is mourning his father's death and he snaps at his mother's attempt to console him. When she asks why mourning "seems so particular with thee?" he snaps back

"Seems, madam, nay it is; I know not 'seems'. I have that within which passeth show."

Hamlet has "that within which passeth show" and Shakespeare makes it his aesthetic ideal throughout the play to contrast this genuine internal affective morality with all the deceits of the Elizabethan court (transparently disguised as Elsinore) that surround this internal decency, seeking to corrupt and suffocate it at every opportunity. When Hamlet says "tis easy as lying" the ubiquitous infiltration of deceit into all organs of Elizabethan society has been incised and exposed with sarcasm's scalpel. He is talking to Rosenkrantz and Guildenstern, "friends" who seem to have quickly embraced their new role as his deceiver. But Hamlet is undeceived. In Act Three, Scene Two, he hands Guildenstern a recorder and asks him to play upon it.

GUILDENSTERN: My lord, I cannot.

HAMLET: I pray you.

GUILDENSTERN: Believe me I cannot.

HAMLET: I do beseech you.

GUILDENSTERN: I know no touch of it, my lord.

HAMLET: Tis as easy as lying: govern these ventages with your finger and thumb, give it breath with your mouth, and it will discourse most eloquent music. Look you, these are the stops.

GUILDENSTERN: But these I cannot command to any utterance of harmony; I have not the skill.

HAMLET: Why, look you now, how unworthy a thing you make of me! You would play upon me; you would seem to know my stops; you would pluck out the heart of my mystery; you would sound me from my lowest note to the top of my compass: and there is much music, excellent voice, in this little organ; yet you cannot make it speak. 'Sblood, do you think I am easier to be played on than a pipe? Call me what instrument you will, though you can fret me, yet you cannot play upon me

(*Riverside Shakespeare*, 1996)

Freud (1905) cited this passage in his early paper *On Psychotherapy* by way of chiding those who "practiced" psychoanalysis without realizing that there was a skill that needed to be mastered before putting the pipe to the lips, so to speak! Etymologically, character deriving from a marking instrument that cuts or scratches the symbol it wants to portray, goes deeper than personality which is a derivative of the Greek "prosopon", a mask. Personality suggests something more theatrical or seductively engaging than character, whose deeper implications are reserved and not on display for social acclaim. Psychologically speaking, character refers to the deep music of humanity, "the heart of the mystery" as Hamlet calls it, not the mouthfuls of air that are blown more casually through the holes of personality's pipe. Hamlet returns to this image of the pipe in Act Three, Scene Two when he addresses Horatio as his trusted true friend.

HAMLET: Horatio, thou art e'en as just a man as e'er my conversation
           coped withal.

When Horatio protests, Hamlet insists he is not flattering but speaking what he knows to be true.

HAMLET: Since my dear soul was mistress of her choice
           And could of men distinguish, her election
           Hath sealed thee for herself; for thou hast been
           As one, in suffering all, that suffers nothing,
           A man that fortune's buffets and rewards
           Hast ta'en with equal thanks: and blest are those
           Whose blood and judgment are so commingled
           That they are not a pipe for fortune's finger
           To sound what stop she please. Give me that man
           That is not passion's slave, and I will wear him
           In my heart's core, ay, in my heart of heart
           As I do thee.

This praise of his friend does bring to mind Hamlet's assessment of his own dead father: "He was a man, take him for all in all, I shall not look upon his like again." The ideal father or friend is passionate without being passion's slave. Such men of well-commingled blood and judgment are not a pipe for fortune's finger to sound what stop she please. If blood is Shakespeare's word for instinct, the ideal Shakespearean compromise seems to be well commingled blood and judgment, not too dissimilar from Freud's marriage of ego and id in his celebrated phrase "where id was, there ego shall be" (1933). The man of well commingled blood and judgment handles fortune's buffets and rewards with character and aplomb and acts like one who "in suffering all" suffers nothing, a Shakespearean depiction of heroic character that seems Greek and Freudian all at once.

Hamlet insists that fate and superstition must be dismissed. He does not wish to be "a pipe for fortune's finger to sound what stop she please." A man's character must embrace the sense of readiness that prepares him to "encounter the reality of experience for the millionth time" as Joyce puts it, whatever it may send his way (1916). Shakespeare seems to equate this kind of readiness to tackle whatever the human condition throws our way with maturity. In King Lear Shakespeare's word for "readiness" seems to be "ripeness". In Hamlet this kind of alert psychological courageous maturity is called "readiness". Surely it is the same kind of unflinching psychological courage that is being extolled in both of these extraordinary tragedies (Lear and Hamlet). It is heroic and yet frail and human also, blood and judgment commingled in the ferocious tenderness of love and survival.

How has Shakespeare crafted such complexity of character in a fictional hero whose blood seems as instinctual as his judgment seems the embodiment of ripeness and readiness? This is an aesthetic question to be sure but I think it has psychoanalytic implications and reverberations also. Bloom makes an extraordinary statement about Shakespearean characters when he suggests that they seem to overhear themselves on stage, thereby presenting the illusion that they could change course at will, make up their own lines so to speak rather than the author's. An author who can create this kind of aesthetic illusion of free-associative spontaneity is in a class of his own. Hegel called Shakespeare's characters "free artists of themselves" (1807). If the free-associative spontaneity that Hegel cites is indeed one of Shakespeare's most creative aesthetic flourishes I believe that Shakespeare's use of parapraxes in his plays is an example of even more unconscious seeming spontaneity.

A deeply significant, but seemingly casual parapraxis occurs in the first soliloquy. Hamlet, having scolded his mother in the "I know not seems" dialogue, is alone. Now, in a self-lacerating suicidal soliloquy, the hatred is directed inwardly. He makes a slip when he imagines that his father has been dead for two months. He immediately corrects himself.

HAMLET: But two months dead: nay, not so much, not two.

Hamlet has made a computational error: his father has not been dead for two months. It's less than that, he realizes, a realization full of dynamic meaning in my opinion. Hamlet is questioning his own memory and Shakespeare is surely questioning the whole concept of memory also, its reliability, its durability, and its fallibility, not to mention its doubts about itself as a stable witness of its experience. Surely this anticipates Freud in a way that Freud would have applauded, given his own extraordinary interest, not only in Hamlet, but in the topic of screen memory also. If Hamlet is actually imagining that his father had died even earlier than the actual date of his demise, has Hamlet not stumbled on his own wish to dispatch his father even earlier than Claudius did? In other words, has Hamlet not encountered in himself the Oedipus complex about 2000 years post-Sophocles and 300 years before Freud discovered it? What an extraordinary dramatic moment Shakespeare has created here in a casual parapraxis most people do not even notice! Hamlet is doubting his own memory. Shakespeare is shedding a very subtle light on memory as a reliable or unreliable witness of its own experience. Obsessional thinking is one symptom that can emerge from this conflicted memory. In a later soliloquy (Act Four, Scene Four) Hamlet ridicules this kind of obsessional defensiveness that delays him from the execution of what he believes to be the right course of action.

HAMLET: Now whether it be
            Bestial oblivion, or some craven scruple
            Of thinking too precisely on the event—
            A thought, which, quarter'd, hath but one part wisdom
            And ever, three parts coward—I do not know
            Why yet I live to say this thing's to do
            Sith I have cause and will and strength and means
            To do it.

Hamlet questions the nature of defensiveness in this soliloquy, repudiating it for making him waver from his true purpose. A few lines later he goes beyond repudiation and self-ridicule and makes a profound comment on the nature of character itself. "Rightly to be great, / Is not to stir without great argument, / But greatly to find quarrel in a straw / When honour's at the stake." Honor, which in psychoanalytic parlance could be called character, is being defined here as the opposite of obsessional doubting which paralyzes action. Shakespeare suggests that greatness of character reflects on instinct and impulsive action, and on reflection changes instinct and impulse into the maturity of decision making. (If Shakespeare extols honor in Hamlet, in Henry IV he is perfectly capable of poking fun at it, as Falstaff ridicules honor as a useless commodity.)

I would like to return to a previously quoted passage in which Hamlet is itemizing those qualities in Horatio that he believes has made the two friends such soulmates.

HAMLET: Since my dear soul was mistress of her choice
          And could of men distinguish, her election
          Hath sealed thee for herself …

Here Hamlet characterizes his soul as female and he seems as comfortable with this metaphor of femininity as he is with the image of himself as swashbuckling male in other instances. From a psychoanalytic point of view one could argue that positive and negative Oedipal identifications are well integrated and harmonized, that passive and active aims have been well fused or that masculine and feminine strivings are not in conflict with each other. Character at its most mature would seem to be the heir of such positive and negative Oedipal resolutions. If superego and ego-ideal are the heirs of positive and negative Oedipal identifications (respectively), character itself could be thought of as the summation of the psychological attributes of all structures, expressed in experiential functioning. Character pathology, which is not my central topic, could then be viewed as the outcome of arrested or compromised development of structuralization as expressed in executive functioning. In other words, borderline psychopathology, where the patient seems to be unable to get beyond separation-individuation issues into a more developed psychological world of Oedipal drama and post-Oedipal stability, would indicate poorly developed and/or poorly integrated psychic structures and their executive failures.

Returning to Hamlet again there are several instances of bisexual conflict and playfulness that illustrate his characterological integration of these issues. For instance, in Act Four, Scene Three, Hamlet addresses Claudius as "mother." In this scene, irony is everywhere. Claudius has decided to send Hamlet to his doom in England. Hamlet sarcastically says "Good." Claudius responds: "So it is, if thou knows't our purpose."

Hamlet who is on to this treachery says: "I see a cherub that sees them. But come / for England. Farewell, dear mother." Claudius corrects Hamlet: "Thy loving father, Hamlet." Hamlet immediately counter-punches: "My mother: father and mother is man and wife, man and wife is one flesh—so my mother. Come, for England."

This is Hamlet's bitter mockery of the healthy bisexual resolution identification with both parents makes possible at the time of "dissolution" of the Oedipus complex, when the facilitating environment "facilitates" a good enough Winnicottian and Freudian outcome. But the facilitating environment in Hamlet is anything but facilitating. It is treacherous. "There is something rotten in the state of Denmark" and it is at the core of governance and makes "normal" development impossible.

In the previously cited passage, in which Hamlet declares that "readiness is all", there is a misogynous moment I would like to draw attention to. Hamlet and Horatio are discussing the upcoming clash between Hamlet and Laertes without knowing all the literally poisoned mischief Claudius and Laertes have pre-planned. Hamlet has some presentiment of the treachery and the whole dreadful, inevitable denouement perhaps.

HAMLET: Thou woulds't not
           Think how ill all's here about my heart—but it is no matter.
HORATIO: Nay, good my lord—
HAMLET: It is but foolery, but it is such of gaingiving, as would perhaps
           trouble a woman.
HORATIO: If your mind dislike anything, obey it. I will forestall their repair
           hither, and say you are not fit.

Gaingiving is an archaic word for misgiving, a superstitious, histrionic trait Hamlet is applying to women as if the affect contained in "how ill's all here about my heart" were foolish and feminine as opposed to wise and masculine. It is an intuition after all about the future clash with Laertes and the whole bloodbath at the play's ending, an intuition that should have been embraced rather than caricatured as gender suspect. Hamlet is clearly repudiating a presentiment that Horatio counsels him not to dismiss. ("If your mind dislike anything, obey it.")

Hamlet's disobedience, his disavowal of his own "feminine" intuition will cost him his life. The point I am stressing, of course, is that while Hamlet was comfortable identifying his soul as feminine earlier ("Since my dear soul was mistress of her choice" etc.) in this instance he seems to need to deride it.

Shakespeare's creation of Hamlet's character is subtle and complex. If Shakespeare seems to stress Hamlet's honesty and maturity of character as opposed to all the character pathology that surrounds him (Rosenkrantz and Guildenstern, Claudius, Polonius) he knows that character is part of the conflict and ambiguity of the human condition, a condition that cannot be "perfect". To render it so would be un-Shakespearean. It would misrepresent it. When the ghost of his father implores Hamlet to remember with the haunting words "Remember me" Hamlet vows that he will "as long as memory holds a seat in this distracted globe." Repressed memory may be Hamlet's undoing, however, of course as the earlier cited parapraxis in Act One, Scene Two suggests. For if Hamlet harbors, in his unconscious fantasies, the same crime Claudius enacted in reality, the appetite for revenge may be dulled by the rumblings of neurosis, and memory may falter in its conflicted purpose. Character at such moments is called into question as it attempts to keep memory alive, to witness all, even when memory itself, in an anguish of self-doubting, mistrusts its purpose. When an ego function falters (memory), does the whole ego have to rally to remind itself that "perfect memory" is not the issue, tragic "good enough" conflicted memory can get the job done. It may take five acts to mull things over, but anyone who believes that Hamlet's inaction is other than a tragic mulling over of all the ingredients of the human condition seems to miss the whole point of Shakespeare's complex subtleties. In a profound sense, character is a deep gouge into the mystic writing pad of conscious and unconscious memory, a deep self healing wound of experience, a witness of not only what needed to be repressed, but of what also needed to be re-pressed back into functional adaptive executive usage. Character could be called the guardian of the repressed, the witness that insists on its re-pressing itself into the complicated living of life. If Hamlet was repressed in Act One, his unconscious eventually ghosted itself into consciousness, a return of the repressed that may have paralyzed him for a few acts. But by Act Five, when he re-presses all of the information he had partially hidden from himself and allows himself to know that "the readiness is all", his capacity to act in his own self interest and in the interest of all, no longer eludes him. He insists that Horatio not kill himself, since Horatio is a character witness that must survive to set the record straight and proclaim that Hamlet's character was the equal of his father's, a character "taken for all in all, we shall not look upon his like again."

Just as Schafer (1968) has shown how defense not only dampens down instinct but expresses it indirectly as well, character not only represses instinct, but expresses it also. It must have been such complementarity between instinctual repression and expression, the conflict between the wish to repress in a shunning manner, and the wish to re-press in a redressive, expressive manner (see Chapter One) that allowed Freud to see the connection between character and anal erotism in the first place. Once Freud opened the eyes of all the investigators who followed him, the absolutely obscure became the absolutely obvious. Child analysts have been able to almost catch the moment when instinct heading for instant gratification changes course and becomes a reaction formation of delayed gratification instead. Nagera has captured such a moment on film where a little girl, gleefully contemplating the sinking of her hands into the paint she wants to smear with, decides to wash her hands instead before her fingers ever reach the paint! Lustman (1962) has given great thought to such moments in his classic paper *Defense, Symptom and Character*. He extracts from his four-year analysis with Wendy many clinical examples of a symptom (cleansing) and a character trait (bravery). Lustman was impressed "with the striking degree of discharge and impulse gratification in both symptom and character trait" (1962). He tried to conceptualize which defense mechanism lent itself more readily to symptom formation as opposed to character development. He describes his analysis with Wendy who had a symptom of obsessive cleanliness, side by side with a remarkable spunky character of bravery. Lustman states that "in Wendy, reaction formation, reversal, undoing seem to be equally involved in either symptom formation (cleanliness) or character trait (bravery)." However, rationalization as a defense seemed "much more clearly related to the possible development of a character trait." Lustman is quite convincing on that point. When he questioned Wendy about the defensive nature of her bravery, she would have none of it: she became a "house lawyer" as Lustman charmingly puts it, defending her bravery with rationalization after rationalization. However, when he questioned her about her often rigorous, symptomatic doll cleansing, she would fall silent even though she might have invoked the rationalization that they were dirty or soiled and needed to be cleaned. In other words, bravery seemed ego-syntonic and defendable, whereas "cleansing" was ego-dystonic, given its closer more intimate relationship with instinct.

The relationship between instinct in both symptom and character may be more obvious in child analysis than in adult analysis and yet there are adults whose characters are more sphincter rigidities than sublimated disguises. In the vice of their company one feels squeezed, controlled, toilet trained, rather than engaged in spontaneous, mutually reciprocal dialogue. In the clutches of such characters one feels sphinctered like faeces rather than related to like a mature object.

Returning to Hamlet, it is clear that his character is not always in control. It is hard not to view his treatment of Ophelia as other than symptomatic. He is abusive, sarcastic, and demeaning and the excuse that she is a mere object of displacement for affects that are meant for his conniving assailants (Claudius, Gertrude, Polonius) hardly justifies such behavior. The only mitigating circumstance would be the toxic environment Hamlet must conduct his grieving in: as Lessing said "the man who does not lose his reason under certain circumstances has no reason to lose" (1867).

By choosing Hamlet's character as the subject matter of this chapter, I am trying to stress that a perfect character, whatever that might be, might not be the ideal, adaptive, good enough model for development to be striving towards. Perfectionism may well be more symptom than character trait! If good enough, resilient, playful, affect embracing, rigidity rejecting, resourceful spontaneous character is the goal, how is it formed and maintained? The question Shakespeare poses about fancy and where it is bred could also be posed in regards to character: "Oh tell me, where is character bred, or in the heart or in the head. How begot; how nourished"? In regards to Hamlet we can say that Shakespeare is the begetter and I have been trying to fathom how he did it. Keats might say it was done with what he called "negative capability" (1970), by which Keats meant a great artistic ability to tolerate ambiguity, contradiction, spontaneities and free associative imaginings: a mind, in other words, that does not demand premature closure but is comfortable with a mess of ideas, that need not be cleaned up prematurely so that there is time for it to get re-pressed into a new remarkable version of itself. Mess becomes message, artistic communication that finds resonance with all humanity and the existential mess all "mewling and puking" emerged from. If we consider all erotogenic zones as contributors to this primal mess, this inchoate curriculum all childhoods must graduate from, character could be conceptualized as the great synthesizer that gathers all developmental components into a cohesive, relatively stable matrix. In a sense, character is the objective correlative or should one say the subjective correlative of the ego, the representation in behavior of the ego's abstract executive functioning (agency). This would be consistent with Glover's definition of character as "a set of organized behavior reactions founded on and tending to preserve a stable equilibrium between id-tendencies and submission to Reality ... characterized by more or less satisfactory adaptation along lines of displacement" (1929). I have stressed the Winnicottian "good enough" rather than Glover's "more or less" but the two are quite similar in form and spirit. Character seems to be the voice of passion and reason "commingled". It counsels itself: "To thine own self be true, and it must follow as the night the day, thou canst not then be false to any man." By putting such lines in the mouth of Polonius as he bids the departing Laertes adieu, only to have him (Polonius) connive later with Reynaldo as to how best to spy on his son, Shakespeare is reminding us that what seems like decency of character may be only a mask of deceit in certain instances. This kind of character seems more symptomatic than characterful, bringing to mind again Lustman's point about "the striking degree of discharge and impulse gratification" he observed in both symptom and character trait (1962). The synthetic, integrative work of the ego and its observable manifestation in smooth characterful functioning is an achievement of the utmost importance not only for the individual but for society at large. Polonius is a typical "political" character, a necessary cog in the wheels of Elizabethan society as depicted at Elsinore. Such cogs are part of all Machiavellian systems then and now and perhaps always. But Shakespeare is skewering the hypocrisy of such a system, Hamlet's decency acting as the foil that accentuates this glaring contrast. This brings us back to the aesthetic question of how Shakespeare managed to fathom the illusion of a character of such depth and complexity: for even though Hamlet has taken on a semblance of reality for all theatre-goers and readers for hundreds of years, he is, after all, only a piece of fiction. The aesthetic question can never be answered. "Before the genius of the creative artist psychoanalysis must, alas, lay down its arms" as Freud reluctantly remarked. The psychoanalytic enquiry is not too easy to address either, but it is the question this chapter has posed itself.

Baudry, (1989) in a comprehensive review and thoughtful critique of the evolution of the concept of character in Freud's writings, shows convincingly that what Freud believed character to be, depends on which phase of Freud's theoretical deliberations is being considered. Just as the concept of repression was put through its changes as Freud's clinical and theoretical ideas grew more complex throughout the decades of his life (well-documented by Brenner in 1957), Baudry has examined an equally complex course of shifting theoretical points of view, as character was considered and re-considered over the many phases of revisionism that characterize the evolution of Freud's thinking.

If character is a creation of an abstraction called ego, how is its essence constructed and maintained? Ego syntonicity and attunement to the dictates of the reality principle seem equally crucial. As defense mechanisms are being "chosen" with these guiding principles of compromise between internal psychological reality (ego) and the actuality of an external phenomenal reality to guide them, synthesis and integration of these adaptive clusters of defensive reactions will make for an abiding characterological identity, as experience confirms adaptive and utilitarian merit and success over failure. Failure would be announced by regression, success by stability and enduring progress. When it comes to a consideration of concepts such as decency, moral fibre, or courage and grace under pressure, some very smooth integration of ego-ideal, superego restraint and ego subtlety needs to be invoked; but the invocation begs the question of course; it does not supply a definitive answer. Perhaps there can be no answer to such highly complex questions other than to say that a place has to be found in any definition of character for ambiguity, respect for the experiential, developmental, constitutional imponderables and unpredictable vicissitudes of the human condition and man's abiding, philosophical attempt to internalize some stability culled from the chaos of it. As Novalis put it "chaos, in a work of art, must shimmer through a veil of order" (1995). Kant's modesty helps us also when he asserts, "out of the crooked timber of humanity, nothing straight can ever be made" (1998). In that sense, character is a crooked thing the ego makes to guide it on its journeys and detours through all the straight and crooked pathways of psychological life. The aesthetic chaos that Novalis talks about that needs to be put in order by artistic rigor is akin to the infantile polymorphous perversity that characterizes early development and needs to be put in order by the maturing ego. Character is the experiential extension of the ego, an attribute of mental resilience and integration that is informed always by the passions and instincts it masters and transcends. Character without that juice of instinct palpable in some affective manner in its make up and expression would be caricature more than character and would thereby fail in its overall goal to represent all the sexual zones of the body and their derivatives in the mind. Hamlet, for all his flaws and failings, is such a character, and it is for that reason that I have chosen him to represent the achievement of character in general, the conflicted achievement of everyman in his ageless confrontation with the trials and tribulations of existence. Wendy too struggles with character traits that are not so strikingly different from her symptoms. Her spunk and bravery is a characterological transformation of the same instincts her symptoms struggle with, when her character falters at times. This is an ambiguous definition of character. Nothing human is alien to it: it transcends the instincts that challenge it but it never dishonors them. Conscience may make cowards of us all, but cowardice integrated into a measured, as opposed to a reckless, counter-phobic bravery is an attribute Hamlet admired in Horatio, but exhibited also in his own deeply conflicted, deeply layered and in the end, deeply accomplished character.

In summation I would like to suggest that character, not unlike play, repression, insight, transference, screen memory and dream is a hybrid of instinct and renunciation, a structure of manifest stability and integration that is nonetheless intimately connected to a wilder, symptomatic side of its nature that can, under duress, pull an instinct out of repression and plunge a rapier through an arras of defensive stability that seemed all but impregnable. Maybe character wouldn't be all that it's cracked up to be if it didn't house this deep-seated unconscious vulnerability within.

CHAPTER TEN

Mourning, dreaming, and the discovery of the Oedipus complex

He will not go behind his father's saying.

—*Robert Frost*

Insight such as this falls to one's lot but once in a lifetime.

—*Sigmund Freud*
Preface to the Third (Revised) English Edition of
The Interpretation Of Dreams, 1931

This book began with a group of three year olds mourning their painted guinea pig. I want to end this book with the role mourning and concomitant dreaming may have played in Freud's discovery of the Oedipus complex. Freud had embarked on his self-analysis in July 1897, according to Ernest Jones. His father died in October 1896. Despite the profound effect this death had on him, Freud would not try to conceptualize his own particular grieving reaction, or the whole subject of mourning in general until 1915. This of course does not mean that the process of Freud's mourning was postponed. In fact I want to argue that mourning and dreaming, two psychic processes that consciousness or will power has no control over, can rake the depths of the unconscious, producing rich, provocative, if painful raw material, especially for the creative mind. Freud was in the middle of his own tortured self analysis, delving free associatively into childhood memories, breaking down barriers of repression singlehandedly, Fliess the only transferential, long distance sounding board in sight. Mourning and dreaming must have been constantly "feeding" his self-analysis with turbulent affect and memory. I want to argue that it was out of such creative torment that the Oedipus complex emerged in October 1897.

Let me acknowledge from the outset that this is of course an exercise in imaginative speculation. By imaginative speculation, I do not mean to imply that I will not use the historical data available to us as I try to piece together Freud's state of mind as the discovery "came" to him. Freud has left us a record (reluctantly as we know; without Marie Bonaparte's intervention we would not have access to it at all) of his self-analysis. We know some of what he was thinking, feeling and dreaming and discovering as he tried to construct the new "science" of psychoanalysis. But even though I reconstruct from data available to all of us, I speculate also and I want to acknowledge that. No matter how prepared for it we are from prior readings, I believe it always comes as a shock to read Freud's letter of October 15th, 1897 to Fliess that begins "... my self analysis is in fact the most essential thing I have at present. And it promises to become of the greatest value to me if it reaches its end." Freud continues: "to be completely honest with oneself is good practice. One single thought of general value has been revealed to me. I have found, in my own case too, falling in love with the mother and jealousy of the father and I now regard it as a universal event of early childhood ..." Five months earlier, in letter sixty-four enclosed with draft N, dated Vienna, May 31st, 1897 Freud wrote: "it seems as though this death wish is directed in sons against the father and in daughters against their mother." Strachey and Jones have commented that this may be the first mention of the Oedipus complex in Freud's writings.

Before getting into the details of Freud's self-analysis and the role of mourning and dreaming within it, I want to comment on mourning and dreaming per se. If one stresses that mourning is a merciless, even ruthless act of re-presenting the absent dead object in consciousness the better to strip it of its libidinal investment, so that the psychic energy can be reinvested in other living objects; the whole process, especially when the father is the object being mourned, has an Oedipal cast to it.

It is as if the stricken mind is proclaiming (protesting even): "I kill the object over and over by summoning it to the table of consciousness so that I can divest it of its psychic energy." If the dead object's wife is still alive and if the mind is investing psychic energy in her that has been retrieved from the attachment to the husband, is this characterization of mourning not entirely Oedipal? If we imagine Freud in early October 1897 not yet in possession of his discovery of the Oedipus complex, but very much possessed by his mourning, isn't it ironic that he had the seeds of his discovery in his hands without recognizing them? In a way his mourning not only held the dead father's absence in its startled hands but the discovery of the Oedipus complex as well.

Dreaming, on the other hand would seem be the opposite of mourning. If mourning insists on the reality of death and the need to deal with it realistically, dreaming's raison d'etre is wish-fulfillment. Dead objects can come to life again in the illusion of dream. Awakening can of course be conceptualized as another kind of mourning: the spoils of dreams have to be recognized and relinquished as the illusions that they are, the reality principle thumbing its nose at wish fulfillment and illusory pleasures. Is it possible that both of these processes (mourning and dreaming) going on from October 1896 (the date of Jacob Freud's death) to October 1897 (the date of the discovery of the Oedipus complex) fed the crucial insights into Freud's self analysis (Jones dates its inception from July 1897) that made the momentous discovery possible one year after the death of Freud's father, a yahrzeit of great significance. The end of Freud's self analysis is left undated by Ernest Jones. His comment is instructive: "Freud told me he never ceased to analyze himself, devoting the last half hour of his day to that purpose" (1981).

Let us try to piece together what these seminal insights might have been. Freud has acknowledged that the writing of *The Interpretation of Dreams* was a reaction to his father's death. In thanking Fliess for his letter of condolence Freud wrote: "by one of the dark ways behind the official consciousness my father's death has affected me profoundly. I had treasured him highly and had understood him exactly. With his peculiar mixture of deep wisdom and fantastic lightness he had meant very much in my life. He had passed his time when he died, but inside me the occasion of his death has reawakened all my early feelings. Now I feel quite uprooted" (1897).

This uprooting led to *The Interpretation of Dreams*. In his preface to the second edition (1908) Freud said that it was only after finishing the book that he could connect it to his father's death. "It revealed itself to me as a piece of my self-analysis, as my reaction to my father's death; that is, to the most important event, the most poignant loss, in a man's life". Is there not a denial of the discovery of the Oedipus complex in this estimation of *The Interpretation of Dreams*, without an equal emphasis being placed on the discovery of October 15th, 1897? Is there not a similar relative diminution of emphasis on the role of mourning in the discovery of the Oedipus complex in Freud's not writing his classic text on *Mourning and Melancholia* until 1915? If my thesis is correct, that mourning in its very form and structure resembles the Oedipus complex in an uncanny way, was Freud unwilling to acknowledge the gift of insight contained in it? Perhaps he was in no mood to be deferential towards such a universal process as mourning and acknowledge his biological debt to it at a time when he was discovering his own particular Oedipal hubris and did not want to be indebted to filial piety and dependency any longer. Like Hamlet confronted with Gertrude's rebuke: "grief is universal, Hamlet. Why seems it so particular with thee?" the Hamlet in Freud responds: "I know not "seems", madam." Freud had gone deeper than "seems" into the very core of re-pressed Oedipal desire itself; and one further manifestation of his Oedipal triumphant discovery might have been his wish not to acknowledge the lineage of his insights and the role that an uncontrollable, unconscious, unwilled, biological process such as mourning had in it. If he were unwilling to surrender to the psychological authority of parents in his new-found Oedipal defiance, why would he be willing to surrender to the kind of uncontrollable process of biology mourning implied?

From a developmental point of view the original resolution of the Oedipus complex in children at approximately six years of age relies mainly on repression and identification to steer the Oedipal child out of seemingly unresolvable conflict into the relative quiescence of latency. (There are other factors besides repression and identification, including a neglected cognitive factor that I cited several years ago.) (Mahon, 1991). But now I want to stress an aspect of mourning that is involved when a child relinquishes his Oedipal conquest of one parent even as fantasy runs off with the prize of the other. This developmental drama is almost completely covered up, the infantile amnesia a kind of painting over of instinct and the replacement of it with the great Eriksonian "industry" of latency. Development and cognitive maturities assist the latency child with his "mourning" of Oedipal desire and his new acceptance of the reality principle that society, and "social hypocrisy", as Freud mischievously called it, demanded of him. If the inevitable developmental demand for a resolution of the Oedipus complex confronts the child with a kind of mourning, it is the actual experience of mourning in later life that re-introduces the adult to the repressed Oedipus complex. In Freud's case, before the Oedipus complex was first formulated by him, it was the experience of mourning and the return of the repressed that made his great insight possible for him to grasp. At least that is one of the main arguments of this chapter.

Let us imagine Freud formulating for himself in 1897 the insights he published in *Mourning and Melancholia* many years later. Earlier I suggested that mourning, as Freud defined it in 1917, seems to encapsulate the Oedipus complex in its very form and structure. In that remarkable paper Freud describes how, after reality has declared the object to be dead, psychology, which drags its feet at first in accepting the painful loss, does eventually, in a piecemeal fashion, sever its attachment to the object. Essentially the work of mourning "kills" the object intrapsychically at a slower pace than reality which finishes the object off in one fell swoop. Comparing mourning and melancholia Freud writes: "Just as mourning impels the ego to give up the object by declaring the object to be dead and offering the ego the inducement of continuing to live, so does each single struggle of ambivalence loosen the fixation of the libido to the object by disparaging it, denigrating it and even as it were *killing* it." (italics added). Freud asks why there is no phase of triumph after the work of mourning is done, no sense of triumph comparable to the mania that sets in when melancholia has severed its ties to the object. "I find it impossible to answer this objection straight away" Freud writes. If my thesis is correct Freud's triumph may have been repressed or sublimated into the masterwork his mourning had instigated. I am referring to *The Interpretation of Dreams* and a little later I will outline several of Freud's own dreams that played a key part in his discovery of the Oedipus complex. In my own clinical experience, a child whose father died when the child was five years old said "good riddance" on hearing the news. "Now I can have my mother all to myself." The child's initial sense of triumph was however replaced in later years with a sense of guilt that compromised his adult life until analysis addressed all the complex vicissitudes of Oedipal conflict. As I commented earlier Freud's triumph may have been sublimated into his masterwork *The Interpretation of Dreams*. I am suggesting that the discovery of the Oedipus complex and the paper on *Mourning and Melancholia* are masterworks also that belong contextually alongside the dream book when the history of psychoanalytic ideas is being considered comprehensively.

So far I have stressed the role of mourning in Freud's discovery of the Oedipus complex, but I believe there were many other factors such as Freud's self analysis, the "transferential" role Fliess played, the recovery of crucial childhood memories, and the remarkable interpretation of several seminal dreams. There are probably a host of other ingredients Freud's genius was comprised of that cannot be fathomed or even formulated. "Before the genius of Freud's creativity, psychoanalysis must alas lay down its arms": I have co-opted Freud's phrase from Dostoyevsky and Parricide to make a point about Freud himself. But since I cannot delineate all the unfathomable ingredients of Freud's creativity I will next examine the crucial role I believe dreams played in his great discovery. Mourning and dreaming were the two engines that fueled the creativity in my opinion, mourning doggedly insisting on engagement with and submission to reality, dreaming embarked on its unconscious mission of mining the past but disguising it out of all recognition in the interest of replacing reality with the hegemony and magic of the infantile wish. These two forces (mourning and dreaming) pulling at the mind from opposite sides, so to speak, must create a confusion, an ambiguity, a ferment that confounds the realistic psyche perhaps, but energizes the creative imagination in complex ways. If mourning insists that the libido invested in dead objects must be re-cycled in practical new engagements with the living rather than the dead, dreams re-envision, resurrect the dead in manifest and latent illuminations of the past that ignore reality as they dramatize and people the oneiric landscape with their bewitching and bedazzling artistic flourishes. Awakening from such dreams and accepting drab reality again is an act of mourning in itself unless one is able to interpret and inform and strengthen reality testing with new, dream-gleaned insights. It is such dream-gleaned insights I now want to turn to.

Before Freud's letter of October 15th, 1897 in which he announced the news of his discovery to Fliess there are a dozen well-documented dreams that could be thought of as stepping-stones on the road to discovery. 1. The dream of Irma's injection (July 24th, 1895). 2. The Close The Eyes Dream (October 25–26th, 1896). 3. The Four Rome Dreams (January, 1897). 4. Uncle with Yellow Beard Dream (February, 1897).

5. Villa Secerno Dream (April 27th and 28th, 1897). 6. The Hella Dream (May, 1897). 7. Running Upstairs Undressed (May, 1897). 8. The Sheep's Head Dream (October 3rd and 4th, 1897). 9. One Eyed Doctor Dream (October, 1897). If we omit the dream of Irma's injection (July 24th, 1895), the other eleven dreams were dreamt in the year between the death of Freud's father and the discovery of the Oedipus complex. These dreams have been well-analyzed by Freud himself and later by Grinstein and Anzieu, whose scholarship I have leaned on and learned from. These eleven dreams were some of the essential raw materials of Freud's intense self-analysis during that most fruitful year, nocturnal gifts he extracted from sleep and his capacity to remember his dreams. But while he was awake there was an essential context to be considered also. Freud was not only examining himself after all: he was treating patients as well and some of what he discovered in his analysands complemented and even stimulated his own burgeoning hypotheses. "The poem is everywhere" the great Greek poet Elytis said, and for Freud I believe psychological raw material was everywhere also, in his dreams, in his analysands, even in his own grief. Just before Freud describes the Oedipus complex, in *The Interpretation of Dreams* he mentions one of his patients, a very obsessional young man who was afraid to go out into the street for fear of killing everyone he met. "The analysis" (which eventually led to the patient's recovery, Freud writes) "showed that the basis of this distressing obsession was an impulse to murder his somewhat over-severe father." (1899, p. 260). Later in *The Interpretation of Dreams* (p. 458) Freud describes his "identification" with this young man, suggesting and even confirming perhaps my earlier point that Freud's clinical work with his patients was, along with his dreams and his mourning, a crucial factor in his voyage of discovery.

Another significant factor was his relationship with Fliess, his secret sharer, whom he idealized, but also felt very ambivalent about, an attitude that eventually could not be contained and led to the end of the relationship. But there is no question that Freud, who was conducting an analysis on himself, without the benefit of an objective professional, found a sounding board in Fliess, who in a way became a transferential therapeutic figure. In the history of science in general has there ever been such a comparable moment? One would be hard pressed to find an equal moment in the annals of science in which the raw material itself emerges from relationship and through relationship. Freud's great discovery of transference, discussed at length in Chapter Three, is after all, the product of a remarkable insight about the nature of relationship itself. What Freud realized was that people are constantly projecting imagined reactions onto the people they are in contact with, as if subjective reality could become a casualty at any moment of what projected imagination needed to dramatize, in the interest of displacing the past rather than facing up to it. Ironically, by displacing the past in this transferential manner, it can be examined in its projected form if one is able to recognize what prompted the projection of it in the first place. Freud's abandonment of hypnosis allowed him to recognize that you didn't have to induce sleep to recover the past; it was there in the transferential ways people reacted to each other all the time. In the privacy of the consulting room, psychoanalysts have exploited this new discovery of transference in very profound ways for more than a hundred years.

Freud was dispatching "letters" to Fliess that contain not only a personal note but also "drafts" of Freud's most original discoveries. These drafts are astonishing to read more than a hundred years after they were written. That Fliess was not always aware of the momentous contents of these drafts and did not always respond to them by return letter began to irritate Freud more and more, sometimes "paralyzing" his ongoing progress. When Fliess eventually did respond, Freud's creative energies would return and the voyage of self-discovery would pick up steam again. In comparison to the usual analytic procedure, which depends on the reliability and predictability of an ongoing free-associative engagement between analyst and analysand, what Freud was subjected to in this quasi-analytic relationship must have been exasperating. It was an exasperation out of which extraordinary products emerged and the history of ideas is indebted to it. If we try to track Freud's unconscious affects from the Irma dream to the One Eyed Doctor dream I believe we will be like the ancient audience at Sophocles' *Oedipus Rex* awash in dramatic irony as they witness the doomed hero (Oedipus) doggedly and innocently insisting on pursuing a truth that only the audience knows will destroy him! Freud of course was not destroyed by his discovery, like Oedipus, but enlightened.

I will try to summarize the dreams and their main affects as I try to depict the structure of the Oedipus complex as it slowly emerges from the mists of ignorance. I will treat the sequence of dreams as if their partial insights eventually coalesce to make the ultimate creative eureka of insight possible. I will assume that the reader has a certain familiarity with these dreams, and that memory can be refreshed, if necessary, by access to the original text and subsequent commentary (Freud; Anzieu; Grinstein to name a few).

The Irma Dream is probably the most famous of Freud's dreams, brilliantly deconstructed by Freud himself, and the subject of much further exegesis by a host of subsequent investigators. I will make one comment only: the predominant affect is guilt about the botched surgery, Freud's reluctance to blame Fliess directly for his obvious surgical mismanagement of the case and Freud's wish to exonerate himself from guilt by association. The elements of an Oedipal triangle are all there, a damaged woman (Irma), a guilty man (Fliess), a child witness (Freud); but Freud has no inkling of their Oedipal meaning yet. His mind seems focused on the challenge and complexity of the dreaming process and how to make sense out of it.

The Close The Eyes Dream is obviously about Jacob Freud's death since we know it was dreamed either immediately before the death or very soon thereafter. The manifest content is stark: "You are requested to close the eyes (or close an eye)." This sentence, like an announcement on a signpost, is the only content of the dream. The conflict seems obvious: should Freud recognize his guilt about his father's death, face it squarely or close an eye to it, wink at it?

The Four Rome Dreams: if we compress these most complex dreams together they express the wish to get to Rome, a very over-determined desire of Freud's, to get to Rome like Hannibal (a one-eyed hero) and thereby overcome the shame he felt when his father was humiliated on the street by a Christian. Freud has described that childhood humiliation as follows:

> I may have been ten or twelve years old, when my father began to take me with him on his walks and reveal to me in his talk his views upon things in the world we live in. Thus it was, on one such occasion, that he told me a story to show me how much better things were now than they had been in his days. "When I was a young man," he said, "I went out for a walk one Saturday in the streets of your birthplace; I was well dressed, and had a new fur cap on my head. A Christian came up to me and with a single blow knocked off my cap into the mud and shouted: 'Jew! Get off the pavement.'"
>
> "And what did you do?" I asked. "I went into the roadway and picked up my cap," was his quiet reply. This struck me as unheroic

conduct on the part of the big, strong man who was holding the little boy by the hand. I contrasted this situation with another which fitted my feelings better: the scene in which Hannibal's father, Hasdrubal, made his boy swear before the household altar to take vengeance on the Romans. Ever since that time Hannibal had had a place in my phantasies (p. 197).

Freud later recognized his error: he has confused Hannibal's father Hamilcar Barca with Hannibal's brother Hasdrubal. This parapraxis is comparable to the one Freud made when he describes his discovery of the Oedipus complex for the first time in his letter to Fliess of October 15th, 1897. Freud is comparing Hamlet and Oedipus Rex. Freud writes that Hamlet is "positively precipitate in murdering Laertes." A close reading of Shakespeare makes it clear that the "positive precipitate" murder refers to Polonius, not Laertes. A father and a son are being confused in this slip. Could it be that the discoverer of the Oedipus complex flinches as he imagines the Oedipal death of his own father and that his guilt-inspired slip unconsciously dispatches himself (Jacob's son) instead, Polonius' son Laertes an unconscious stand-in for Freud himself? The fact that all of this was first adumbrated in a letter to the transferential Fliess adds to the Oedipal irony in question.

The Uncle with the Yellow Beard Dream: Freud's ambition to become a professor is the core affect of this dream.

The Villa Secerno Dream. Obvious growing ambivalence toward Fliess and toward his own father begins to emerge more clearly in this dream. Secerno refers to hiding or secreting, the conflict about knowing and not knowing; opening the eyes or closing them continues to be unresolved.

The Hella Dream. Freud's sexual feeling for his daughter Mathilde is the main affect of the dream. Jones maintains that this dream led to Freud's abandonment of the seduction hypothesis. This is a major advance: sexual instincts must be acknowledged as opposed to projected or disavowed.

Running Up the Stairs Undressed Dream. This is the dream along with other staircase dreams that leads to the recovery of a most significant memory of Monica Zajic, the nurse who took care of Freud in Freiberg. This nurse could be rough. As Freud sarcastically puts it: "her treatment of me was not always excessive in amiability." So if the Villa Secerno dream allows Freud to embrace his ambivalence toward

Fliess and his father, this retrieved memory puts him in touch with ambivalence toward a woman. The two poles of the Oedipus complex (positive and negative Oedipal attitudes toward parents) are beginning to come into view.

The Sheep's Head Dream. Here is the manifest content:

1. "I took out a subscription in S. and R's bookshop for a periodical costing twenty florins a year."
2. "She was my teacher in sexual matters and complained because I was clumsy and unable to do anything …. At the same time I saw the skull of a small animal and in the dream I thought "pig", but in the analysis I associated it with your wish (Fliess) that I might find as Goethe once did, a skull on the Lido to enlighten me. But I did not find it. So I was a 'little block head' (*Ein kleiner schafskopf*, a little sheep's-head)."

This dream leads to the memory of the nurse who bathed him in red water (she was menstruating). She also stole twenty zehners, a "crime" Freud first took on himself. Later his mother confirmed the details of his retrieved memory but corrected his distortion. The nurse was found out and subsequently spent ten months in prison. Freud was clearly affected by the loss of this significant primary object (just as Alex was, whose "catch up" strivings I have described in Chapter Four). Freud, trying to assess this significance of a recently recovered memory writes: "I said to myself that if the old woman disappeared from my life so suddenly, it must be possible to demonstrate the impression this made on me. Where is it then? Thereupon a scene occurred to me which in the course of twenty-five years has occasionally emerged in my conscious memory without my understanding it." Freud is knocking on the door of the Oedipus complex, so to speak, and the door is about to be thrown open. Freud continues, remembering the frantic affects of the scene that returns to consciousness again and again without being fully understood. "My mother was nowhere to be found: I was crying in despair. My brother Philipp (twenty years older than I) unlocked a wardrobe (Kasten) for me, and when I did not find my mother inside it either, I cried even more until, slender and beautiful, she came in through the door." There is a poignant congruence here between a child trying to open the mystery of his own distorted magical misunderstandings and a genius trying to make science out of that distortion many years later. Freud did eventually make sense out of this memory and its condensation of the nurse being locked up in prison and his mother locked up in the prison of his own imaginings. Freud had feared that his mother was pregnant and was relieved when she appeared "slender and beautiful" and therefore decidedly not pregnant.

The components of the Oedipus complex were slowly falling into place, Philipp the twenty years older brother, Freud's mother and Freud himself locked in an Oedipal unconscious "box" that only insight, and a most transgressive insight at that, could unlock. When one considers Freud's letter to Fliess of October 3rd, 1897 (which contains the Sheep's Head Dream in a post-script) it is clear that Freud's self-analysis had helped him to recover very early memories from the first three years of life. In that letter he admits to feeling jealous of his father, even if he had failed to find any evidence in the coffers of retrieved memory of sexual seduction on the part of his father. He acknowledges sexual feelings for his *matrem* whom he had seen "nudam" on a journey to Vienna with her when he was between "two and two-and-a half years." The need to describe his memory in Latin surely suggests his discomfort with the affects his Oedipal conflict was arousing in him. In that same letter Freud describes the birth of his brother Julius and the ill wishes he felt toward him. When Julius died a few months later Freud's guilt must have been intense. Recounting all of this to Fliess in October 1897, on the verge of discovering the Oedipus complex, one senses that Julius was the prototype of Oedipal hatred toward the father, given the telescopic, tendentious nature of memory.

The One-Eyed Doctor and Schoolmaster Dream. Here is the manifest content:

> "I had a dream of someone who I knew in my dream was the doctor in my native town. His face was indistinct, but was confused with one of my masters at the secondary school, whom I still meet occasionally."

Freud had much resentment toward the childhood doctor. Freud's ambivalence is displayed by juxtaposing the hated doctor and the beloved schoolmaster. These condensations became clearer when his mother explained to Freud that both doctor and schoolmaster were one-eyed! Freud seems very reluctant to interpret this dream fully when he first describes it to Fliess. It is only in later editions of *The Interpretation of Dreams* that Freud allows himself to disclose how he had fallen as a very young child and injured his chin. The castration fear aspect of the Oedipus complex was too much to be incorporated into the complexity of Freud's emerging philosophy at this time. His mother reminded him of the reason the one-eyed doctor had been called in the first place. It is tempting to condense the one-eyed doctor and the closing of one eye in the earlier "It is necessary to close the eyes/an eye, dream." Freud's Oedipal hatred of the one-eyed doctor and father can only be insightfully seen with both eyes open. Closing one eye or two at this point would be a denial of an extraordinary insight at the moment of incipient triumph. Freud's question in *Mourning and Melancholia* is relevant in this context. "Why, then, after it has run its course, is there no hint in its case (Freud is referring to mourning, and when the work of mourning is completed) of the economic condition for a phase of triumph?" Freud immediately writes: "I find it impossible to answer this objection straight away." If I am correct in my thesis that mourning contains in its very form and structure the architecture of the Oedipus complex itself, (the very discovery Freud was on the verge of granting himself in October 1897) he must have felt it almost impossible to experience any sense of triumph, especially if that triumph were in any way related to the Oedipal "good riddance" triumph I described earlier in one of my own patients. "Ahahs" of excitement, Eureka's of self-congratulation usually accompany great discovery. In Freud's case was it necessary to close the eyes to such Oedipal dancing on his father's grave? Freud insisted on depicting the Close The Eyes Dream as a two-fold text: to close one eye (to wink) is juxtaposed with the closing of both eyes. To wink at someone has an Oedipal meaning that I would like to emphasize. Freud did not focus on this, nor did subsequent scholarship, to the best of my knowledge. If one deconstructs the drama of one person winking at another in the presence of a third it becomes clear that an Oedipal motif is being enacted. Winking is usually triadic. I wink at you, both of us in a collusion of supposed superiority over a third party who is left out of our mutual comic conspiracy against him. Isn't winking a drama of ironic subtlety, a cruel version of the Oedipus complex in comic dress, two "informed" members lording it over an unwitting third?

There is one other "incident" prior to Freud's discovery of the Oedipus complex that is analogous to winking and closing the eyes or keeping them insightfully open. Between October 4th and 15th Freud made a professional blunder. He used to see an old woman daily to put a few drops of eye lotion (collyrium) into her eye and give her a morphine injection. (Is it not striking how prominent eyes are in Freud's mind as he approaches this most momentous discovery, as if he needs to blind himself like Oedipus even as he dares to retrace the footsteps of Sophocles' tragic protagonist?) This particular morning he put morphine in the eye instead of collyrium. It was only years later in the Psychopathology of Everyday Life that Freud explained his symptomatic act. It was a memory of a patient's dream that made it possible for Freud to understand the meaning of his self-destructive, mal-practical parapraxis.

I was under the influence of a dream which had been told me by a young man the previous evening and the content of which could only point to sexual intercourse with his mother. (...) While absorbed in thoughts of this kind I came to my patient, who is over ninety, and I must have been on the way to grasping the universal human application of the Oedipus myth as correlated with the Fate which is revealed in the oracles; for at that point I did violence to or committed a blunder on "the old woman" (date).

Freud was aware in October 1897 that he was "on the way to grasping the human application of the Oedipus myth", but he seemed to need to blind, not only the old woman whom he transgressed against, but himself as well by damaging his own professional status in a kind of Oedipal blinding of himself. His tragic identification with Oedipus seems total at such moments of blinding insight, even as his scientific integrity insists on staying the course.

In retrospect it would seem that symptomatic acts, parapraxes, dreams, mourning, screen memories, transference (in relation to Fliess), and clinical work with the daily raw material of his patients' unconscious minds led to the remarkable discovery of the Oedipus complex in October 1897. In the final analysis what is crucial of course is the fact that Freud was able to open both eyes in an act of triumphant, transgressive insight and make the Oedipus complex a cornerstone of psychoanalytic thinking for the last 115 years and a major contribution to the history of ideas for all the years to come.

I have suggested that mourning and dreaming assisted Freud in his extraordinary odyssey into the mysteries of the unconscious mind, especially into that aspect of the mind subsumed under the concept of the Oedipus complex. If the Oedipus complex is the precipitate in the mind of complex interpersonal dynamics between a child and his parents, a precipitate that is rendered unconscious by powerful forces of repression culminating in the infantile amnesia at age six or seven, the repressed can re-press itself into symptomatic repetitions of itself that can startle current adaptation with its pathological replications. But it can also become a revenant in dreams and mourning, two non-pathological phenomena that can enlighten, and lead to extraordinary insights if the mind is prepared to greet the revenants as ambassadors of knowledge rather than fearful specters of superstition.

The Oedipus complex is so repressed that it seems like a dark secret that reveals itself in uncanny ways. The return of the repressed is always greeted ambivalently as if the mind wants to be reminded and doesn't all at once. Mourning seems to insist on a brutal confrontation with reality; dreaming seems to need to disguise truth in an elaborate finery of self-deception. Working together they seem to churn the mind, by appealing to reality and fantasy all at once, an ambiguous state of affairs that genius, in its most creative iteration in the mind of Sigmund Freud, exploited with extraordinary results. When dreaming learns to fathom its own disguises and mourning learns to bury its own guilt with its dead, so to speak, reality testing is enhanced and even the confounding affects of the Oedipus complex can be integrated into a good enough adaptation of fantasy and reality. Freud went beyond Sophocles in the sense that he insisted on opening the eyes even as he closed the eyes of the dead father, an act of courageous, visionary, Oedipal hubris that does not need to blind itself, even as it re-presents its guilt to itself, in the fierce tenderness of human insight.

EPILOGUE

I have tried to depict the mind as odyssey, each individual mind, possessed of its own unique consciousness, on a journey of self-discovery. If there were no such thing as the unconscious mind, consciousness, in and of itself, would be baffling. If the evolution of complex multi-cellular organisms out of primal atomic matter is somewhat understandable, though still quite astonishing to contemplate, the evolutionary leap from matter to consciousness itself has never been adequately explained. Neo-Darwinism, sophisticated as it is, cannot explain it. From an elemental periodic table to the complexity of the ribosome's replicability, the journey from the inanimate to the animate can be conceptualized, but the biochemical, molecular steps from the animate to self-consciousness remain a mystery. The concept of an unconscious portion of the mind posits a depth psychology beneath "our official consciousness" as Freud once called it, thereby making the voyage of self-discovery all the more difficult to chart (1897). In a sense, the history of ideas could be considered a never-ending voyage of Eastern and Western philosophical and psychological thought from Lascaux to the Louvre, from Buddha to Breuer and Freud. There are probably as many odysseys as there are individual minds to make them. In his contempt for psychology, Joyce, as mentioned earlier, sneered: "Psychology! What can a man know but what passes through his mind" (Ellmann, 1982). And yet what passed through Homer's mind passed through the mind of James Joyce, as both "imagined" the human condition as an evolving odyssey.

Each analysand conducts his/her own voyage in the company of a psychoanalyst. If there is no such thing as a baby, as Winnicott famously observed, by which he meant that the mother-child relationship is indeed a relationship from childbirth on, there is no such thing as an analysand either, given that psychoanalytic odysseys represent a dyadic journey, not a solo flight. If the devoted mother puts her own selfishness aside in the interest of creating the ideal facilitating environment for her infant, the devoted analyst, and his evenly hovering attention, promote the facilitating psychoanalytic environment that allows a free-associative psychoanalytic odyssey to proceed. The free-associative odyssey of ideas that emerges in each unique analysis I have tried to represent with complex cross-sections of analytic experience. I have chosen to focus on mourning, repression, insight, play, dream, screen memory, symptom, character, and the discovery of the Oedipus complex, to give some impression of the vastness of the odyssey each psychoanalytic process contends with. No doubt there are many ports of call this book ignored. A journey is a finite thing after all, time-bound, limited, daring, yet realistic. If there are more things in heaven and earth than are dreamt of in our philosophies, a single journey can only address the vastness of such mysteries partially and incompletely. If this psychoanalytic odyssey has whetted the appetite for further travel in these intriguing regions of human experience, its mission will have been accomplished.

REFERENCES

Abraham, K. (1913). A screen memory concerning a childhood event of apparently aetiological significance. In: Editor (Ed.), *Clinical Papers and Essays on Psychoanalysis* (pp. 36–41). New York: Basic Books, 1955.

Abrams, S. & Neubauer, P. B. (1976). Object orientedness. *Psychoanalytic Quarterly 45*: 73–99.

Alexander, I. E. & Adlerstein, A. M. (1958). Affective responses to the concept of death in a population of children and early adolescents. *Journal of Genetic Psychology 93*: 167–177.

Anthony, S. (1940). *The Child's Discovery of Death*. London: Routledge & Kegan Paul.

Anthony, S. (1972). *The Discovery of Death in Childhood and After*. New York: Basic Books.

Auden, W. H. (1968). *Secondary Worlds*. New York: Random House.

Baudry, F. (1989). Character, character type and character organization. *Journal of the American Psychoanalytic Association 37*: 655–686.

Berlin, I. (1998). *The Crooked Timber of Humanity*. Princeton: Princeton University Press.

Bernan, L. (1985). Primal scene significance of a dream within a dream. *International Journal of Psycho-Analysis 66*: 75–76.

Bloom, H. (1998). *Shakespeare: The Invention of the Human*. New York: Riverhead.

Blos, P. (1979). *The Adolescent Passage*. New York: International University Press.

Bolt, R. (1990). *A Man For All Seasons*. New York: Vintage.

Bonaparte, M. (1928). L'identification d'une fille a sa mere morte. *Rev. Fran. Psychanal.* 2: 541–565.

Brenner, C. (1982). *The Mind in Conflict*. New York: Int. Univ. Press.

Carroll, L. (1872). *Alice in Wonderland and Through the Looking Glass*. Kingsport, TN: Grosset & Dunlap, 1946.

Costain, T. B. (1998). *The Silver Chalice*. Cutchogue, NY: Buccaneer Books.

Deutsch, H. (1932). *Psychoanalysis of the Neuroses*. London: Hogarth Press.

Deutsch, H. (1937). Absence of grief. *Psychoanalytic Quarterly* 6: 12–22.

Eissler, K. (1975). Personal Communication.

Eliot, T. S. (1963). *Four Quartets: Collected Poems (1909–1962)*. New York: Harcourt, Brace & World.

Ellmann, R. (1982). *James Joyce*. New York: Oxford University Press.

Empson, W. (1966). *Seven Types of Ambiguity*. New York: New Directions.

Falzeder, E. & Brabanr, E., (Eds.) (1996). *The Correspondence of Sigmund Freud and Sandor Ferenczi, Vol. 2, 1914–1919*. Cambridge, MA: Harvard University Press.

Fenichel, O. (1927). The economic function of screen memories. In: Editor (Ed.) *Collected Papers* (pp. 113–116). New York: Norton, 1953.

Ferenczi, S. (1952). *A Little Chanticleer. First Contributions to Psycho-Analysis*. New York: Brunner/Mazel.

Flavell, J. H. (1963). *The Developmental Psychology of Jean Piaget*. New York: Van Nostrand Reinhold.

Frank, A. (1969). The unrememberable and the unforgettable. *Psychoanalytic Study of the Child*, 24: 48–77.

Frazer, J. G. (1959). *The New Golden Bough*. New York: Criterion Books.

Freud, A. (1927). *Introduction to the Technique of Child Analysis*. New York and Washington: Nervous and Mental Disease Publishing Company.

Freud, A. (1958). Adolescence. *Psychoanalytic Study of the Child* 13: 255–278.

Freud, S. (1893a). On the psychical mechanism of hysterical phenomena. *S. E.*, 3: 26–39.

Freud, S. (1897b). Letters 70 and 71. *S. E.*, 1: 261–266.

Freud, S. (1899a). Screen memories. *S. E.*, 3: 301–322.

Freud, S. (1900a). The Interpretation of Dreams. *S. E.*, 4/5: 1–625.

Freud, S. (1901b). The Psychopathology of Everyday Life. *S. E.*, 6: 1–279.

Freud, S. (1905a). On psychotherapy. *S. E.*, 7: 257–268.

Freud, S. (1905c). Jokes and their relation to the unconscious. *S. E.*, 8: 9–238.

Freud, S. (1905d). Three essays on the theory of sexuality. *S. E.*, 7: 125–243.

Freud. S. (1908b). Character and anal erotism. *S. E.*, 9: 169.

Freud, S. (1908e). Creative writers and daydreaming. *S. E.,* 9: 142–153.

Freud, S. (1909b). Analysis of a phobia in a five-year-old boy. *S. E.,* 10: 3–149.

Freud, S. (1910c). Leonardo da Vinci and a memory of his childhood. *S. E.,* 11: 59–137.

Freud, S. (1911b). Formulations of the two principles of mental functioning. *S. E.,* 12: 218–226.

Freud, S. (1914g). Remembering, Repeating and Working-Through, *S. E.,* 12: 145–156.

Freud, S. (1915b). Thoughts for the times on war and death. *S. E.,* 14: 273–302.

Freud, S. (1915c). Instincts and their vicissitudes. *S. E.,* 14: 109–140.

Freud, S. (1915f). A case of paranoia running counter to the psycho-analytic theory of the disease. *S. E.,* 14: 261–272.

Freud, S. (1916–1917). Introductory lectures on psychoanalysis. *S. E.,* 15: 15–463.

Freud, S. (1917b). A childhood recollection from Dichtung und Wahrheit. *S. E.,* 17: 145–156.

Freud, S. (1917e). Mourning and melancholia. *S. E.,* 14: 237–260.

Freud, S. (1918b). From the history of an infantile neurosis. *S. E.,* 17: 3–122.

Freud, S. (1919h). The uncanny. *S. E.,* 17: 217–256.

Freud, S. (1920g). Beyond the pleasure principle. *S. E.,* 18: 3–64.

Freud, S. (1924d). The dissolution of the Oedipus complex. *S. E.,* 19: 173–179.

Freud, S. (1926d). Inhibitions, symptoms and anxiety. *S. E.,* 20: 77–175.

Freud, S. (1933a). New introductory lectures on Psycho-Analysis. *S. E.,* 22: 7–182.

Freud, S. (1937c). Analysis terminable and interminable. *S. E.,* 23: 209–253.

Freud, S. (1937d). Constructions in analysis. *S. E.,* 23: 255–270.

Frost, R. (1983). *The Norton Anthology of Poetry.* New York: W. W. Norton & Company, Inc.

Furman, E. (1974). *A Child's Parent Dies.* New Haven & London: Yale University Press.

Furman, R. A. (1964a). Death and the young child. *Psychoanalytic Study of the Child* 19: 321–333.

Furman, R. A. (1964b). Death of a six-year-old's mother during his analysis. *Psychoanalytic Study of the Child* 19: 377–397.

Glover, E. (1929). The screening function of traumatic memories. *International Journal of Psychoanalysis* 10: 90–93.

Greenacre, P. (1947). Vision, headache, and halo. In: Editor (Ed.) *Trauma, Growth and Personality* (pp. 132–148). New York: International University Press, 1969.

Greenacre, P. (1949). A contribution to the study of screen memories. *Psychoanalytic Study Child* 3/4: 73–84.

Greenacre, P. (1957). The Childhood of the Artist. *Psychoanalytic Study of the Child* 12: 47–72.

Greenacre, P. (1979). Reconstruction and the process of individuation. *Psychoanalytic Study of the Child 34*: 121–144.

Greenacre, P. (1980). A historical sketch of the use and disuse of reconstruction. *Psychoanalytic Study of the Child 35*: 35–40.

Greenacre, P. (1981). Reconstruction. *Journal of the American Psychoanalytic Association 29*: 27–46.

Greenson, R. R. (1958). On screen defenses, screen hunger, and screen identity In: Editor (Ed.) *Explorations in Psychoanalysis* (pp. 111–132). New York: International University Press, 1978.

Hartmann, H. & Kris, E. (1945). The genetic approach in psychoanalysis. *Psychoanalytic Study of the Child 1*: 11–30.

Hegel, G. W. F. (1807). *The Phenomenology of Mind*. Mineola, New York: Dover Publications, 2003.

Jones, E. (1916). The theory of symbolism. *Papers on Psycho-Analysis*. London: Bailliere, Tindall, & Cox 1948 pp. 87–144.

Jones, E. (1961). *Papers on Psychoanalysis*. Boston: Beacon Press.

Joyce, J. (1922). *Ulysses*. New York: Random House, 1961.

Joyce, J. (1916). *A Portrait of the Artist as a Young Man*. New York: Viking, 1969.

Katan, A. (1935). The role of displacement in agoraphobia. *International Journal of Psychoanalysis 32*: 41–50.

Keats, J. M. (1970). *Selected Letters of John Keats*. Cambridge, Massachusetts: Harvard University Press, 2002.

Kennedy, H. E. (1950). Cover memories in formation. *Psychoanalytic Study of the Child 5*: 275–284.

Kris, E. (1956a). The recovery of childhood memories in psychoanalysis. *Psychoanalytic Study of the Child 11*: 54–88.

Kris, E. (1956b). The personal myth. *Journal of the American Psychoanalytic Association 4*: 653–681.

Lessing, G. E. (1867). *Nathan the Wise*. New York: Henry Holt.

Lewin, B. D. (1946). Sleep, the mouth, and the dream screen. *Psychoanalytic Quarterly 15*: 419–434.

Lewin, B. D. (1950). *The Psychoanalysis of Elation*. New York: Norton.

Loewald, H. W. (1968). The transference neurosis. In: Editor (Ed.), *Papers on Psychoanalysis*, (pp. 302–314). New Haven & London: Yale University Press, 1980.

Luria, A. R. (1968). *The Mind of a Mnemonist*. New York/London: Basic Books, Inc.

Lustman, S. (1962). Defense, symptom and character. *Psychoanalytic Study of the Child 17*: 216–244.

Mahler, M. S. (1968). *On Human Symbiosis and the Vicissitudes of Individuation*. New York: International University Press.

Mahon, E. J. (1991). The dissolution of the Oedipus complex: a neglected cognitive factor. *Psychoanalytic Quarterly 60*: 628–634.

Mahon, E. J. (1993). Play, parenthood, and creativity. In: Editor (Ed.) *The Many Meanings of Play* (pp. 229–233). New Haven and London: Yale University Press, date.

Mannoni, O. (1971). *Freud*. New York: Pantheon.

Miller, J. B. M. (1971). Children's reactions to the death of a parent. *Journal of the American Psychoanalytic Association 19*: 697–719.

Muffs, Y. (1992). *Love and Joy: Law, Language and Religion in Ancient Israel*. The Jewish Theological Seminary of America, New York, pp. 1–240.

Nagera, H. (1970). Children's reactions to the death of important objects. *Psychoanalytic Study of the Child 25*: 360–400.

Nagy, M. (1948). The child's theories concerning death. *Journal of Genetic Psychology 73*: 3–27.

Neubauer, P. (1987). The many meanings of play. *Psychoanalytic Study of the Child 42*: 3–9.

Partridge, E. (1959). *Origins: A Short Etymological Dictionary of Modern English*. New York: Macmillan.

Piaget, J. (1945). *Play, Dreams and Imitation in Childhood*. New York: Norton, 1951.

Piaget, J. (1937). *The Construction of Reality in the Child*. New York: Basic Books, 1954.

Proust, M. (2003). *In Search of Lost Time*. New York: Modern Library.

Reider, N. (1953). Reconstruction and screen function *Journal of the American Psychoanalytic Association 1*: 389–405.

Sarnoff, C. A. (1970). Symbols and symptoms. *Psychoanalytic Quarterly 39*: 550–562.

Schafer, R. (1968). The mechanism of defense. *International Journal of Psychoanalysis 49*: 49–62.

Shakespeare, W. (1599). The Tragedy of Julius Caesar. In: *The Riverside Shakespeare* (pp. 1100–1134). Boston: Houghton Mifflin.

Shakespeare, W. (1600). Hamlet. In: *The Riverside Shakespeare* (pp. 1135–1197). Boston: Houghton Mifflin.

Shakespeare, W. (1606). King Lear. In: *The Riverside Shakespeare* (pp. 1249–1305). Boston: Houghton Mifflin.

Shakespeare, W. (1597). The Merchant of Venice. *The Riverside Shakespeare* (pp. 250–285). Boston: Houghton Mifflin.

Silber, A. (1983). A significant dream within a dream. *Journal of the American Psychoanalytic Association 31*: 899–915.

Simmel, E. (1925). A screen memory in statu nascendi. *International Journal of Psychoanalysis 6*: 454–467.

Skeat, W. W. (1910). *An Etymological Dictionary of the English Language*. Oxford: Clarendon Press.

Spitz, R. A. (1965). *The First Year of Life*. New York: International University Press.

Thomas, D. (1952). Do not go gentle into that good night. In: M. Ferguson, M. Salter and J. Stallworthy (Eds.), *Norton Anthology of Poetry* (pp. 1181–1182). Oxford, England: W. W. Norton & Co., 2005.

Valenstein, A. (1983). Working through and resistance to change: insight and the action system. *Journal of the American Psychoanalytic Association, 31*: 353–373.

Waelder, R. (1930). The principle of multiple function. In: S. A. Guttman (Ed.) *Psychoanalysis: Observation, Theory, Application* (pp. 68–83). New York: International University Press, 1976.

Waelder, R. (1932). The psychoanalytic theory of play. *Psychoanalytic Quarterly, 2*: 208–224.

Winnicott, D. W. (1953). *Transitional objects and transitional phenomena* In: Editor (Ed.) *Collected Papers* (pp. 229–242). New York: Basic Books, 1958.

Winnicott, D. W. (1971). *Playing and Reality*. New York: Basic Books.

Wolfenstein, M. (1966). *How is mourning possible? Psychoanalytic Study of the Child 21*: 93–123.

Wolff, P. H. (1967). The role of biological rhythms in early psychological development. *Bulletin of the Menninger Clinic, 31*: 197–218.

INDEX